POLICY
THROUGH
IMPACT ASSESSMENT

Recent Titles in Contributions in Political Science

POLICY THROUGH IMPACT ASSESSMENT

INSTITUTIONALIZED ANALYSIS AS A POLICY STRATEGY

Edited by Robert V. Bartlett

PREPARED UNDER THE AUSPICES OF
THE POLICY STUDIES ORGANIZATION
Stuart S. Nagel, Series Editor
Contributions in Political Science, Number 235

GREENWOOD PRESS
New York • Westport, Connecticut • London

Library of Congress Cataloging-in-Publication Data

Policy through impact assessment : institutionalized analysis as a policy
   strategy / edited by Robert V. Bartlett ; prepared under the
   auspices of the Policy Studies Organization.
      p.   cm. — (Contributions in political science, ISSN 0147–1066
   ; no. 235)
      Bibliography: p.
      Includes index.
      ISBN 0–313–26775–8 (lib. bdg. : alk. paper)
      1. Environmental policy.   2. Environmental impact analysis.
   I. Bartlett, Robert V.   II. Policy Studies Organization.
   III. Series.
   HC79.E5P653   1989
   363.7′0525—dc20   89–2122

British Library Cataloguing in Publication Data is available.

Library of Congress Catalog Card Number: 89–2122
ISBN: 0–313–26775–8
ISSN: 0147–1066

First published in 1989

Greenwood Press, Inc.
88 Post Road West, Westport, Connecticut 06881

Printed in the United States of America

The paper used in this book complies with the
Permanent Paper Standard issued by the National
Information Standards Organization (Z39.48–1984).

10 9 8 7 6 5 4 3 2 1

Contents

Preface

When I first began to study environmental impact assessment ten years ago, I was amazed to discover how little interest in the subject had been manifested by public policy scholars. A huge literature waited to be mastered, but most of it focused on environmental impact assessment as a technique or set of techniques, or on the environmental impact statement as a legal procedural requirement. There were prominent exceptions, to be sure—work for example by Lynton K. Caldwell, Richard N.L. Andrews, Richard Liroff, Geoffrey Wandesforde-Smith, H. Paul Friesema, and Paul Culhane—but these seminal analyses did not exhaust the rich theoretical and empirical possibilities for research on a profoundly significant innovation in the way governments operate. Impact assessment failed to excite large numbers of policy scholars because, like engineers, scientists, and lawyers, they too saw it as technique or nonsubstantive legal procedure or, at most, as a simplistic decision-making reform.

It seemed to me that an essential insight had been provided by Aaron Wildavsky in the 1960s (*The Politics of the Budgetary Process*) when he observed that mandatory cost-benefit analysis made important contributions to the practice of government, but less by way of installing comprehensive economic rationality than through redefining political rationality. This evaluation could be applied to any policy analytic method or approach; practical effectiveness in the real world of policy is determined by the way that internal logic and institutionalization redefine political rationality in a given system. This view, which has provided direction to my own research on environmental impact assessment, seems to underlie several important contributions by others, notably Taylor and Caldwell (see the bibliography).

The idea behind this edited book, then, was to stimulate research into the policy impact of impact assessment generally. In organizing the project and soliciting contributions, I defined impact assessment broadly to include several kinds. I am, of course, not the first person to see commonalities among environmental impact assessment, social impact assessment, technology assessment, risk assessment, cost-benefit analysis, and numerous other existing and proposed types of impact assessment. But the purpose here was not to focus on the commonalities of the techniques, but to explore patterns of institutionalization, the ways policy is determined through impact assessment.

In order to give the project greater coherence, I did draw boundaries, some of them arbitrary. No effort would be made to provide a catalogue of impact assessment approaches. Limited attention would be given to cost-benefit analysis and other highly quantitative approaches to impact assessment. Purely descriptive case studies, or histories, of impact assessment systems would be excluded. The techniques as well as the legalities of impact assessment would be discussed only secondarily. These are all important kinds of research and analysis, all of which complement the kind of work presented in this book. But they are not central to the topic of *policy through* impact assessment.

I owe thanks to a number of people and organizations who have contributed to this project over the last thirty months. The Policy Studies Organization and the International Association for Impact Assessment provided financial and logistical support, which was arranged by Stuart S. Nagel, Frederick A. Rossini, and A. T. Roper, among others. Additional support, in the way of excellent secretarial assistance and other necessary material incidentals, was provided by my institutional home, the Department of Political Science at Purdue University, which also provided an environment conducive to research and writing. I thank four capable department secretaries, Barbara Bergner, Beth Turner, Claire Windler, and Margo Reiss. I thank Cheri Lorenzetti for the index.

I thank all of the authors of this book, who made it what it is. Their punctuality (usually) and responsiveness to suggestions made my job much easier. In addition to their contributions as authors, several served as critics and referees for proposals and other chapters: Geoffrey Wandesforde-Smith, Walter F. Baber, William R. Mangun, William W. Nicholls, Jr., Michael E. Kraft, and Lynton K. Caldwell. Others serving on an unofficial editorial advisory board were James N. Gladden, Miriam Ershkowitz, A. T. Roper, Robert C. Paehlke, William P. McLauchlan, and Joseph Haberer. Their reward is a higher quality book.

Abbreviations

ACIR	Advisory Commission on Intergovernmental Relations
ADC	Animal Damage Control
AEC	Atomic Energy Commission
AID	Agency for International Development
ANILCA	Alaska National Interest Conservation Act
ATAS	Advance Technology Alert System
BLM	Bureau of Land Management
CEQ	Council on Environmental Quality
CRM	Cultural resource management
DEC	Department of Environmental Conservation (in New York State)
DOE	Department of Energy
DOE	Department of the Environment (in the United Kingdom)
DOI	Department of the Interior
EA	Environmental assessment
EC	European Community
ECC	Environmental Compliance Certification (in the Philippines)

EIA	Environmental impact assessment
EIR	Environmental impact report
EIS	Environmental impact statement
EPA	Environmental Protection Agency
FWS	Fish and Wildlife Service
GAO	General Accounting Office
IRG	Interagency Review Group
IUCN	International Union for the Conservation of Nature and Natural Resources
JIA	Judicial impact assessment
JICA	Japan International Cooperation Agency
LNG	Liquified natural gas
MAFF	Ministry of Agriculture, Fisheries and Food (in the United Kingdom)
NEPA	National Environmental Policy Act
NEPC	National Environmental Protection Council (in the Philippines)
NIMBY	Not in my backyard
NPC	National Power Corporation (in the Philippines)
NRC	Nuclear Regulatory Commission
NSF	National Science Foundation
NWF	National Wildlife Federation
NWPA	Nuclear Waste Policy Act
NWR	National Wildlife Refuge
OCRWM	Office of Civilian Radioactive Waste Management
OCS	Outer Continental Shelf
OECD	Organization for Economic Cooperation and Development
OECF	Overseas Economic Cooperation Fund (in Japan)
OTA	Office of Technology Assessment
PIER	Project Impact Evaluation Report
R&D	Research and Development
SEQR	State Environmental Quality Review Act (in New York State)
SIA	Social impact assessment

SIS	Social impact of science
UK	United Kingdom
USGS	U.S. Geological Survey
VIS	Victim impact statement

1

Impact Assessment as a Policy Strategy

Robert V. Bartlett

Impact assessment constitutes a general strategy of policy making and administration—a strategy of influencing decision and action by a priori analysis of predictable impacts. A simple, even simplistic, notion when stated briefly, making policy through impact assessment is in fact an approach of great power, complexity, and subtlety.

Impact assessment clearly is one of the major innovations in policy making and administration of the twentieth century. It has its origins in the historical efforts of some bureaucrats, legislators, and government reformers to analyze the likely consequences of possible government actions prior to adoption and implementation. Classic U.S. examples include the post–Civil War surveys and reports by John Wesley Powell (largely ignored) regarding the physical character of, and likely impact of settlement on, the western United States (Stegner, 1954); the river basin planning techniques of the U.S. Army Corps of Engineers as long ago as 1870 (Rowe et al., 1978); and the emphasis given to future consequences by urban and natural resource planners, beginning in the 1850s with Frederick Law Olmstead (Stein, 1957; Spreiregen, 1971; Udall, 1963; Caldwell, 1988). The Flood Control Act of 1936 firmly established the principle of cost-benefit analysis for water resource development projects; such analysis is now an accepted part of the decision formulae for much of what governments around the world do. Environmental impact assessment (EIA) and technology assessment were invented in the late 1960s; variations have been adopted and implemented widely by national and provincial governments, funding organizations, private firms, and international agencies. Risk assessment and social impact assessment (SIA) are perhaps the best known and most consequential of the numerous impact assessment approaches developed in the 1970s (for a partial list and analysis of others see Taylor, 1984). Proposals for new impact assessment systems, and actions establishing them, are now commonplace (Porter, 1988).

The policy potential of impact assessment requirements and arrangements always has been appreciated quickly by involved political actors—whether legislative, bureaucratic, judicial, executive, or nongovernmental. Once the political potency of institutionalized impact assessment had been manifestly demonstrated, by the early 1970s, thousands of political initiatives subsequently appeared worldwide as reformers attempted to harness the same poorly understood mechanisms in the cause of various substantive values.

If impact assessment is a major innovation in the practice of government in the twentieth century, then the National Environmental Policy Act (NEPA), which established the first requirement for EIA and environmental impact statements (EISs) and thus provided the inspiration and model for most other impact assessment systems, is surely one of the most significant pieces of legislation. Russell Train, who played a role in drafting NEPA and later, as chairman of the Council on Environmental Quality and then as administrator of the Environmental Protection Agency, was instrumental in its implementation, has declared,

I can think of no other initiative in our history that had such a broad outreach, that cut across so many functions of government, and that had such a fundamental impact on the way government does business. . . . I believe I had a unique familiarity with the whole EIS process from inception to implementation and am qualified to characterize that process as truly a revolution in government policy and decision-making.[1]

The substantial significance of impact assessment has been widely recognized by, among others, lawyers, applied biologists, economists, and engineers—and their journals abound with articles. Scholarly research has addressed wide-ranging questions of techniques and procedures, legal implications, background knowledge, communication, and history. But, with few exceptions, impact assessment has yet received little attention from policy scholars—certainly not the kind of attention it deserves.

Two of the most prominent exceptions can be found in books by Caldwell (1982) and Taylor (1984), both of which analyze impact assessment as a distinctive policy strategy. How and why, and under what circumstances, can impact assessment be expected to influence policy? Taylor and Caldwell show that it makes a difference how impact assessment is institutionalized in the policy system; its policy impact is neither simple nor assured. Impact assessment does not influence policy through some magic inherent in its techniques or procedures.

More than methodology or substantive focus, what determines the success of impact assessment is the appropriateness and effectiveness in particular circumstances of its implicit policy strategy.

In the context of the long history of public policy and administration, impact assessment is novel in all the senses of that word: it is new, unusual, and different. It is new, having only a few antecedents prior to the 1960s. It is unusual, being still far less common than other approaches to achieving policy goals such as reorganization, detailed rule making, or resource reallocation. Finally, impact assessment is different, with peculiar weaknesses and limitations and with a characteristic logic to the way it influences policy (Bartlett, 1986a). It falls in the category of policy controls that Gormley labels "catalytic": "Catalytic controls require the bureaucracy to act and direct the bureaucracy towards certain goals but do not rob it of the capacity for creative problem-solving. . . . They prod, stimulate, and provoke bureaucrats but also allow them to be both innovative and efficient" (Gormley, 1987:160).[2]

This is exciting stuff for policy researchers and scholars, offering the possibility for incisive theorizing coupled to fruitful empirical investigation, with such work having immediate relevance to contemporary problems of institutional design. The need clearly exists. Persons who propose new impact assessment systems often assume the policy effects to be automatic and entirely beneficial (e.g., Koshland, 1988). Many of these superficially imitative programs and proposals have "been based on a misreading of how the EIS process works, and almost always on a misunderstanding of what is necessary if an impact statement system is to change agency policy" (Taylor, 1984:7). Critics, on the other side, often see impact assessment as merely symbolic, or diversionary, or obstructionist, or expensive and wasteful, or redundant and unnecessary (e.g., Renwick, 1988; Fairfax, 1978; Bardach and Pugliaresi, 1977). All of these views of impact assessment are simplistic and incorrect if impact assessment is properly viewed as an adjustable *policy strategy*.

Indeed, the purpose of every impact assessment system is to influence policy. Yet exactly how impact assessment systems do affect the course of policy is incompletely and poorly understood. The contributors to this book establish that impact assessment can be, and is, a powerful tool for making policy, but a tool whose users must be sensitive to its requirements and to the political and cultural context in which it is being used. Indeed, it is a tool with many particular designs and variations. The policy analyst who looks only for the dramatic and direct policy impact is likely to be unimpressed; appreciating how policy is made through impact assessment requires acknowledgment that policy decisions are shaped, channeled, learned, reasoned, and structured before they are "officially" made. How impact assessment affects prominent, public, formal policy decisions is only one of the "big" questions (to borrow Geoffrey Wandesforde-Smith's terminology, Chapter 15) about making policy through impact assessment, and not even the most important one at that.

The contributors to this book confirm that understanding impact assessment requires much more than understanding a body of techniques and procedures. Impact assessment is not antipolitical; neither is impact assessment a neutral, value-free mechanism for avoiding the unpleasantness of politics. At the same time, the politics of bureaucracy provides an environment in which the effectiveness of impact assessment can be tempered, subverted, and broken in the absence of adequate provisions for external accountability.

Thus what is called for is a strong dose of institutional policy analysis, which, at its best, is "the application of clear values and systematic empirical research to a problem of institutional design" (Gormley, 1987:165). Such analysis administered to impact assessment is the objective in the chapters that follow. Our aim is neither to summarize all that is known about impact assessment, nor to be certain that every possible topic is treated in a balanced way. Rather, our concern here is to enhance theoretical perspectives on impact assessment, to contribute to the growing body of literature describing how various existing impact systems work, to explore the application of the impact assessment idea to new policy fields, and to evaluate critically some of the little questioned assumptions and implications of impact assessment as presently practiced; to provide, in sum, further insight into the possibilities, effects, and limitations of institutionalized impact assessment as a policy strategy.

NOTES

1. Russell E. Train, correspondence, 15 October 1988.
2. Gormley does label impact assessment, incorrectly I believe, a "coercive" control. As the contributors to this book demonstrate, some small degree of coercion is required to make an impact assessment system work, to avoid its being merely an exercise in symbolic politics (a danger identified by Gormley), but the mechanisms through which impact assessment has a policy effect are basically catalytic, not coercive.

PART I

IMPLEMENTING AND MANAGING: IMPACT ASSESSMENT AS AN INSTRUMENT OF POLICY MAKING

2

Understanding Impact Analysis: Technical Process, Administrative Reform, Policy Principle

Lynton K. Caldwell

Although the following discussion focuses on environmental impact analysis (EIA), a more general term is used in the title. The purpose is to obviate an unnecessary distinction between environmental, social, and economic impacts. All impacts are in some sense environmental. The idea of interactive relationships is implicit in the term "environmental." The application of our most reliable analytic capabilities toward disclosing the probable consequences of human behavior is the essence of impact analysis. Environmental impact analysis in its broader context represents a fundamental change in perceptions of how propositions regarding society's environmental future should be evaluated and how political and economic decisions affecting that future should be made. EIA cannot be fully understood unless it is understood in its several aspects and historical context.

Given this general observation, it follows that environmental impact analysis may be examined from several points of view. It is a technical process, it is a means toward administrative reform, and, more important, it establishes a principle of policy. This final viewpoint is fundamental, not only to impact assessment, but to governance in today's world. The basic purpose behind development of environmental impact analysis was to broaden and strengthen the role of foresight in governmental planning and decision making. The case for foresight was never better stated than by Arthur C. Clarke in *Voices from the Sky*

(1967:162) when he counselled: (1) do not attempt the unforeseeable and (2) do not commit the irrevocable.

Clarke explained that "though these rules have often been broken in the past it seldom mattered; for the damage was confined to the meddler and his immediate vicinity. This is no longer the case; the consequences of meddling are now global and will soon be astronomical."

Time has proved Clarke to be prophetic. As the Strategic Defense Initiative invades an outer space environment previously threatened by the U.S. Defense Department's West Ford and Starfish experiments (1958, 1962) in the Van Allen belts, as various artificial satellites are put into orbit, and as "space junk" accumulates, man's environmental impacts are no longer confined to planet Earth. The growing need for EIA was voiced by James Van Allen at a meeting of the American Association for the Advancement of Science in 1962: "Our failure as a nation to produce a substantial study of the scientific consequences of these tests long before the decision was made that they were to be conducted, is, it seems to me, quite inexcusable. With tests such as this, studies should have been conducted in such a way that they were subject to publication and general scientific discussion" (Van Allen, 1962).

Seven years later and after many comparable, unexamined, environment-threatening propositions and undertakings, the nation and the Congress in effect revolted against technological Russian roulette and enacted the National Environmental Policy Act (NEPA) with its environmental impact statement requirement. The possible effects of the U.S. experiments with nuclear explosions and orbiting copper dipoles in outer space were global and, for all that was known beforehand, could have indefinitely ruined radio telescopy and orbiting satellite communication. It should have been clear a quarter-century ago that impact analysis had become a global imperative. We are only now beginning to recognize the need for its international implementation.

HAS TECHNIQUE DISPLACED PURPOSE?

We now have institutionalized a methodology for analyzing the prospective impact of environment-altering propositions. Impact analysis has developed rapidly and widely as a professional skill. Development of science-based analytic technique has been essential to the reliability and credibility of EIA. Yet the professionalization of EIA entails a predictable risk—the adumbration of purpose by technique.

This overshadowing or displacement of purpose is much less the fault of impact analysts than it is of policymakers and program administrators who have not learned to think ecologically or in multidimensional systemic terms. *Purpose* is the business of the policy planners and decisionmakers. EIA is intended to force them to consider the full and true dimensions of their undertakings. To the extent that they see EIA as an unavailable inconvenient exercise to which they need only give pro forma recognition, the purpose of EIA is defeated—but not by technique. Understanding EIA as technique is nevertheless necessary to its effective integration into the planning and decision processes.

The development of EIA specifically has been influenced by several parallel techniques, notably: (1) rational planning theory, (2) technology assessment, (3) risk assessment, and (4) cost-benefit analysis. The purpose of EIA is to be found in the policy goals of the environmental movement, initially in the United States and subsequently in other countries. In the United States, an additional factor has been a popular and legislative desire to reinforce administrative accountability through disclosure of considerations entering into public decisions by government agencies, supplementing the Administrative Procedures and Freedom of Information Acts (Title 5, U.S. Code, Sec. 551 et. seq.). The significance of EIA as technique, notably in relation to NEPA, may be summarized in the following six points:

1. Beyond preparation of technical reports, EIA is a means to a larger end—the protection and improvement of the environmental quality of life.

2. It is a procedure to discover and evaluate the effects of activities (chiefly human) on the environment—natural and social. It is not a single specific analytic method or technique, but uses many approaches as appropriate to a problem.

3. It is not a science, but uses many sciences (and engineering) in an integrated interdisciplinary manner, evaluating relationships as they occur in the real world.

4. It should not be treated as an appendage, or add-on, to a project, but regarded as an integral part of project planning. Its costs should be calculated as a part of adequate planning and not regarded as something extra.

5. EIA does not "make" decisions, but its findings should be considered in policy- and decision-making and should be reflected in final choices. Thus it should be part of decision-making processes.

6. The findings of EIA should focus on the important or critical issues, explaining why they are important and estimating probabilities in language that affords a basis for policy decisions.

HAS EIA REFORMED ADMINISTRATION?

Cumulative evidence (see the other chapters in this book and the bibliography) indicates that EIA has significantly if imperfectly influenced policy and decision making. One should hardly expect EIA as technique or policy principle to be more effective than other provisions for administrative accountability (e.g., government procurement, fiscal accountability, or honesty in performance evaluation). Public administration is an imperfect aspect of a notoriously imperfect enterprise—governance. Even so, the EIA process as a manifestation of value change in society has affected the kind of propositions advanced in government and has killed or forced revision of a significant number of projects (Caldwell, 1979).

EIA where seriously applied has reformed administrative behavior to a degree reflective of a growth of popular expectation. For example, in response to a query by me regarding impact analysis in the U.S. Corps of Engineers, an officer of the Corps opined that if the Corps were no longer required by law to undertake EIA the practice would be continued nevertheless. Why? Because the public now expects it.

Serge Taylor (1984) is right in observing that supportive forces both inside and outside of government have much to do with the effective implementation of EIA. In democratic societies public expectation, sufficiently focused, does act as a pressure and restraint on public officials. The substantial failure of the Reagan administration's effort to reduce environmental regulation in the United States is a case in point. To the question: has EIA reformed administration, my reply is yes—but as an instrument of a public opinion demanding administrative and policy reform.

To the counterargument that the general public never asked for EIA and was sometimes critical of its use, my answer is that the public wants general outcomes, but seldom fixes on specific procedures. The spread of EIA from the U.S. government to the states, to Canada and abroad, and to international organizations should answer definitively the allegation that EIA was unwanted and unnecessary. That argument has now lost credibility with all but the invincibly uninformed. But EIA cannot reasonably be expected unilaterally to induce environmental sensitivity and foresight in political leadership. Rather the growth of environmental concern in politics will strengthen and extend the process of EIA.

EIA AND POLICY DEVELOPMENT

Development of EIA and its associated analytic techniques demonstrates a capacity for technical learning and, beyond that, for social learning. But this capability fails to achieve its purpose if the qualitative purposes for which EIA was invented are restricted to the exposure of environmentally bad proposals. American experience with NEPA shows how important legislation can be distorted or underutilized. The forward-looking provisions for research, training, monitoring, and forcasting mandated under Title II of NEPA remain largely inactivated. Why?

Among other possible reasons, two are salient. First, people, including public officials, seldom learn what they do not want to know or prefer to regard as unimportant. Second, present-day education, training, and conventional patterns of thought tend to be analytic rather than synergistic. Modern technological societies tend to be stronger on "can-do" techniques than on farsighted thoughtfulness. Here-and-now enthusiasms tend to obscure opportunity costs. EIA should but does not always warn against the foreclosure of future options. Training for EIA is too often limited to learning a marketable, analytic skill. Learning how to think about complex, evolving environmental relationships and their implications is a more difficult task with no obvious patron if the government and the educational institutions decline that role. Evolving circumstances, however, may be forcing—sometimes reluctantly—an acceptance of the role.

Where EIA does not legally predetermine or force an administrative decision, it is not generally regarded as threatening. This is especially so, for example, in Canada, the United Kingdom, the German Federal Republic, and Sweden, where EIA procedures are less formalized and less mandatory than in the United States. The unactivated substantive provisions of NEPA have threatening potential; bureaucratic, economic, and political interests with contrary priorities do not wish to encourage public investigation and monitoring of trends wherein the release of information might itself affect the prospects for preferred policies.

People are reluctant to learn or promote learning when that learning appears to work toward their perceived disadvantage. They also find difficulty in relating the many interconnected aspects of the environment with other aspects of life—for example, relationships between energy utilization, deforestation, climate change, and human life-styles and expectations. EIA and the integrated interdisciplinary approach to policy that NEPA requires implies syncretic thinking that does not comport well with predetermined political objectives which characteristically have been based on single-track perceptions of reality.

Science and schooling have collaborated to structure the formal process of learning along restrictive disciplinary lines. Syncretic thinking, which often leads to synergistic conclusions, is an unusual quality; it is rarely encouraged or encountered anywhere. It seeks a whole that may be significantly different and more revealing than a mere summation of the parts. This type of thinking, seldom regarded as job related, is called for mostly at the policy-forming levels of government and business where it appears to be in short supply. Problem-solving techniques are taught in schools of business and public administration, but they differ in important ways from the kind and content of thinking required to translate the findings of EIA into environmental policy or to consider what values, beyond those of hard data, an adequate EIA should investigate. Much of our leadership in government, education, and the economic sector is handicapped by educated incapacity. As humans we have seldom learned how to think in relation to the kinds of complex problems that our societies have created. Environmental systems are inherently dynamic and nonlinear, and advanced theorists in physical sciences, mathematics, and ecology are only beginning to visualize their behavior.

In a review of EIA in North America and Western Europe, William V. Kennedy of the Organization for Economic Cooperation and Development (OECD) reached the following conclusions regarding the question "What has worked where, how, and why?"

Given the differing approaches that have been taken to EIA in various national contexts, it is difficult to provide a short or simple answer to this question. Generally speaking, however, it would appear that EIA works best when it is instituted in a formal-explicit way. That is to say, it works when there is a specific legal requirement for its application,

where an environmental impact statement is prepared, and where authorities are accountable for taking its results into consideration in decision-making.

In addition, for EIA to be successfully integrated in the project planning process it
would appear that procedures for screening, scoping, external review, and public participation need to be a part of it.

Of course, environmental impact assessment does not have to be a formal-explicit
procedure. Ideally, it can and should happen automatically so that environmental values
are taken into account in decision-making. However, experience in countries where it
has been applied shows that it is rarely put to use unless political pressures demand it.
(Kennedy, 1988:262)

Taking these observations one step further, one might speculate that EIA will
be most effective where environmental values (1) are implicit and consensual in
the national culture and (2) are explicit in public law and policy. Thus EIA is
nowhere as effective as it might be. Consensual circumstances appear to facilitate
a relatively informal use of EIA, for example, in Scandinavia. Insufficient consensus on environmental values in the United States necessitates formalized
mandatory procedures with the possibility of judicial review which is itself limited
by ideological restraints.

Under either of these circumstances, the ultimate effectiveness of EIA could
be enhanced by an explicit statement of the purposes and goals of environmental
policy reinforced by effective sanctions. To declare an environmental standard
against which the actions of government could be compared should clarify the
role of EIA and give direction to its efforts. NEPA sets such a standard for the
United States, and yet its substantive provisions (notably, Section 101) appear
to be regarded as inoperative—they lack the teeth of legal sanctions notable, for
example, in civil rights legislation. These provisions are important nonetheless.
They antedate the EIA requirement; without them, EIA might not have been
invented in the United States. Although rarely invoked, they are not to be flouted.
There is a latent risk that egregious disregard of the Section 101 precepts could
result in reversal of administrative decisions by the courts. In what has thus far
been the definitive judicial interpretation of NEPA, the Court of Appeals of the
District of Columbia declared in the case of *Calvert Cliffs Coordinating Committee* v. *Atomic Energy Commission*:

The reviewing courts probably cannot reverse a substantive decision [of an administrative
agency] on its merits, under Section 101, unless it be shown that the actual balance of
costs and benefits that was struck was arbitrary or clearly gave insufficient weight to
environmental values. But if the decision was reached procedurally without individualized
consideration and balancing of environmental factors—conducted fully and in good faith—
it is the responsibility of the courts to reverse.

WHAT REMAINS TO BE DONE

In the United States, EIA appears to be securely, if imperfectly, imbedded in
the normal processes of public planning and decision making. In practice, there

remains some resistance, particularly among older federal bureaucrats and self-serving politicians. And there is continuing disagreement over the scope of environmental impact analysis—does it or does it not extend to matters beyond the state of the natural environment—for example, to sociological, psychological, and economic impacts? In general, however, this issue seems to be resolving in favor of broader interpretation. A large number of national governments have now adopted some form of EIA, and the International Union for the Conservation of Nature and Natural Resources (IUCN) has published a description of many of these efforts in the so-called Third World countries. The Commission of the European Community has issued a directive to member states on environmental impact analysis, effective in 1988 (see Chapter 4). A great many experiments have therefore been going under various forms of government and socioecological circumstances. A descriptive and analytic literature has been growing, and there are rational grounds for optimism that the decade of the 1990s will see substantial advances in the technique, substance, and implementation of EIA.

As more is learned about the interrelatedness of environmental trends, the scope of EIA will broaden further. As the interconnectedness of our problems is better understood, EIA will be integrated with analysis of socioeconomic impacts. In the long run, impact analysis will be more firmly built into the normal processes of planning and decision making rather than serve as a post facto check upon them. As the complexity of environmental policy problems is increasingly appreciated, integrated multidisciplinarity will necessarily become the expected, conventional approach to planning and decision making. Subject matter "isolationism" in the conventional academic disciplines will need to be overcome through supplementary and interdisciplinary knowledge if higher education is to help society cope with the dynamically complex problems of the larger world of public affairs.

The experience in the United States may not provide the last or best word in the evolution of EIA. Yet the important contribution of EIA in the United States has been the bringing of ecological rationality to a reorientation of policy thinking and to the redirection of administrative decision making (Bartlett, 1986a; Bartlett, 1986b). NEPA, activated by the EIA requirement, brings a new set of assumptions (substantive precepts) into the decision processes of government that the public officials cannot safely ignore even though they may not yet accept them as fully as they must accept the analytic techniques.

Generically, EIA is an aspect of the information revolution of our time in which knowledge is becoming a growing influence. EIA not only forces environmental knowledge into policy processes where it had hitherto been tendentiously employed, neglected, or rejected; it also reveals the insufficiency of the information upon which society and government often propose to act. Hence EIA is a stimulus both to basic and applied science and to education. The answer to the scientific inadequacies of EIA is not to abandon the process but rather to strengthen the substance and methodology of science. There are important technical requirements for the soundness and reliability of EIA, but it should not be forgotten that EIA is more than a technical process. It is foremost an informing and testing of policy alternatives, and this is its role in NEPA or, at least, its intended role.

EIA, in principle, is now universalized, and governments and other environmental impacting organizations everywhere may benefit from the interchange of experience. Comparative studies of national experience conducted in adequate depth and breadth should be undertaken to advance the prospect that this important contribution to rationality in public policy will fulfill its potential, especially in view of intensifying societal problems. There are abundant signs that modern societies everywhere are in trouble. We see our problems as economic, political, behavioral, demographic, and even environmental—but few see their interconnections. Attempts to solve some of them separately often worsen the others. Examples are colonization schemes in which governments try to cure poverty (or at least remove its presence) by settling poor people on virgin land, destroying forests and irreplaceable biotic resources to relieve a momentary social pressure certain to build up again in the near future unless preventative policies are introduced. Other examples are afforded by large river development projects, especially high-level dams constructed with little regard for socioecological consequences, or famine relief without reforms in agriculture and population growth.

Internationalization of EIA is one established fact; its convergence with other forms of impact analysis is another. In principle, studies undertaken by the International Joint Commission pursuant to references from Canada and the United States approximate the EIA process. The formation of the International Association for Impact Assessment is building a worldwide network of professional analysts, which should facilitate communication across national boundaries. The technical aspects of impact analysis seem certain to improve and to induce a strengthening of their scientific bases. The larger challenge to EIA is not technical; it is political (Caldwell et al., 1983). If EIA is to be more than a ritual, further change in the attitudes and behaviors of political leaders and public officials will be necessary. That this is occurring is suggested by the rise of environmental issues to prominence in the 1988 presidential election in the United States and by the demands for environmental reform spreading throughout the Soviet Union. Growing receptivity to environmental considerations is evident in most developed countries and in many that are less developed. And yet an unsubstantiated faith in solving society's problems through economic growth continues to obstruct consideration of the basic causes of those problems and of alternative ways to cope with them. Thus the most significant development of EIA in the future could be to strengthen and enlarge its role in the policy-making process. But the development has less to do with EIA than with the reorientation of politics and public administration toward meeting the unavoidable challenges of the postmodern age.

We should understand that EIA is not the only, nor a sufficient, answer to coping with the environmental problems of modern society. EIA has been essentially responsive and reactive. It does not initiate policies except by way of alternatives to the proposals investigated. In the United States, NEPA provides a set of positive goals and principles but, other than the EIA process, has no means to activate them. The cutting edge of environmental policy is found where people are afraid—for example, of toxic substances, atomic radiation, or severe environmental degradation in their immediate vicinity. For the present, the governmental response has been regulatory legislation. The root causes of the dangers are not addressed; to do so would imply radical changes in the economy. Yet as people gradually come to understand the more pervasive, longer range, and irreversible effects of "greenhouse gases" and the loss of ozone protection from dangerous solar radiation, a new level of environmental politics is reached. The prompt U.S. Senate ratification of the Montreal Protocol on the ozone layer shows how rapidly latent apprehension can give rise to affirmative political action.

Beyond EIA at least three courses of action are needed to realize the goals stated in NEPA, or in such global efforts as the World Conservation Strategy.

The first is education or, more frankly, indoctrination. Enough is known about man-environment relationships to demolish the argument that humanity is well served by leaving man's beliefs and behaviors to unguided personal choice. The aim of environmental education should be not only knowledge but informed belief. This belief need not be arbitrary or dogmatic; it should assume the need to change with changing evidence. But it should afford the consensual base for public policy that is now relatively weak and which allows the shifts in policy that follow changes among elected governments.

The second need is for a stronger base in law for environmental policy. A legal equivalent to an amendment to the U.S. Constitution is required if the judiciary is to afford more than procedural protection to environmental policies. Canada has moved ahead of the United States in consideration of an environmental bill of rights and crimes against the environment. In the late 1960s, an environmental bill of rights was proposed for the United States, but the nation did not appear to be ready for anything so basic at that time. The provision of "a right to a healthful environment" was deleted in the House-Senate conference from the Senate version of the National Environmental Policy Act. What is not possible today may be possible in the future. One ought not forget that the U.S. Constitution once protected human slavery. When public opinion reaches a point of recognition that human behavior in relation to the biosphere is critical to human welfare and survival, environmental protection will become a fundamental constitutional principle.

Third, the recognition derived from science-based understanding of the life-support systems of the biosphere will extend environmental policy beyond national frontiers. The internationalizing of EIA has already been noted. This recognition will also ultimately be institutionalized in some transnational arrangement. Antecedents of this development have already appeared. The National Environmental Policy Act declares a national purpose "to promote efforts which will prevent or eliminate damage to the environment and biosphere." The Vienna

Treaty and Montreal Protocol for the ozone layer forecast the future internationalization of environmental policy. The EIA directive from the Commission of the European Community to member states exemplifies the internationalization of EIA. The extension of NEPA requirements, including the EIA provisions to actions beyond U.S. territorial jurisdiction by U.S. governmental agencies, further exemplifies the recognition that the ultimate environment of Americans and of all life on Earth is planetary and substantively indivisible.

Unless present global trends in population growth, environmental contamination, deforestation, desertification, and depletion of soil fertility and fresh water are soon arrested and reversed, the world faces an immense tragedy not only for humans, but for nearly all life. Understanding the purpose of EIA in its conceptual and political context is a prior condition for containing these trends. Institutional mechanisms for implementing the understanding is no less necessary. The drafting of the National Environmental Policy Act of 1969 afforded a rare opportunity to infuse an action-forcing procedure of revolutionary potential into the political processes of public planning and decision making. The initial function of EIA was to place a governor on the exuberant expansionism of an unguided technological society. Its dominant function in the future is likely to be in ascertaining the hazards and opportunities that are now being overlooked. It is in this historical context that the significance of EIA is best understood.

3

Making Technology Assessment an Effective Tool to Influence Policy

Vary T. Coates and Joseph F. Coates

Technology assessment, the most general form of impact assessment, is best understood as a subcategory of public policy analysis that emphasizes the anticipation of second- and third-order effects of technological change in the society or economy. This chapter concentrates on the institutionalization of the assessment concept in the U.S. Congress's Office of Technology Assessment (OTA). Some identifiable reasons for OTA's success can be found in its operating practices, compared to those of other institutions and practitioners. The origins of the concept and the history of the OTA (Ferwerda, 1976) are not considered in this chapter; rather, we offer a snapshot and analysis of a functioning activity.

SOME DEFINITIONS

Technology assessment is a class of policy studies that provides decision-makers and stakeholders with a base of information about the possible societal consequences—planned and unplanned, direct and indirect—of the development of new technology or of significant changes in existing technology. As practiced by OTA, it is usually not concerned with a specific project, location, or facility, or with details of a proposed government action, regulation, or law. Technology assessment is an open-ended search, through a variety of qualitative and quantitative techniques, for potential impacts on the economy, the environment, the polity, and social behavior and institutions. It may examine the need for or feasibility of government interventions either to stimulate or to control the development of technology. It maps the uncertainties involved in such interventions and lays before decisionmakers an ordered set of alternative or complementary policy options together with their long-range implications.

Technology assessment uses the methods and approaches of the natural and social sciences and may draw upon analytical algorithms such as cost-benefit analysis, systems analysis, and operations research. Technology assessment draws also on techniques developed for futures research.

After the introduction in 1966 of the concept of technology assessment, a conceptual framework and a considerable body of experience and shared learning were developed. The U.S. Congress established OTA in 1973 as a research and policy analysis unit. Many U.S. agencies established technology assessment programs and in-house technology assessment capabilities at about the same time.

Most of these executive branch experiments no longer exist as organizational entities and the term technology assessment is seldom applied to any U.S. agency practice or program outside of OTA. The Reagan administration was not noted for encouraging futures-oriented policy studies in general, and impact assessment may have had about it an aura of citizen participation and activism too reminiscent of the 1970s. At any rate, formal technology assessment activities tended to be early victims of the budget tightening of the 1980s. Still, federal agencies have been forced by pressure from constituents, as well as by the mirror of critical OTA studies, to continue to pay some attention to downstream effects of their actions.

Under government sponsorship, many university teams have developed experience in technology assessment and, particularly under the auspices of OTA, many private organizations and not-for-profit study organizations have done work in support of technology assessments. In general, nongovernmental research institutions have often been insufficiently sensitive to the needs of political decisionmakers. Assessments must ultimately be judged by the criteria of usefulness to those who would act upon them and reliability in guiding decisions.

THE CONSTITUTIONAL BASES FOR OTA'S SUCCESS

Throughout the 1960s, awareness of the need for better anticipation and management of the consequences of technology was stimulated by the growing complexity of technology and a steady crescendo of technological shortfalls. These contributed both to the environmental movement of the 1970s and to the establishment of OTA. The constitutional separation of powers in the U.S. government made an organization such as OTA timely and practical. A strong trend had developed after World War II for increasing expertise to be concentrated in the hands of the executive relative to the legislature. A further, more pernicious development was that the executive agencies, in justifying their projects and programs, were increasingly likely to mislead Congress about associated risks or social costs. This was true even when the White House and congressional majority were held by the same political party; doubly so when they were not.

Within the Congress itself, there have always been wide differences in the orientation, ambience, skill level, and traditional practices of the House and Senate. Neither speaks with one voice nor do they reflect the same time perspectives, constituents, or interests. Congressional committee staffs are limited and overworked. The Congressional Research Service, doing a massive job of information provision, is intrinsically limited in the attention it can give to any problem. Its tradeoffs and functions favor breadth rather than depth and conventional wisdom rather than critical insights. The General Accounting Office primarily performs an inspector general function, repeatedly addressing the question, "Has the will of the Congress been wrought?" It is primarily constituted to look to the past rather than to the future.

The reliance of Congress on special interest groups as the primary source of external information is another major problem. Even if not biased and distorted in their presentation, such groups collectively present a partial and unintegrated picture of the policy choices facing the Congress.

OTA's charter, the Technology Assessment Act of 1972, says that OTA is to provide Congress with "early indications of the probable beneficial and adverse impacts of the applications of technology and to develop other coordinate information which may assist the Congress." As an organization that exclusively serves the needs of Congress, OTA has been structured and designed to mirror the concerns of Congress in a highly reliable way and to prepare reports which closely fit the congressional processes. These tailored reports are the basis for policy effectiveness.

The organic act gives OTA breadth and flexibility; its operations are not prescribed. The structure of its governing body, the Technology Assessment Board, provides broad political balance and an assurance of evenhandedness and neutrality. Six members from each chamber and six from each party, with a chairmanship and vice chairmanship alternately rotating between chamber and party, assures fairness. The mechanism for the selection of the board is the same as for the selection to committees, which give OTA status. Making the director a nonvoting member gives him status but leaves him little room for independence.

The board process for releasing documents has become an effective mechanism for certifying the process by which the reports are produced. The board does not certify the accuracy of the reports, but it tells the public that the process and outcome were not politically determined. By having decisions as to what project will be undertaken made by the board, the full Congress is alerted to the fact that OTA reflects its interests.

Making committee chairmen or the ranking minority members the primary source of requests for projects again guarantees that narrow political needs of individual members do not dominate OTA's agenda, as they can in other congressional agencies. The most significant operating unit of the Congress, the committee, is the unit to which OTA responds. On the other hand, the requirement for board approval gives assurance that a project is important.

The board itself can originate projects, but, since the early days of OTA, such action has been unusual. That saves OTA from being a playground for an individual member of the board. The director can initiate projects (with board approval), but that has also become rare, again because there is a rich enough menu that his intrusions are not necessary to fill out an agenda.

The operation of OTA is marked by several things beneficial to the practice of technology assession. OTA has roughly twice the budget that it is permitted to expend on internal staff. This assures extensive involvement of outsiders, and it acts as a brake on creating a constantly increasing permanent staff with all the consequences of rigidity that implies. The lean hierarchy—a director, three assistant directors, and nine program managers—is a minimum bureaucracy between the working level projects and the board and primary clients (the committees).

A fellows program brings in sophisticated and skilled outsiders. The extensive use of contractors also contributes to freshness. Quality control is achieved by complementary mechanisms: every project has an advisory panel representing, in principle if not always in fact, a broad spectrum of stakeholders or groups with a direct interest in the issue. The panel also includes academic experts and public interest representatives. Their advice is frequently drawn upon in project formulation, work-plan formulation, review, and the final endorsement of the project report.

The review process is critical. OTA is precluded from making recommendations. The purpose of this restriction, reflecting the needs of the Congress, is to keep OTA from becoming just another special interest with whom committees must deal. OTA's function is to provide balanced, evenhanded analysis of the facts, the situations, and the views of stakeholders. Early in the history of OTA this created some problems, since the customary practice throughout government is to provide reports that attempt to homogenize divergent points of view and paper over difficulties. OTA strategy is the reverse: to lay out the pros and cons and the supporting basis for divergent points of view.

The review of a draft report may involve over a hundred reviewers. That review process reflects a broad spectrum of stakeholder interests; it checks the report's scope, comprehensiveness, objectivity, and analysis; and it provides further exposition of alternative points of view. Even when merely presented as the front matter in the report, the list of reviewers itself demonstrates the attempt to achieve balance and evenhandedness in the document.

Time is the essential factor in high-quality complex work. OTA reports are generously funded and are usually given an extended deadline: a year to a year-and-a-half is typical. Hence, there is ample time to orchestrate the elaborate process described. The procedural rules for accomplishing that effectively make it clear that OTA is buffered from the committees that it serves through the endorsement, certification, and quality control mechanisms of the board. The staff is not permitted to solicit work, although much exchange goes on and a great network of informal relationships exists between the committee staffs and the OTA staff and management.

There is a general openness between the committees and OTA. Staff and members of Congress are invited to sit in on OTA meetings, workshops, and seminars as observers. Meetings are broadly announced and open to the public, so that all stakeholders concerned have access to what is going on.

SOME SHORTFALLS IN OTA

OTA probably rates a general grade of "B" in its performance, in a policy milieu that is generally operating at "C." The shortfall from a grade of "A" results largely because OTA mirrors the wishes of the Congress, which, in spite of the statements of the Organic Act, are sharply and strongly limited. Congress does not necessarily want new, imaginative, bold, or fresh policy options. What it is looking for and what it gets from OTA is an understanding of the issues on the table, who the stakeholders are, and what their concerns are. Consequently, OTA reports generally do not produce fresh or new policy options.

Although Congress claims it is interested in the future, its future tends to be narrow, sectorial, and short term. Consequently, OTA rarely looks broadly at a ten-, twenty-, or fifty-year future. That depth of field could on occasion be political dynamite.

Congress has a multifaceted concern with technology as buyer, user, policymaker, and regulator. It authorizes and appropriates huge sums for technological systems to be used by government in administration, in the delivery of services, and in national defense. Yet Congress is not generally concerned with technology forecasting, and, except perhaps for military and space technology, it does not want "forefront technology." It prefers tried and proven technology, off the shelf, for which there are many competitive vendors.

Congress is also concerned with technological trends in making law and formulating policy. Currently it is much concerned with encouraging scientific research and technological development to ensure our international competitiveness and industrial strength. But this does not imply a need for technological forecasting; Congress has consistently, for example, refused to adopt an industrial policy that would earmark emerging technologies for special encouragement or aging technologies for phasing out.

Finally, Congress regulates technology in the public interest. It considers regulation when technology appears to impinge on public health and safety, or when a change in technology may significantly redistribute costs and benefits and thus generate political conflict. In spite of the recent trend toward deregulation, there is still a strong assumption that technology must operate under constraints necessary for the general welfare, such as protection of the natural environment and conservation of resources.

It was this imperative that led the Congress to establish the Office of Technology Assessment. But neither OTA itself nor the congressional committees that it serves have been willing to push this mandate very far. One of the most frequent and consistent criticisms of OTA has been that the time horizon for its studies is too short; OTA does not often look far beyond technological changes that are already of concern to Congress. This criticism is well founded, and the interest of Congress probably suffers from its institutional shortsightedness.

Nevertheless, as a general strategy, emphasis on the short- and midterm future is justified. Congress is concerned chiefly with political conflict. It should act only when issues fall within the domain of federal responsibility, when they cannot be resolved at lower levels of government, and when they fall outside of already established regulatory domains. Legislative action is ponderous, inflexible, and hard to reverse. A new law quickly becomes overlaid with an administrative and regulatory apparatus that takes on a life of its own. Thus, it is often wise to avoid legislative action where problems are still being clarified and may be transitory and transitional. This drives Congress toward emphasis on the midterm, where the institutional, economic, behavioral, and social context of technological change can be analyzed.

Congressional interest in the future may be increasing. There is a trend for congressional committees to build and maintain expert and stable staffs to deal with the increasingly specialized technical subjects affected by public policy. The expertise available to Congress through OTA and other support agencies also makes it increasingly able to benefit from information about structural, technological, economic, and social trends affecting the society.

There are several congressional activities in which a longer horizon is increasingly desirable. One is the need for budgetary or legislative initiatives to support efforts by the executive branch to deal usefully with global problems such as acid rain and the greenhouse effect or, more realistically, to use congressional oversight to force a reluctant executive branch to respond to such long-range concerns.

The area in which Congress most clearly needs a long-range technological perspective, however, is in the funding of research and development. There is a growing appreciation of the critical importance of science to our international market competitiveness, national security, and public health (see Chapter 9). This may give Congress a stronger interest in long-range anticipation of technological developments.

THE INDIRECT POLICY EFFECTIVENESS OF OTA

The insulation of OTA from the partisan politics of the presidency and from the partisan and nonpartisan politics of Capitol Hill have, through the late 1980s, made it the best policy analytic organization in Washington. As a consequence, OTA has *indirect* policy effectiveness beyond that which would normally accrue to a well-functioning policy organization. The executive agencies have become attuned to OTA as a factor that is not necessarily hostile to the activities of the agencies. It has become, in many cases, an alternate channel for staff who find a problem in breaking through to their own upper management.

Both special interest groups and public interest groups have gained respect for OTA. The antitechnology bias frequently imputed to OTA in the early days proved false. There is a general awareness that OTA is an effective organization and that cooperating with it gives interest groups a voice in the material that reaches Congress.

Having established clear links to the committees, OTA enjoys high prestige in recruiting people to its advisory panels and as consultants or contractors. The work of contractors and consultants is acknowledged in the documents but generally appears in reports only as thoroughly reworked and integrated by the staff. In spite of that anonymity, OTA still draws the best people into the game, a good measure of the effectiveness of OTA.

LIMITED EFFECTIVENESS OF TECHNOLOGY ASSESSMENT ELSEWHERE

Many other U.S. agencies, notably the National Science Foundation (NSF), have attempted programs of technology assessment, which by and large have been either abandoned or transformed into a more dilute and narrow version of assessment.

The NSF program is particularly interesting because it was well funded over nearly a decade, from 1969 to about 1977, but the NSF is primarily a research funding organization. Its primary clientele, the university community, has few incentives to respond to policy issues. The strength of the NSF program was largely exploratory but exemplary in the development of methods and paradigms (Arnstein and Christakis, 1974; Porter et al., 1980; Armstrong and Harmon, 1980).

Executive agencies have generally shied away from assessment; several were burned early in the process. They discovered the hard way that technology assessment, when taken seriously, can often reveal implications and consequences uncongenial to the preconceptions or already implemented plans of the agency. Nor has technology assessment caught on at the state level, although there have been occasional forays in that direction by various legislatures. State legislatures tend to be more politicized in the very narrow sense of the word, less professionally committed, and less experienced in using outside resources than Congress. We believe that situation will change, albeit slowly.

TECHNOLOGY ASSESSMENT IN THE REST OF THE WORLD

There were repeated attempts during the mid–1970s to establish technology assessment mechanisms in the United Kingdom, France, West Germany, the Netherlands, Sweden, Japan, and other countries (Coates and Fabian, 1982).

These attempts faltered or failed. The mechanisms proposed were modeled after the U.S. OTA. In parliamentary countries, parties not in power often favored a parliamentary OTA because it could give them access to information used by the ministries in developing projects and programs for the governing party—including impact assessments that pointed to undesirable secondary effects. Governing parties, not surprisingly, opposed establishment of OTAs for the same reason.

In spite of this, some excellent assessments were carried out: in the Netherlands and West Germany by national ministries of science or development; in Great Britain by a Programmes Analysis Unit established jointly by two government agencies; in Sweden by a special sercretariat within the prime minister's office; and in Japan by the Ministry of International Trade and Industry. A Canadian Royal Commission (the Berger Commission) assessment of the potential impacts of an oil pipeline across Canada (Berger, 1977) was widely recognized as an outstanding model for comprehensive social and environmental impact assessments. There is a voluminous literature on technology assessment in other countries (von Thienen, 1983).

In the mid–1980s, when governmental support for technology assessment was at very low ebb in the United States, a new wave of active interest surfaced in Europe.[1] France established a parliamentary OTA (Office Parlementaire d'Evaluation des Choix Scientifiques et Technologiques), which is still developing its programs and has therefore kept a very low profile during its early years. In West Germany, a movement to establish a parliamentary OTA faltered when a key parliamentarian failed to win re-election, but the Ministry for Research and Development has committed $50 million annually to assessment. Great Britain has a parliamentary committee working on plans for a technology assessment mechanism, likely to begin as a committee staff function but with the possibility of enlargement if it proves useful. The Netherlands established an Office of Technology Assessment as a nongovernmental foundation with support from the Ministry of Education and Science. Austria has an independent technology assessment institute. Switzerland and Sweden have begun technology assessment projects. Discussions and debates about establishing technology assessment institutions are also in progress in other countries. Both the European Parliament and the Commission of the European Community have functioning, productive technology assessment programs.

In developing nations, the concept of impact assessment in international development has been gaining ground (see Chapter 7 and Chapter 8 in this book). It is clearly needed in projects related to river basin development, reforestation, land reform, industrial development, housing development, population resettlement, hazardous waste disposal, and tourism development. Guidelines for impact assessment have been promulgated by international institutions such as the Organization of American States, the World Bank, and the United Nations. (e.g., Organization of American States, 1984). Much of the emphasis has been on project-specific environmental impact assessment, but a major role for technology assessment is evolving as well (Wolf, 1988). The UN Centre for Science and Technology for Development encourages the use of impact assessment. The centre has established an Advance Technology Alert System (ATAS), which it describes as "a think tank and coordinator of [assessment] efforts" (UNCSTD, 1988). The British Commonwealth Science Council has a program to encourage technology assessment in former British colonies.

PROSPECTS FOR THE FUTURE

The outlook for a reinvigorated technology assessment movement in the United States is improving. The example of other nations, growing recognition of the greenhouse effect, and a change of political administration may stimulate a renewed interest in technology assessment mechanisms in the U.S. government. The challenge of alternative institutions for and approaches to technology assessment would be a positive benefit for OTA, which has had a tendency to grow complacent and unadventuresome in its work; it would be an even greater benefit for the nation and its government. But as the experience of the last fifteen years demonstrates, technology assessment is not automatically useful in policy making even if it is technically well done. It must be institutionalized in ways that facilitate and encourage its use. Simultaneously it must be recognized that structures and processes in turn determine the kind of technology assessment that will be done and how adequate it will be as a tool for informing choices about a technological future.

NOTE

1. These developments are only partially reported and described in published literature as yet. The most comprehensive current description in English is a multivolume report on activities in nineteen countries, published jointly by the Dutch Ministry of Education and Science, the FAST Programme of the Commission of the European Communities, and The Netherlands Organization of Technology Assessment and Organization for Applied Scientific Research, based on a European Congress on Technology Assessment held in Amsterdam (Dutch Ministry of Education and Science et al., 1987). Another source, not available in English, is a study for the Austrian Academy of Sciences, Technology Assessment Unit (Rakos, Braun, and Nentwich, 1988).

4

Implementing Supranational Policy: Environmental Impact Assessment in the United Kingdom

Peter Wathern

In the evolving relationship between the United Kingdom (UK) and the European Economic Community—now commonly known as the European Community (EC)—environmental impact assessment (EIA) may yet be seen to occupy a pivotal position. Previously, the UK has successfully contained EC policy initiatives not seen to be in the immediate national interest. EIA procedures, however, have been adopted during an important period of reform in EC practice with respect to environmental policy. As a consequence, the UK has failed in its attempt to use a tried and tested strategy in dealings with the EC.

Over EIA, the UK has been forced to retreat from a position, held since the 1970s, that there would be no mandatory EIA provisions in UK planning law. The concessions made by the UK during formulation of the EC EIA provisions are reviewed in Wathern (1988b;1988c). Further concessions, probably of greater significance, were wrested during the implementation phase. In this chapter, it is argued that implementation of the EC EIA provisions will effect a major change in UK environmental policy. Indeed, when seen in conjunction with the evidence in Macrory (1986), this may represent part of a more fundamental shift in the UK environmental policy style.

UK PRACTICE IN IMPLEMENTING EC ENVIRONMENTAL POLICY

The EC is a form of supranational government currently comprising twelve member states. Member states have chosen, with varying degrees of enthusiasm, to cede some of their sovereign powers to the Council of Ministers, the decision-making body of the EC. Ceding power to the EC has always been viewed by some UK Parliamentarians with great suspicion. It is considered a fundamental erosion of UK independence, even though, constitutionally, the Council of Ministers comprises the twelve foreign ministers of the member states. Clearly, one function of any member of the Council of Ministers is to balance carefully national interests against the broader concerns of the EC as it moves toward full integration. The UK is sometimes seen to set its own narrow national interests above those of the EC and is considered a less than enthusiastic member of the EC.

In terms of adopting EC legislation, however, the UK record is exemplary. In contrast, certain other member states, such as Italy and Greece, have great difficulties, verging on apparent reluctance, in adopting EC requirements, and thus often appear before the European Court charged with a failure to adopt individual EC measures. Rarely has the UK even been threatened with court action. Paradoxically, despite this record, it is the UK which is perceived as the reluctant participant when it comes to EC environmental policy.

UK administrative procedures are generally closed to outside scrutiny, which makes it impossible to piece together the rationale for a particular decision and even more so to elucidate the bargaining which may have taken place within ministries, between ministries, and between the UK and the EC in the period leading up to that decision. Often the decision stands as the sole indication of intent. Only rarely will evidence more substantial than hearsay and unattributed leak come to light. With respect to implementing any EC provisions that impinge upon the environment, there is some evidence to suggest that the UK government has sought to sustain the status quo and the retention of its established administrative procedures.

Directives are the favored administrative device for EC environmental policy (Haigh, 1984). A directive sets binding policy objectives, but leaves the means for realizing these objectives to be devised by each member state. It is seen as a flexible policy instrument that takes account of the diverse administrative systems that exist in the various member states. EIA was introduced into the EC by means of a directive (Council of the European Communities, 1985).

The adoption of EC environmental policy by member states, therefore, involves two stages. First, the directive must be incorporated into national law. Second, it must be implemented. The consistency of the UK in adopting EC measures can be explained largely in terms of its legislative style. Much UK legislation can be described as "enabling" in that it sets relatively broad policy objectives and then empowers ministers to adopt the necessary instruments to achieve them. There is a tendency to elaborate procedures for decision making rather than to define express goals to be achieved. Consequently, change may be effected by secondary means, such as statutory instruments and government circulars, which can be formulated and adopted rapidly. Regulatory powers are often consolidated into large pieces of cornerstone legislation. For example, most pollution control and wildlife conservation powers are found in single pieces of legislation, the Control of Pollution Act 1974 and the Wildlife and Countryside Act 1981, respectively.

One consequence of this legislative system is that often the powers to implement EC environmental policy already exist in related domestic legislation. For example, the various facets of the EIA directive have been adopted under provisions contained within the Town and Country Planning Act 1971, the Agriculture Act 1986, the Forestry Act 1967, the Coast Protection Act 1949, and the Land Drainage Act 1976. EC directives, however, sometimes require the exercise of powers not currently available under domestic legislation. Even in these instances, new primary legislation is unnecessary, as Section 2(2) of the European Communities Act 1972 provides a vehicle for their rapid adoption. This explains why the UK's record in adopting EC provisions has been so good. Legally, the process is an easy one.

The strategy adopted by the UK to defend national interests over EC environmental policy is a dual one. In part, the strategy depends upon paring away elements of proposed policies which are seen to be against the national interest during the formulation stage, so called preadoption emasculation. Formulation of the EC EIA directive was a protracted affair which began with the presentation of a proposed draft to the EC Commission—the EC bureaucracy—in 1976 (Lee and Wood, 1976). During the nine-year period spent refining the directive—it was finally adopted in 1985—individual member states were able to effect significant changes (see Wathern, 1988b; 1988c).

In part, UK strategy also involves nullifying the effects of a policy through the procedures adopted to implement it, so called postimplementation deflection. Wathern et al. (1987) have argued against reliance upon a purely legislative review in assessing compliance with EC provisions.

UK IMPLEMENTATION OF THE EIA DIRECTIVE

The ways in which individual member states were able to curtail the scope of the EIA directive during its formulation are discussed in Wathern (1988c). From the perspective of the UK, there appeared to be no outstanding issues to resolve during implementation. It seemed likely that implementation procedures could be drawn up rapidly and without controversy, but in fact the process has presented some difficulties and has raised some important issues. The primary concern has been the so-called Annex II projects. These are the categories of projects listed in Annex II to the directive which, under Article 4(2) "shall be subject to an assessment . . . where Member States consider that their characteristics so require." To this end, "Member States may . . . specify certain types of projects as being subject to an assessment or may establish the criteria and/ or thresholds necessary to determine which of the projects of the classes listed in Annex II are to be subject to an assessment" (Article 4[2]).

Development of the implementation procedures has been marked by four main events. When it became apparent that the Council of Ministers would adopt the directive at its June 1985 meeting, the UK government began to develop implementation procedures, with a view to having them in place long before the official compliance date, 3 July 1988. Thus, in April 1985 a working party was set up with the mandate of formulating guidelines for central government on how the directive should be implemented. The working group comprised representatives of central government departments, primarily the Department of the Environment (DOE), local government officials representing district and county councils, industry, and an amenity society. It was anticipated that the group would report fairly rapidly so that central government could issue a consultative document for public review in late autumn 1985.

The notable absentee from the working group was the Ministry of Agriculture, Fisheries and Food (MAFF). Traditionally one of the powerful, high-spending ministries within government, the relationship of the DOE to MAFF can be described as one of long-standing subservience. When the original town and country planning legislation was enacted in 1947, MAFF was able to secure the exclusion of most forestry and agricultural practice from its provisions. Similarly, much agricultural practice is statutorily exempt from the Control of Pollution Act 1974. Over the years, the environmental lobby has made many attempts to persuade central government to extend the jurisdiction of planning legislation to all aspects of agriculture and forestry. All have foundered. Most have simply been ignored by MAFF, content that its preserve was safe from environmental interference. Even though certain agricultural projects are included in Annex II, MAFF did not participate in the working group, secure in the knowledge that, in the past, similar problems had simply disappeared provided they were ignored.

Although the report of the working group has never been published, it is clear that some of its suggestions were unpalatable to central government. Annex II projects, however, did not appear to be an issue, for the confidential report of the working group stated that the UK government did not intend to extend mandatory EIA to Annex II projects. In effect, the UK interpretation of the directive was that the government could foresee no circumstances where such projects would warrant EIA. If the UK could sustain this interpretation, there would be no extension of mandatory EIA procedures to agriculture and forestry, thereby vindicating MAFF's decision not to join the working party.

DOE's consultative document on implementation was not released until April 1986. Of the issues raised, only those related to Annex II are discussed here. Its main conclusion was that the "requirements of the directive can be met within the context of existing planning system" (Department of the Environment, 1986:2).

In the words of a senior civil servant involved in developing the implementation procedures, the assumption that "it would be open to the Government not to make Assessment compulsory for Annex II projects" (Fuller, 1986:7) clearly underpins the consultative document. With respect to Annex II provisions, the document states that the UK government did not "foresee that it will be necessary to make carrying out of formal assessments mandatory" (Department of the Environment, 1986:3). Instead, it was proposed that the secretary of state should be empowered to require the preparation of an assessment for "particular Annex II projects which are so substantial in their environmental impact that a formal assessment should be carried out" (Department of the Environment, 1986:3). Implicit is that such developments were unlikely in the UK.

As well as wishing to curtail the extension of formal EIA procedures in the UK, central government was intent on preventing local authorities from using the directive to extend their powers. Consequently, planning authorities were advised that it would not be appropriate for them to request assessments from a developer, except for Annex I projects (under Article 4[1] of the directive, EIA for such projects is mandatory). Clearly, the UK government was intent on retaining a central constraint on the proliferation of EIA.

From the consultative document, it appears that the UK government intended to implement the EC directive in such a way that no material change in established practice would occur. The first indication that this strategy was not permissible came in September 1985 when a senior official of the commission outlined the view that Annex II was not considered optional by the commission. There is a clear conflict between this statement and the UK position as expressed in the consultative document. If the commission's view prevailed, the UK would be required to determine those Annex II projects that would be subject to mandatory EIA.

Member states are required to advise the commission of the provisions that will be adopted to implement a directive. After publication of the consultative document, there was another protracted delay during which the UK was informed by the commission that its intended procedures would not comply with respect to Annex II projects. At this stage, the UK seems to have accepted this ruling. Had it not done so the commission could have instigated procedures to enforce compliance. This involves a series of official warnings issued by the commission followed by the ultimate sanction of an appearance before the European Court. The court can order compliance after a ruling in favor of the commission. The UK elected not to "tough out" adherence to its view.

In January 1988, the impact of the commission's interjection became apparent when the DOE issued a second consultative paper detailing the mechanisms to give effect to the directive (Department of the Environment, 1988). The minister proposed to issue regulations to be set before Parliament in a statutory instrument, a form of secondary legislation. In addition, it was proposed that departmental circulars would be issued advising local authorities how the regulations should be interpreted. The consultative document consisted of a draft of the proposed circular; draft procedures for implementing the regulations; criteria and thresholds for determining which Annex II projects would be subject to assessment; and proposals by MAFF and the Forestry Commission (covering agriculture and forestry), the Department of Transport (highways and ports), the Department of Energy (power stations and transmission lines), and the Crown Estate Commissioners (mineral extraction and fish farming) to cover Annex II projects outside planning legislation.

As a result of these consultations, the UK government drew up its formal procedures for implementating the directive. In the remainder of this discussion only those provisions that relate to developments under the planning acts and to agriculture and forestry projects are considered. The provisions are specified in statutory instruments set before Parliament on 12 June 1988—to come into effect on 15 July 1988—with, in the case of projects falling under the planning acts, a supporting departmental circular released on 12 July 1988 (Department of the Environment, Welsh Office, 1988).

Appendix A to the circular specifies thresholds for Annex II projects. Whereas the draft issued for consultation in January 1988 contained thresholds for agricultural projects, extractive industries, local roads, airports and other infrastructure projects, and waste disposal facilities, the circular has been extended to include a major section on defining thresholds for urban developments projects. Thus, there has been a constant expansion in the interpretation of the applicability of the directive's provisions.

Whereas the secretary of state initially intended to reserve for himself these powers (Department of the Environment, 1986), the circular makes it clear that for Annex II projects "it will fall initially to local planning authorities to consider whether a proposed development requires environmental assessment" (Department of the Environment, Welsh Office, 1988:3). The key test is whether they are likely to lead to significant environmental effects. The circular advises planning authorities that these conditions are likely to be met for "major projects which are of more than local importance . . . occasionally for projects on a smaller scale which are proposed for particularly sensitive or vulnerable locations . . . [and] . . . for projects with unusually complex and potentially adverse environmental effects, where expert and detailed analysis . . . would be relevant to the issue of principle as to whether or not development should be permitted" (Department of the Environment, 1988:4).

IMPLICATIONS FOR EIA IN THE UK

The UK government has always had an ambivalent attitude toward EIA. While arguing consistently that there was no need for formal EIA procedures, government departments began to fund research on EIA as early as 1973. The results of this research (Clark et al., 1976) were published in such a way that DOE could commend EIA as a methodological approach to project assessment, without being formally committed to adopting EIA procedures. That the UK sought significant changes in the EC directive during its formulation is consistent with this position. These modifications were designed to ensure that there would be no significant change in UK practice (Wathern, 1988c). Yet, at the time that this bargaining to curtail the directive was taking place, one government department, the Ministry of Defence, was already changing its procedures by preparing an EIA for the redevelopment of the Faslane nuclear submarine base. Furthermore, Foster (1984) has argued that this EIA would have complied with the directive then under discussion. Clearly, one ministry was taking out insurance.

During the early 1970s, the UK was grappling with a whole new complex of development proposals associated with the emerging North Sea oil and gas industry. Planners in central and local government had little experience with such developments and, perhaps, viewed EIA as a powerful weapon to redress somewhat the inequality in information between the planners and the developers over such projects. EIAs began to be produced on an ad hoc basis. The first EIA undertaken in the UK was partly funded by central government.

The subsequent history of EIA has been one of dual evolution. While central government was advocating a cautious approach to EIA and the Confederation of British Industry was arguing for a rejection of formal EIA procedures, developers were quick to realize the full potential of EIA. British Gas was, perhaps, the first major developer to adopt EIA procedures voluntarily on a regular basis. Its reason for doing so was not to protect the environment nor to lead to better decisions on development proposals, but simply as a means of facilitating the decision-making process. In the context of "time is money," British Gas considered EIA a wise and cost-effective investment. Over the years, numerous other developers have come to the same realization.

The reality of EIA in the UK prior to the implementation of the EC directive, therefore, was a situation in which EIA was carried out for many developments. Consequently, the question must be raised as to whether the EC directive was necessary and whether the UK has made any significant concessions in the implementation procedures adopted during July 1988. In both cases it appears that the answer must be "yes," although time will provide the definitive judgment.

The reason given by developers for producing an EIA, namely that it accelerates the decision-making process, should never be the justification for a measure which is essentially an element of preventive environmental policy. With implementation of the directive, the initiative for deciding that an EIA should be prepared has been wrested from the developer. In the future, the justification for EIA in a particular situation will be the anticipated improvement in the quality of the decision.

Developers may welcome the UK decision to accept the need for Annex II thresholds as it may remove some uncertainty from the process. A developer with a proposal above the threshold will know that the planning authority may require an EIA. Furthermore, the procedure which permits developers, prior to the submission of an application, to obtain a ruling from the planning authority on whether an EIA will be required should also help to remove uncertainty.

This procedure should encourage greater contact between the developer and the planning authority during project formulation. Although this should lead to a more focused EIA, the lack of any formal scoping procedures involving the public at the preapplication stage still remains a weakness of the UK system. This can only lead to confrontation when EIAs are produced without public involvement.

Perhaps time will reveal that the most significant amendment incorporated into the directive had nothing to do with the UK. When Denmark secured the exclusion of all projects authorized by an act of national government, immense scope for evasion was opened up. Two of the most environmentally significant development projects in the UK in the past decade have been authorized along this route. The Windscale reprocessing plant (see Clark, Bisset and Wathern, 1981) and the Channel Tunnel (see Wathern, 1987) were authorized as a result of hybrid bills enacted by Parliament and, as such, would not have been subject to the provisions of the directive. The advantage of such hybrid bills is that they are exempt from the formal public consultation required under Article 6(2) of the directive. In the case of the Channel Tunnel, public consultation consisted of the presentation of ''evidence'' before a select committee of Parliament, a procedure that was over in a matter of days and left the participants dissatisfied.

The normal method of public consultation on major developments in the UK, the public inquiry, may be a protracted procedure. For example, the proposal to build the first pressurized water reactor nuclear power plant in the UK, Sizewell B, was delayed by more than two years by a public inquiry. In the future, the attraction of using hybrid bill procedures in order to avoid long delays will probably prove irresistible for projects, such as the Channel Tunnel, which carry a high degree of government commitment.

Over the course of a short Parliamentary debate, it would be impossible for the environmental effects of a project to be given adequate consideration. If the debate were drawn up along party political lines, it is likely that environmental considerations would carry little weight. Those looking to the EC directive to further their hopes for enhanced influence of environmental considerations in the decision-making process will be frustrated in their aspirations whenever hybrid bill procedures are used. The threat from hybrid bills is not confined to major developments, for the procedures have been used over a long period to authorize many more mundane projects. For example, the state railway company, British Rail, almost invariably uses this route.

The Danish amendment, however, poses another threat. Development authorization is often sought from Parliament using another devise, so-called private bills. Any individual or organization can petition Parliament to enact a private bill. Developments authorized in this way would be outside the scope of the directive. Hampshire County Council, for example, recently attempted to use a private bill to obtain permission for a road through part of the New Forest, an area of great cultural, historical, scenic, and wildlife importance in an attempt to cut across a complex legal situation and to circumvent established planning procedures. It is essential, therefore, that private bills be scrutinized very carefully, for many developments are authorized on scanty environmental evidence.

As well as these potential hazards, there are major benefits from implementing the directive. Of note are the important changes that have occurred in the assessment of some categories of development. Thus, for the first time since town and country planning legislation came into effect, certain agricultural and forestry developments are subject to formal environmental assessment procedures. The directive has forced MAFF to compromise the position that it had been able to sustain throughout the postwar period. EIA will be mandatory, for example, for major agricultural drainage projects, many of which have been criticized for their environmental impact. Similarly, both public and grant-aided private sector large-scale afforestation in particularly sensitive areas, such as national parks, will require EIA.

The political strength of the farming lobby has been eroded somewhat in the past three or four years as a result of vast surpluses of produce and a spiralling agricultural budget which consumes most of the available EC resources. The UK treasury, intent on severely curtailing public expenditure, has identified environmental arguments as a valuable bolster to its position. MAFF, therefore, was not in a strong position to resist the imposition of EIA procedures on certain of its activities.

For another state organization, the Crown Estate Commissioners, the provisions of the directive may even prove to be a welcome additional reponsibility. The commissioners are responsible for licensing certain activities in coastal waters. Of greatest environmental significance are mineral extraction (in particular, dredged aggregates) and offshore salmon farming. There has been a dramatic rise in the number of salmon farms in coastal waters in recent years, particularly in the deep sea lochs of the west coast of Scotland. Environmentalists have been concerned about the possible environmental effects, mainly visual impact and pollution from food residues and pharmaceuticals.

By 1 August 1988 the Crown Estate Commissioners had not produced final implementation procedures, but it is clear that new salmon farms will require EIAs when located in particularly sensitive locations. This will probably include most of the west coast of Scotland, much of which has been given "preferred conservation status." Thus, there will be an onus on the developer to investigate possible impacts as a prerequisite to licensing. At present there is a dearth of information with which to address the concerns of the environmentalists, but the EIA directive will stimulate research on this topic. At least one government agency, therefore, is being required formally to consider environmental matters in decision making for the first time.

CONCLUSION

In Wathern (1988c) the ways in which the UK eroded the provisions of the EC EIA directive during formulation were highlighted. When that paper was written (January 1988), the procedures for implementing the directive were still evolving. Past experience suggested that the UK would employ a dual strategy to contain the impact of a directive which was seen to carry significant administrative costs, but few political benefits. There was no reason to believe that a combination of preadoption emasculation and postimplementation deflection—successful in the past—would not be used again. The first part of the strategy was indeed successfully applied, but the UK encountered difficulties in its attempt to adopt neutral implementation procedures.

This failure can be explained primarily in terms of a change in EC practice. It is clear that the commission has now resolved to discourage mere legislative compliance. In three recent instances, the UK has been threatened with court action over the bathing beach directive, and has complied; it has been warned that its nitrate standard would not give compliance with the drinking water directive, and has adopted a more stringent one; and it has been prevented from exempting Annex II projects in the EIA directive from mandatory assessment.

Even the first part of the dual strategy now looks far from secure. The UK preadoption emasculation approach was developed to deal with a perceived threat to the national environmental policy style, and it depended upon the veto which, at that time, was available to every member state. EC procedures, however, evolve, and the ability of any member state to operate a veto, as the Danes and the UK, among others, did so successfully with the EIA directive, has now disappeared. In 1985, the Council of Ministers, frustrated by UK resistance to a directive concerned with the use of growth regulators in animal husbandry, adopted the measure on a majority vote. The procedure was almost certainly illegal at that time, but the UK, outmaneuvered, felt compelled to adopt its provisions. The Council of Ministers has since decided to adopt majority voting procedures for enacting environmental provisions. Whether the UK can continue to use its preadoption emasculation approach successfully in the future, therefore, is also being called into question.

5

Environmental Assessment, Science, and Policy Failure: The Politics of Nuclear Waste Disposal

Bruce B. Clary
and Michael E. Kraft

Five years after its enactment, the Nuclear Waste Policy Act (NWPA) of 1982 was demonstrably a case of policy failure. The ambitious plan of the U.S. government to survey and evaluate possible sites for permanent, mined geologic repositories for high-level radioactive waste ran into the formidable barrier of public fear and opposition and seemingly the familiar not-in-my-backyard (NIMBY) syndrome. Public officials in all of the affected states were quick to align themselves with that public sentiment. In the face of such massive public and state resistance to the preliminary site evaluation process, mounting lawsuits against the Department of Energy (DOE), and concern over the political fallout of those events in an election year, the Reagan administration put the act's implementation on hold in late May 1986; in effect, it acknowledged that the NWPA could not be implemented as originally designed, and it looked to Congress for redirection. Congress responded in December 1987 with a midcourse correction to the act that it hoped would save the waste disposal program and produce an operational repository early in the twenty-first century.

Our interest here is in the impact assessment process built into the 1982 act, which called for a systematic and objective survey of hundreds of possible sites in the nation and an elaborate environmental assessment of the approximately two dozen sites considered most suitable for a repository. In its policy revision of late 1987, Congress abandoned the initial requirement of evaluating multiple sites for a repository for a simpler, less costly, and more politically attractive evaluation of a single site at Yucca Mountain, Nevada. Should DOE's review of that site indicate that it is not technically suitable, the department once again will have to turn to Congress for guidance (Davis, 1987). Given these recent decisions, analysis of the role of the environmental assessments (EAs) in the act's implementation from 1982 to 1987 should tell us much about their potential, limitations, and effects in this case while also speaking to the broader question of how impact assessments affect the policy process.

We are concerned with several questions: What kind of assessments were mandated by the 1982 act, and how were those provisions implemented? What did the assessments indicate about the possible environmental impacts of repository siting, and how were those conclusions received by state officials, Indian tribes, and the public in the affected states? What can be said about the major effects of the assessments on the policy process? In particular, in what ways was the assessment process a positive contribution to DOE's implementation of the act? To what extent was it a constraint on implementation, leading to increased opposition to DOE's efforts? We begin with an overview of the NWPA itself and then turn to the assessments conducted in both the western and the eastern United States and their impact on the policy process.

THE NUCLEAR WASTE POLICY ACT OF 1982

Formulation of a national policy on nuclear waste disposal became possible only with a series of developments in the early 1970s. Until then one might best characterize the federal government's handling of the nuclear waste problem as neglect; it was viewed as a nonproblem or a back-door problem by all of the key policy actors in the subgovernment that dominated the nuclear power arena: the nuclear industry, the Atomic Energy Commission (AEC), and the congressional Joint Committee on Atomic Energy. This relatively small and homogeneous group shared a confidence that simple technical measures would be sufficient to solve the waste problem and that there was no urgency to adopt a national policy (Carter, 1987). This orientation is evident in a 1960 report by the AEC: "Waste problems have proved completely manageable in the operations of the Commission and of its predecessor war-time agency. . . . There is no reason to believe that proliferation of wastes will become a limiting factor on future development of atomic energy for peaceful purposes" (U.S. Atomic Energy Commission, 1960). Consistent with this pattern, when a National Academy of Sciences report (1957) called for policy action in the mid–1950s, it had no discernible effect on the prevailing technological optimism and complacency.

The politics of nuclear waste began to change in the early 1970s. There were many reasons for the shift, but chief among them were (1) the mounting quantity of nuclear waste; (2) increasing public fear of the risks associated with nuclear power and waste, attributable in part to problems of leakage at some military storage facilities (e.g., in Hanford, Washington) and difficulties with early efforts to locate a waste repository near Lyons, Kansas; (3) organized opposition by environmental groups concerned about continued reliance on nuclear power itself; (4) apprehension in the nuclear power industry (largely sparked by state actions, such as a referendum in California, which linked future development of nuclear power to solving the waste problem) that, without a quickly approved national solution, the future of commercial nuclear power would be in jeopardy; and (5) the decision made by the Carter Administration to terminate reprocessing of nuclear waste, which implied a much larger quantity that would have to be stored or disposed of in some manner (Kearney and Garey, 1982; Graham, 1984; Downey, 1985). The combined effects of these changes were to push the issues from the back to the front burner, to broaden significantly the set of participants in policy making, and to introduce more critical perspectives on the problem of radioactive waste.

Perhaps the most important of these factors in shaping the new policy climate was the rapid increase in the amount of waste being generated, especially after the decision to end reprocessing. The stock of commercial spent fuel rods (the major component of civilian high-level waste, which in turn is the largest component of nuclear waste measured by radioactivity) in 1982 totaled some 10,000 metric tons, and by 1985 was accumulating at about 3,000 tons per year; by the year 2000, the amount was expected to grow to about five times the 1985 total, and by the year 2020 reach some 130,000 metric tons (U.S. Council on Environmental Quality, 1986:353). Although stored successfully in surface, water-filled basins at commercial reactor sites for close to twenty years in some cases, such storage is widely considered to be insufficient for long-term needs. Thus a permanent disposal method was sought, one that could be relied on to isolate these wastes from the biosphere for thousands of years (Gould, 1983).

An equally important factor affecting formulation of the 1982 act was public fear of nuclear waste and the anticipated NIMBY reaction.[1] Nuclear waste is perceived as far more threatening than most other societal risks, and public attitudes on the issue have proved difficult to change (Slovic and Fischhoff, 1983). Yet experience with the location of hazardous waste facilities shows that some degree of public acceptance of the siting process is needed if major delays and possibly defeat of the siting proposal are to be avoided. Hence the act had to be written to consider public concerns and to provide suitable mechanisms for public and state participation. The impact assessments were a key part of this policy design; the information they contained, along with what was to be a rigorous technical screening process, was intended to reinforce the credibility of DOE's site evaluation procedures and to build confidence in, and promote acceptability of, the final siting decisions. As might have been anticipated from the federal government's experience with environmental impact statements (EISs), however, such information may also stimulate opposition to the siting process by increasing public concern about the safety or environmental impact of the repositories.

The factors noted above shaped the general political climate for nuclear waste disposal. The particular design of the 1982 act was set during the late 1970s as an outgrowth of the Carter administration's efforts to formulate a comprehensive national energy policy. Carter established an Interagency Review Group (IRG) in 1977 to assess the scope of the nuclear waste problem and to devise a national plan of action (see Colglazier, 1982). After an elaborate study and wide circulation of its draft recommendations, the IRG report became the basis for Carter's recommendations to Congress in February 1980 (Interagency Review Group, 1979). Congress struggled with a number of different bills on low-level and high-level waste over a period of several years. In 1980 it approved the least controversial part of the Carter proposal as the Low-Level Radioactive Waste Policy Act, which gave states (through the formulation of regional compacts) the responsibility for disposal of low-level waste produced by private industry (see Kearney and Stucker, 1985). After another two years of intense controversy, centering on the authority of states to veto placement of a repository within their borders, the NWPA was approved on 20 December 1982, the last day of the 97th Congress.

Signed by President Reagan on 7 January 1983, the NWPA (Public Law 97–425) established a comprehensive national program for the permanent disposal of high-level commercial and military radioactive waste in mined geologic repositories. It created an Office of Civilian Radioactive Waste Management (OCRWM) within DOE to implement the program, and it established a selection process for two disposal sites that included extensive state and public involvement. A detailed schedule for the repository siting process was set out in the act. The secretary of energy was required to study five potential sites for the first repository, to conduct environmental assessments of them, and to recommend three of the sites to the president by 1 January 1985, to be followed by further site characterization. Five more potential sites, at least three of which were not in the first group, were to be studied and three of them recommended to the president by 1 July 1989, for a second repository. Other guidelines were set for DOE to follow in locating a site, including holding hearings in the vicinity of each site being considered. Although not specified in the act, one of the key congressional compromises was that one site would be in the West and the other in the East or Midwest, to avoid placing the risk entirely on one state or region as well as to secure sufficient agreement to pass the act.

The president was to make his recommendation to Congress on the first site by 31 March 1987, and for the second site by 31 March 1990; the deadlines could be extended for one year at the discretion of the president. A full EIS was required only when a site was selected by DOE for recommendation to the president as a repository, and the facility was also to be fully licensed by the Nuclear Regulatory Commission (NRC). Prior to that time, the less comprehensive and less rigorous EAs were thought to be sufficient. In addition, judicial review was allowed for any final decision or action of the secretary of energy, the president, or the NRC in selecting a site for and constructing a repository, and the completion of an EA was defined in the law as such a final action. As is evident in even this brief summary, many points of likely contention, review, appeal, and thus potential delay were built into the siting process (see U.S. Office of Technology Assessment, 1985).

We will concentrate here on the environmental assessments and their impact on the siting process for the two disposal sites under NWPA. The act was specific about how these sites were to be assessed—and what contribution the EAs were expected to make to decision making; the EAs were considered critical for successful implementation of NWPA. The assessments in the West and East were different in many respects, but there were similar technical and political expectations. The most important of these was that multiple sites were to be evaluated using a rigorous set of technical guidelines. The assessments were to address physical, social, and environmental impacts of site characterization (the actual testing of a potential site), repository siting, construction, and operation, making use of both the natural and social sciences. These assessments, like EISs, were to be subject to review and comment through a conventional hearing process, which was expected to encourage public and state acceptance of the overall repository program.

The site assessment process did not work the way the policy's designers and DOE imagined it would. Political response to the EAs was colored to a considerable extent by public fear of nuclear waste and by the prevailing attitude among state officials and Indian tribal leaders with whom DOE was required to negotiate under NWPA's "consultation and cooperation" provisions; the position of state and Indian leaders was described by one DOE official as one of "unalterable opposition and dedication to stopping us [which didn't] leave any room for negotiation." Eventually, this political stance forced Congress to revise the act.

Potentially, the assessments could have provided credible technical data to address concerns over the environmental and social impacts of a repository program. This was not the result, however, in either the West or the East. In both cases, the assessments were attacked as scientifically unreliable and biased. That outcome was to some extent anticipated by representatives for a number of federal agencies (including the Environmental Protection Agency [EPA], the U.S. Geological Survey [USGS], and the NRC) during congressional hearings on the act in 1981. They argued that insufficient time would be provided under the act's fast-track schedule to conduct proper assessments. For example, the USGS representative noted that, although the technical information needs for repository evaluation were fairly well understood, many of the geologic, hydrologic, and engineering test procedures had yet to be developed. The agency believed that it was highly unlikely that adequate earth-science information would be available by the proposed deadlines to allow DOE to make an objective decision about potential sites (U.S. Congress, 1981). Concerns about such scientific deficiencies were not as salient as other issues, however, and there were intense pressures (especially from industry) to adopt a rapid siting schedule. As a result, Congress decided to leave the proposed schedule largely intact.

By the mid–1980s, when the EAs for the western sites were being prepared, it became clear that the requisite scientific developments for the program to be implemented on schedule had not occurred. DOE found itself in the unenviable position of having to balance the political demands of Congress against the ability of science to provide an answer regarding how a site should be assessed and what technology of nuclear waste isolation should be employed. Congress failed to appreciate that public fear of nuclear waste in combination with the weak scientific base for the assessments would likely undermine the act's implementation, especially in light of criticism of DOE's prior record for handling waste.

We do not know, and can only speculate on, whether assessments that were more scientifically defensible would have altered this outcome. Conceivably, they would have been no more successful in alleviating public fears and stemming what seemed to be inevitable state and local opposition to siting a repository. At a minimum, however, a slower process of site evaluation would have provided more time for the necessary scientific information to be collected and analyzed, and assessments prepared under such circumstances probably would have fared better in the harsh light of public scrutiny. Presumably, they would have been less susceptible to legal challenge as well.

THE FIRST ROUND SITING PROCESS

EA Methodology and Findings

At the heart of the repository siting process is a sequence of five decision points which lead to the location of a facility: site screening, site nomination, recommendation for characterization, site characterization, and site selection. Only the first three stages are pertinent given the five-year life of the original act. Under the 1987 revision, however, the fourth stage, an elaborate characterization of the Yucca Mountain site, began in 1988, and will take almost five years to complete, will cost over $1 billion, and will involve about 800 scientists. This new and comprehensive assessment effort puts the earlier analyses into a useful comparative perspective; they were far more modest in scope, relied heavily on secondary data, and involved many uncertainties about how to evaluate the environmental risks of siting a repository. These limitations in the first assessment process proved to be highly significant factors in the political response to DOE's efforts.

The first of the three stages in the original siting proces was determination of whether a location is potentially acceptable as a repository site. This decision is based on an evaluation of largely pre-existing sources of information. Detailed geological data are not collected until a site has actually been recommended for further study. While a reasonable procedure from a scientific perspective, because this stage of the analysis is clearly preliminary, the political ramifications of the approach were significant. DOE studies were continually criticized for a lack of site-specific information, leading to more general assertions that the agency was not doing a thorough analysis.

Site nomination for characterization was the second stage of the evaluation process. This part of the act requires the preparation of environmental assessments. In December 1984, DOE issued nine draft EAs for public comment for what became known as the First Round of repository siting. These EAs involved sites in six states: Washington, Nevada, Texas, Utah, Mississippi, and Louisiana. Over 20,000 comments were received on the EAs, an unmistakable indication of the saliency of the nuclear waste issue in these states. From this list of nine sites, DOE selected the final three candidate sites for the first waste repository: Yucca Mountain, Nevada; Deaf Smith County, Texas; and Hanford, Washington.

The EAs were similar in scope and content to EISs, and all were quite long, averaging nearly 1,000 pages. The findings, presented in largely narrative terms, were divided into four major parts. First, a site was described in very general terms to answer the question of why it was being considered for nomination. Second, site characterization was discussed from two perspectives: the effects on public health, safety, and the environment from conducting site characterization (e.g., the drilling of exploratory shafts), and whether a site was suitable for characterization. Third, the question of repository development was considered. Finally, the sites were evaluated comparatively. This last part of the analysis was quite complex and required that important value judgments be made about site characteristics. Many public comments on the inadequacy of the EAs focused on this section of the assessments.

There were a number of similarities in the findings on the potential impacts of the three final sites. For the environmental effects of site characterization and the regional and local effects of repository development, the conclusions across the three sites were generally the same: no major land-use or ecosystem effects were predicted. In all three cases, however, contamination from transportation of radioactive materials was raised as a possibility. This problem later proved to be a major concern of citizens, as evidenced in public comments on the EAs.

The EAs for these three sites differed most in the environmental problems seen as likely to be encountered once the repository was filled and sealed. In each case, the geology of the site created some risk of eventual leakage of radionuclides and thus contamination of the biosphere. The specific problems varied across the sites because of differences in their geologic structure. For the Deaf Smith site, concern centered on the possibility of salt dissolution, a problem that has developed with the Waste Isolation Pilot Project in New Mexico. For Yucca Mountain, the main problems envisioned included oxidation by groundwater (where water and oxygen in the tuff formation combine and might dissolve spent fuel) and earthquakes (especially if the magnitude of earthquakes increases in the region). Given the location of the repository in the unsaturated zone, however, the problem of oxidation was considered to be minimal, and earthquakes, which do occur in the site area, were seen as unlikely to alter the natural characteristics of the unsaturated zone, the primary natural mechanism for controlling radionuclide migration. The Hanford site was in basalt, a highly fractured and jointed rock medium which presents complex problems in understanding the geohydrological system; this was a particularly critical problem because of the site's proximity to the Columbia River.

The significance of these findings about the limitations of the various geological media was that DOE was unable to say with certainty that there would be no environmental contamination. As is usually the case with risk assessments, only probabilistic estimates could be made. These conclusions did little to reduce the anxiety of local residents and opponents of the program. They expected greater certainty in these analyses: either the facility would leak or it would not. To them, low levels of risk were unacceptable—a judgment characteristic of how the public responds to nuclear risks (see Slovic and Fischhoff, 1983:123–27; also Chapter 13 in this book).

At the base of the comparative evaluation across the sites was the division of each of the nineteen siting criteria into one or more major dimensions. Comparisons between the sites were made on the basis of these groupings. For example, geohydrology was broken down into four categories: groundwater travel time and flux, changes in geohydrological processes and conditions, ease of characterization and modeling, and presence of suitable groundwater sources. Under each dimension, favorable and potentially adverse conditions were identified. The sites were then compared on the extent to which positive or negative site characteristics were present. To aggregate the rankings, three different quantitative methods were employed. Criticisms of this approach later led DOE to use a single method, multiattribute utility analysis, to arrive at the nomination of the final three sites (U.S. Department of Energy, 1986b).

Criticisms of the EAs

As observed in many public policy disputes over the last several decades, scientific information is often the subject of debate and controversy. It is not unusual to find experts on both sides of an issue and little agreement on the wide range of issues, from interpretation of scientific information to the policy implications of the data. Criticisms are frequently directed at all steps in the scientific process: the scope of analysis, the variables chosen for study, the methodologies employed, the data collection procedures, and the conclusions reached (see Kraft, 1988; Masters and Kantrowitz, 1988).

Public reaction to the EAs fits this general pattern. A large portion of the comments on the draft EAs was directed at what was perceived to be the inherent subjectivity of site evaluation when the broad characterizations were made. The identification of major dimensions and the judgment of whether a favorable or potentially adverse condition existed necessitated site decisions that were quite general and not always supported with appropriate technical information; hence, the decision was potentially subject to bias. Many criticisms of the EAs dealt with the appropriateness of making comparisons among sites on the basis of such limited anaysis (U.S. Department of Energy, 1986c).

Similar objections were raised to other components of the analysis. For example, DOE had to make assumptions about how to estimate some of the parameters affecting environmental risk. It chose to do so conservatively, a scientifically reasonable procedure for decision making under uncertainty, but it nevertheless subjected the impact assessment process to criticism of incompleteness. These kinds of limitations of existing methodologies often resulted in what the General Accounting Office (GAO) called a "trial-and-error" assessment process (U.S. General Accounting Office, 1985b:49).

The effect of such methodological weaknesses was clear enough in a range of responses to the EAs. In one congressional oversight hearing in 1985, evidence was presented indicating that the EPA, Interior Department, and NRC all claimed that at least some of the conclusions in the assessments were not supported by existing data. Although presumably less neutral about the findings, the director of Texas's Nuclear Waste Program office asserted that the "draft EAs are so filled with technical errors, omissions, and arbitrary determinations as to be an insult to the reader." He attributed the errors to time schedules which "sacrificed" technical competence. Other criticism concerned procedural issues, particularly the lack of transcripts or working papers from DOE sessions where sites were ranked (U.S. Congress, 1985).

Negative comments were also directed at the way DOE organized the research process. The primary responsibility for drafting the documents was given to DOE field offices under rather loose guidelines and with some competition among the offices (which apparently were encouraged to speed the process along), hence contributing to the doubts about the quality of scientific data and the erosion of DOE's credibility (Salisbury, 1985).

Finally, the conclusions themselves were often challenged as inconsistent with DOE's stated guidelines. For example, the ranking system used by the agency in selecting sites for further consideration had the Hanford location as the most expensive and least safe of the final sites evaluated in the First Round. Nevertheless, it was one of the three recommended to the president for additional study. Because Hanford is already a site of defense-related waste storage, many of DOE's critics suspected that the agency favored the site largely because local residents are both more familiar with the nuclear waste problem and presumably less likely to resist the siting of a repository.

The cumulative effect of the many perceived limitations in DOE's analysis was the frequent charge that it was "playing politics" with the site nomination process. In a typical comment, the director of Nevada's Radioactive Waste Project complained that the "process is rigged: It's prejudged, predetermined, and DOE is just filling in the data to fit" (Salisbury, 1985). This kind of criticism was echoed in comments by public interest groups; for example, in September 1986, the newly formed National Nuclear Waste Task Force, representing twenty-seven citizen groups in states being evaluated for waste sites, complained that DOE's site selection process was based on "expediency and politics, not science" (Environment Reporter, 1986a:782). Members of Congress representing candidate states or neighboring states were also sharply critical of DOE; for example, Rep. James Weaver (D–Oreg.) characterized DOE's decision making "as usual [showing] little regard for technical advice and much regard for politics" (Environment Reporter, 1986b:1155).

Given the way the environmental assessments were conducted, the substantive findings, the comparative rankings of sites, and the criticisms of the analysis and conclusions, what can we say about how the EAs affected the policy process in this First Round? The major effects were to stimulate state and public opposition to DOE's efforts, including the instigation of numerous lawsuits, much of it turning on the quality of the scientific analysis. For example, within six months of the first site nominations, all three states were challenging the legality of the designation process, and several environmental groups joined in the legal fray by attacking the assessments themselves. As noted, distrust of DOE and skepticism about its technical competency were already prevalent, especially in the West, due to a long history—not easily separable from that of the old AEC— of false starts, mistakes, and suppression of critical information on the waste issue (Salisbury, 1985; Abbott, 1979). However, the EA process sharply altered the level and type of public protest.

THE SECOND ROUND: PUBLIC PROTEST MOUNTS

DOE encountered similar disapproval in its search for a second repository site. The Second Round assessments differed in two important respects from the First Round. The exploration for a second repository focused on crystalline rock bodies, which meant that midwestern and eastern states would be the study areas. Additionally, the methodology used by DOE in this analysis was less thorough because the assessments were even more preliminary than the First Round EAs; as a DOE official explained in late 1987, "they were not meant to be as rigorous as an EA" (U.S. Department of Energy, 1987b).

In the Second Round, the site screening process involved focusing on progressively smaller land units in an attempt to identify acceptable sites. Initially, a national survey was completed, which led to recommendations that the Lake Superior, Northern Appalachians and Adirondacks, and Southern Appalachians be considered for further study. Seventeen states had land that fell within these regions. These 235 sites were further narrowed through regional and area surveys to twenty locations in seven states: Wisconsin, Minnesota, Maine, New Hampshire, Virginia, Georgia, and North Carolina.

The criteria and methodology for evaluating the environmental impact associated with the twenty sites were similar to the western EAs since the preparation of both was governed by the NWPA and DOE regulations (U.S. Department of Energy, 1986a). Thus the assessments in the Second Round were subject to many of the same kinds of objections. For example, to approach the area survey (initial identification of potentially acceptable sites) more rigorously, DOE conducted a series of workshops to develop weights for the variables to be used in the screening. This effort at systematizing the process, with the appearance of quantitative analysis, was still based on subjective judgments, opening the methodology to criticism. In its comments on the draft Area Recommendation Report for the Second Round sites (which was to be followed by a more elaborate environmental assessment), the State of Maine (1986a) argued that the weights were highly skewed toward geologic variables, to the detriment of population and environmental factors. While such a weighting might be justified by the scientific considerations involved in the long-term geologic storage of nuclear waste, it was the more immediate social and environmental impacts that concerned the residents of areas under study.

The result of DOE's weighting scheme was to recommend areas such as the Sebago Lake Batholith in Maine, which is located near a metropolitan area with a large transient summer population and lies under the water supply for Portland, the state's largest city. It was these kinds of factors that received low weighting compared to the geologic ones in the assessments. Consequently, as Luther Carter (1987) notes, the assessments did not address the issues of greatest concern to the local citizenry. The political response in Maine as elsewhere was predictable. Meetings were held throughout the state to protest DOE's proposed action, and local newspaper editorials strongly criticized DOE for gaps in its siting criteria. The state's Advisory Commission on Radioactive Waste, in its comments on the draft assessment, stated: "We have found that DOE has failed to create public confidence in the siting process, and that the draft Area Recommendation Report issued on Jan. 16, 1986, has many errors and omissions" (State of Maine, 1986b).

A similar response to DOE's assessment efforts in the East was seen in public hearings on the draft report. DOE conducted thirty-nine briefings and thirty-eight public hearings in fifteen states during a three-month period in the spring of 1986. All told, some 18,000 people attended these sessions, and another 3,200 individuals and organizations provided written comments (U.S. Department of Energy, 1987c). In some cases, particularly in Maine and Wisconsin, the hearings and briefings were attended by thousands of impassioned citizens and state and local officials.

An extensive content analysis of the public testimony at these hearings in four states—Wisconsin, Maine, North Carolina, and Georgia—has been reported elsewhere (Kraft and Clary, 1988). For present purposes it is sufficient to note that the environmental assessment process did little to alleviate public concern about DOE's ability to dispose of nuclear waste safely. The assessments in the Second Round and the hearings on them led to much the same result as in the First Round states: there was widespread public rejection of the agency's implementation plans, which eventually forced Congress to revise the entire siting process.

The Impact of the EAs within DOE

Any evaluation of the role of these assessments on the policy process would be incomplete without consideration of their effect within DOE. Although the major impact on the external political environment was clearly adverse for DOE's implementation of NWPA, within DOE the EAs and Area Recommendation Report were viewed much more positively. Given the five-part site selection process noted above, this is not unexpected. These assessments were considered by DOE to be early and very preliminary evaluations of sites that were to be examined much more thoroughly during site characterization, as was under way with the Yucca Mountain site by 1988.

When asked in late 1987 about the impact these assessments had on DOE itself, one key policy official in the agency described them as follows: "[They are] valuable tools [for] guiding us to the next step in the site characterization plans. They are certainly tools we put a lot of good work into and we continue to draw upon the scientific information in them as planning documents leading us forward" (U.S. Department of Energy, 1987b). He drew a clear distinction between their value in a complex, multistage process of site evaluation, which DOE was (and still is) mandated to pursue, and public response to them. The public's reaction was seen as a reflection of its fear of nuclear waste and its strong disinclination to accept a waste repository nearby, thus creating a severe political liability for DOE given the siting process it was obliged to implement. Hence in 1987 the agency looked to Congress to repair the process. And Congress responded with the Nuclear Waste Policy Amendments Act of 1987, which restricted the search process to the Yucca Mountain site and withdrew authorization for the second repository.

As site characterization proceeds at Yucca Mountain, DOE should find the earlier assessments helpful, if only for better appreciating the research questions, methodological difficulties, and problems in data collection that need to be addressed in the far more comprehensive characterization process—and the challenge of communicating technological risks in the policy area. As noted above, one can only speculate on whether a different public response to the EA process might have occurred had better information been available or had DOE established better relations with the state. The same official in OCRWM, quoted above, who has been deeply involved with the repository siting process, believed that the assessments themselves were not at fault for DOE's political tribulations. In late 1987, he volunteered that "no matter how rigorous, how complete those [early] assessments might have been, I don't think the outcome would have been any different" (U.S. Department of Energy, 1987b). Partly for that reason, the assessments in both the West and the East were considered useful exercises for an agency that will have to provide more exhaustive and credible scientific studies of environmental risk over the next decade.

CONCLUSION

Policy analyses are typically viewed as efforts to improve the quality of decision making through the provision of information on the consequences of public policy or of policy alternatives. However, it is often difficult to determine whether such information is utilized, by whom, in what ways, and with what effects. Analyses may be intended for one group or one purpose (e.g., to assist agency officials in policy implementation) but used by others for different purposes (e.g., by state officials and the public to challenge the agency's decisions). They may also be intended for multiple purposes, as are EISs. Under certain circumstances, the immediate consequences for policy implementation may be distinctly adverse, even if the longer term effects may be more positive for achievement of policy goals.

For the case of the NWPA, we need to distinguish between these short-term and long-term effects. In the short term, the major effect was policy failure; DOE was unable to achieve its original objectives under the act. However, the impact assessment itself did not fail. The *technical* assessments were not well conducted and could not have been because of the state of scientific knowledge. The *process* of impact assessment was successful in that it revealed many deficiencies in our knowledge of repository siting and its impact on the environment.

This outcome parallels what one sometimes finds for the EISs required under the National Environmental Policy Act (Caldwell, 1982). One of the purposes of the assessments, like EISs, is to force public officials to consider information on the possible environmental consequences of siting decisions and thus to contribute to a more rational selection of waste repository locations. More specifically, such assessments require an interdisciplinary and integrated use of both the natural and social sciences in order to foster ecological rationality in bureaucratic decision making (Bartlett, 1986a; Taylor, 1984).

Yet as we have shown, the environmental assessments had other effects on the policy process beyond their presumed scientific contribution to agency decision making—effects which are nevertheless consistent with another purpose of impact assessments more generally: to improve society's ability to solve problems effectively. The most important of these for the NWPA were political in character: the assessments increased the visibility and salience of agency decision making and thereby expanded and broadened the set of participants and perspectives in what otherwise would have been a largely technical decision-making process dominated by the DOE officials and staff. In particular, the assessments helped to mobilize, organize, and represent the interests of citizen activists, Indian tribal leaders, and state and local policymakers; to equip them with critical technical data and arguments with which they could redefine the policy problems, introduce new issues, and challenge DOE statements on environmental risks; and ultimately to contribute to a shift in opinion against the siting procedures specified in the 1982 act, which led to the 1987 revision.

There were some obvious short-term consequences for the NWPA. It could be implemented only with a major change in the site review process that made it less vulnerable to political opposition at the state level. These short-term negative effects of the EAs and the Area Recommendation Report may obscure more positive, long-term impacts of building such assessments into the decision-making process. In this case, despite much criticism of the technical quality of the assessments and their contribution to mobilizing opposition forces, they were clearly helpful to DOE. They improved the understanding of technical issues and uncertainties which will surely affect the agency's extensive characterization of the Nevada site. Thus one could say the environmental assessment process provided a vehicle for institutional learning.

Moreover, the very failure of the EAs and the Area Recommendation Report to build confidence in the initial siting process forced Congress to reformulate the act in a way that may result in more successful implementation over time. In this sense the impact of the assessments is consistent with the larger function of promoting effective resolution of the nuclear waste problem. Of course, whether DOE achieves that outcome will depend on how much it learns from the experience of the past five years and its capacity to devise appropriate strategies for what remains a highly complex, difficult, and controversial public policy.

NOTE

1. The NIMBY problem is the subject of several studies of public response to the siting of hazardous waste facilities. It is also becoming a focus of concern for students of nuclear waste repository siting. For analyses of the policy implications of this attitude, see O'Hare, Bacow, and Sanderson, 1983; Morell and Magorian, 1982; Kraft and Clary, 1988.

6

Environmental Impact Assessment as a Tool for Wildlife Policy Management

William R. Mangun

INTRODUCTION

This research represents one of the first efforts to describe and evaluate the environmental impact assessment process as a policy tool for wildlife management with particular attention to the U.S. Fish and Wildlife Service (FWS). The National Environmental Policy Act (NEPA) made considerable changes in the way federal agencies conducted their business after 1970. A prominent question concerning NEPA and impact assessment is whether the process has truly made a positive change in the way agencies make their decisions or has simply created busywork for agency employees. The primary purpose of this research was to identify through case studies and a historical overview of the impact assessment process in the FWS what types of changes in agency policy actions have actually resulted.

The analysis was based on current FWS impact assessment documents to assess changes in policy decisions or implementing actions, past impact assessments to determine any general trends or patterns over time, and interviews with agency managers in order to assess whether their perceptions of how the impact assessment process functions correspond with the apparent patterns that have been demonstrated in the decision-making process in the past and at the present time.

Policy in a resource management agency like FWS is dominated naturally by the availability of scientific information in the decision-making process. As a policy tool the FWS environmental impact assessment (EIA) process has evolved from basically a procedural requirement limited mostly to biological concerns in earlier years to a more comprehensive process involving social and economic considerations today. The greater attention given by the FWS to the latter issues largely results from the 1978 Council on Environmental Quality revisions to the NEPA guidelines. For example, through the scoping requirement, FWS policy alternatives have been modified to accommodate greater citizen input which promotes more sound policy decisions. Furthermore, in contrast to other resource management agencies which tend to have site-specific EIAs due to their development orientation, the FWS EIA process tends to have a broad programmatic orientation. Consequently, the EIA process tends to engender broader political constituencies for the FWS to deal with than is the case for other resource management agencies.

BACKGROUND

Responsibility for fish and wildlife management policy in the United States is distributed across all levels of government as well as numerous agencies at any one level. Generally, resident species are dealt with under state and local regulations; migratory species fall under federal and international law. Resident species such as white-tailed deer and pheasants are regulated under state laws because these species are presumed to reside within state boundaries. Migratory species such as waterfowl and salmon are managed under federal law and international treaties inasmuch as these species routinely cross state and national political boundaries. Endangered and threatened species are covered by the federal Endangered Species Act if they have been listed by the U.S. Fish and Wildlife Service. Species also may be threatened or endangered only within a particular area within a specific state and thus subject to state endangered species regulation if they do not appear on the federal list.

At the federal level, each land management agency such as the U.S. FWS, the National Park Service, the Forest Service, the Bureau of Land Management (BLM), and the Bureau of Indian Affairs has its own fish and wildlife management regulations, and each is required to implement appropriate federal laws pertaining to fish and wildlife. Further complications occur in the management of resident species on federal lands. Such species are managed by federal agencies in accordance with state regulations; likewise, state and local agencies must manage migratory species on their lands under federal and international laws. In light of the above delineation of responsibilities, it is important to remember that the Council on Environmental Quality (CEQ) environmental impact assessment regulations apply to major *federal* projects and actions likely to have a significant impact on the environment. Some states have their own environmental impact assessment requirements, but most environmental assessment related to fish and wildlife is conducted by federal agencies. Yet virtually nothing has been published on the role of environmental impact assessment concerning fish and wildlife management (Mangun, 1988).

The Fish and Wildlife Service differs fundamentally in policy orientation from other federal resource management agencies. The Army Corps of Engineers (Corps), Forest Service, and BLM have a market or development orientation; FWS does not. Consequently, the EIA process in FWS tends to be directed toward broad management actions, not projects—with the exception of the sixteen National Wildlife Refuges (NWRs) in Alaska where the Alaska National Interest Conservation Act of 1981 (ANILCA) requires EIAs. For example, predator damage control strategies, migratory bird hunting regulations, use of lead shot for hunting migratory birds, and translocation of southern sea otters are all management actions. In contrast, the Corps builds water control projects; the Forest Service conducts timber harvests and builds roads to specific cutting projects; and BLM harvests timber and sells grazing permits and mineral mining rights. These natural resource agencies are required to conduct environmental assessments and develop environmental impact statements (EISs) on a site-by-site basis.

Although FWS does not have a market orientation, occasionally the agency gets involved in management situations concerning market activities on NWR lands. For example, following a controversy over grazing on the C.M. Russell NWR, FWS had to write a site-specific EIS. The controversy arose because FWS refuges are managed for a dominant purpose, i.e., provision of habitat for the protection or enhancement of an animal or plant species under specific refuge-authorizing legislation or other mandates such as the Endangered Species Act or the Migratory Bird Treaty Act. Under some circumstances, Congress or the president may identify alternative uses that may occur on refuge lands. The executive order creating the C.M. Russell NWR contained such a provision that permitted grazing activities. Although a decision was made to permit grazing on the refuge, the EIA process that was conducted in order to determine how best to manage the refuge resulted in the identification of less environmentally damaging management practices including a significant reduction of grazing activities. Grazing interests resorted to the courts to oppose any reduction in grazing opportunities. The district court supported grazing interests. However, in 1983, the appellate court overturned the district court and ruled that wildlife has priority in access to forage resources of the C.M. Russell NWR and that the range is to be administered under the Refuge Act. The ruling of the appellate court reaffirmed the criteria followed in the preparation of the draft EIS.

In contrast to FWS, other resource management agencies administer their lands under substantially different mandates. BLM and the Forest Service are managed under a multiple-use approach. Under this approach, the agencies are to manage their lands in a manner that promotes a harmonious relationship between competing land uses such as recreation, timber harvesting, and grazing. Consequently, a conflict may develop at any particular site managed under the multiple-use approach where potentially incompatible uses occur. A decision to clear-cut a particular National Forest area may conflict with aesthetic enjoyment of the area by hiking or wildlife-oriented enthusiasts. Because two or more parties may differ as to the appropriate use of public lands among competing uses, these resource agencies tend to have numerous site-specific environmental impact assessments.

Hence the political environment of the EIA process for the FWS tends to differ from that of other natural resource management agencies. FWS tends to have broad programmatic EISs that affect wide geographic areas. The migratory bird hunting regulations and use of lead shot EISs, for example, affect hunting on refuges across the United States. The sea otter EIS affects most of the western coast of the United States. Exceptions to this rule-of-thumb are EIAs associated with specific wildlife refuge master plans such as the Chincoteague NWR. This means that the political environment of FWS more often involves national or broadly based regional constituencies. Consequently, the political constituencies concerned about FWS environmental impact assessment may be more national or regional in scope representing potentially greater political clout. In contrast, the geopolitical structure of BLM, the Forest Service, and the Corps tends to consist of microenvironments with considerable variability from one region of the country to another (Taylor, 1984). This might mean that EISs are more efficacious as policy tools for FWS under such circumstances.

CONTROVERSIAL FWS ENVIRONMENTAL IMPACT ASSESSMENTS

Because of the broad-based nature of the assessments conducted by FWS, the agency frequently is involved in highly visible, confrontative situations. Part of the problem is the large political constituency a broad-based issue can engender. In addition to the extensive number of people a large constituency has at its disposal, the aggregate wealth of the group tends to be larger; and together, they equate to political power.

When politics get out of balance with science, NEPA has some capacity to put things back into balance through the information gathered in the EIA process. Even when a decision has been made before the analysis, the shortcomings of a decision are often brought out during the impact assessment process, and corrective action is taken. In the EIS process, public comments are often used to shape the preferred alternative and, thus, the decision-making process. The highly controversial decision to translocate 250 endangered southern sea otters from their current range along the California coast to San Nicolas island produced tremendous political pressure on FWS from oil and fishery interests as well as environmentalists. In the case of the southern sea otter, FWS identified a wide range of social, economic, and biological issues through the EIA process. Appropriate risk analyses were subsequently undertaken to provide decision makers with the information necessary to make responsible decisions regarding the sea otter translocation.

Interviews with agency personnel indicate that it is accepted as more cost effective to take public comment into consideration and to modify the preferred alternative, if need be, than to persist with a pre-made decision that goes against popular opinion and forces the agency to go to court and incur litigation costs. Natural resource agencies do not always modify the environmentally preferred alternative based on public comment or threat of litigation. In the case of the 1987 Arctic National Wildlife Refuge Alaska Coastal Plain Resource Assessment, Secretary of the Interior Donald Hodel selected alternative A, full leasing, as the environmentally preferred alternative for management of the area. This decision was based on the belief that alternative A would best meet the nation's goals and responsibilities. The potential $79 billion to $325 billion contribution to the nation's economy from the area's estimated oil resources and the favorable effects on the U.S. balance of trade and national security were cited as the principal reasons for supporting the preferred alternative. Previous experience at Prudhoe Bay led FWS employees to suggest that the potential detrimental effects of oil production could be avoided substantially.

Major environmental organizations do not agree with the FWS assessment and are likely to pursue litigation to challenge the Department of the Interior (DOI) decision to pursue full leasing on the Arctic NWR Coastal Plain. Six environmental groups accused DOI of misleading the public about the chances of finding oil and gas under the refuge (Darst, 1986). The groups complained that the report did not state that there was only a 19 percent chance that an economically recoverable reserve of oil lies under the reserve. The National Wildlife Federation (NWF) (1987) challenged the Arctic NWR study and issued its own report to Congress rebutting the conclusions of the FWS study point by point. DOI released the environmental assessment in November 1986 along with a recommendation that the entire study area be leased for oil and gas development. The NWF report indicates that the study is seriously flawed because it fails to address critical resource questions, contains faulty conclusions, and discounts or disregards pertinent scientific information about the negative impacts on the internationally important Porcupine caribou herd. In this instance, it would appear that the environmental impact assessment process failed to balance the political position of energy development interests against sound scientific opinion.

IMPACT ASSESSMENT METHODOLOGY

Current research suggests that environmental impact assessment should be conducted through interdisciplinary teams (Burdge and Opryszek, 1983). Early environmental impact assessment efforts in FWS appear to lack any integration of interdisciplinary teamwork. More recent efforts such as the 1979 EIS on "Mammalian Predator Damage Management for Livestock Protection in the Western United States [i.e., Animal Damage Control (ADC)] " and the 1987

EIS on "The Translocation of the Southern Sea Otter" represent good examples of interdisciplinary teamwork. The interdisciplinary ADC EIS resulted in a major policy revision in the manner in which FWS controlled damage to livestock caused by predatory animals, primarily coyotes, in the West.

Among the major shortcomings of the attempts to establish an interdisciplinary team of biologists, economists, and sociologists to conduct impact assessment are (1) establishment of budget suballocations, (2) data compatibility, (3) developing an effective decision-making structure, (4) working at the interfaces between discipline and project segments, and (5) enforcement of understandings between participants (Burdge and Opryszek, 1983).

Despite such obstacles, interdisciplinary approaches can produce effective results. For example, through the joint efforts of biologists, economists, social psychologists, and resource management specialists, FWS conducted a twenty-one-month review of the federal role in controlling damage by predators. Livestock groups maintained that the economic impact of predator losses was staggering. These groups advocated increased use of all current control techniques and emergency use of the toxicant Compound 1080. In contrast, many wildlife interest groups and citizen activists strongly opposed the reintroduction of Compound 1080, preferring increased emphasis on nonlethal coyote control methods and a policy of taking only offending animals. The latter groups were interested in the humaneness of control techniques and were concerned about nontarget animals. A communications research technique—content analysis—was used to analyze public comment on the draft and final EIS. Results of the content analysis were combined with preliminary findings from a national survey on public attitudes toward critical wildlife and natural habitat issues (Kellert, 1978) as well as pertinent biological analyses in order to provide the basis for changes in predator control policy.

The mere existence of an interdisciplinary team does not ensure equal treatment of disciplines. Burdge and Opryszek (1983) assert that approaches within the EIS authors' disciplines are often presented in a sophisticated and knowledgeable manner, while less familiar disciplines are treated more generally. This assertion is partially demonstrated in the EIS concerning the translocation of sea otters. FWS established a review group consisting of recognized experts in the fields of benthic ecology, marine mammal biology, marine resource economics, physical oceanography, and the physics and chemistry of pollutant transport. Although this constitutes an interdisciplinary team and although the final EIS report bears detailed information that represents each field, very little is included on sociological impacts. For example, there is no analysis on the potential impacts on the lives of the abalone and razor clam fishermen, even though the potential biological consequences on the shellfish and the economic consequences on the shellfish industry are well identified. The primary authors of the sea otter EIS were biologists, economists, and ecologists. Consequently, the level of analysis related to the biological, economic, and ecological issues appears to be substantially greater than the analysis of sociological and other issues. To be truly effective, an interdisciplinary team must include representative experts on all components of the problem from the social as well as the life sciences. FWS seldom has the fiscal and organizational resources necessary to staff fully such interdisciplinary teams.

The Fish and Wildlife Service has a strong biological orientation consistent with its mandates to protect and enhance fish and wildlife populations. FWS conducts biological assessments on major projects of other federal agencies that are likely to have an impact on fish and wildlife under the authority of the Fish and Wildlife Coordination Act; FWS then provides advisory opinions to the agencies with recommendations for mitigation actions if necessary. Partially as a result of this responsibility, early EISs were concerned almost entirely with biological issues and the impacts of the proposed alternative actions on animal populations with virtually no consideration of social impact assessment. For example, the 1975 EIS on the "Issuance of Annual Regulations Permitting the Sport Hunting of Migratory Birds" casually addresses the impact of the regulations on hunters, the nonhunting public, the economy, and private landowners whereas the impact on individual avian species is given considerable detailed coverage.

In contrast, the 1987 EIS on "Translocation of Southern Sea Otters" contains extensive analyses on the potential economic impacts of the translocation on commercial and sport fisheries as well as on oil and gas resource development on Outer Continental Shelf (OCS) lands. Similarly, a social impact assessment was conducted to help decisionmakers select the management alternative in the master plan for the heavily visited Chincoteague NWR, in Virginia. The purpose of social impact assessment was to ensure that federal management actions produced the least negative impact on both human uses of the refuge and the economic vitality of the surrounding region while preserving the area for wildlife protection and enhancement. Thus we can see that over the years impact assessment methodology in FWS has evolved substantially from an almost exclusive EIA approach with heavy emphasis on biology to a more balanced approach integrating EIA and social impact assessment.

A possible explanation for the change in methodological approaches and, therefore, the better integration of economic and social considerations in FWS impact analyses lies in the CEQ NEPA regulations. The CEQ "guidelines" became regulations in 1978. These regulations stipulate that a "scoping process' should be conducted to identify the most significant issues to be considered in the environmental assessment. The purpose of the scoping process is to solicit input from interested parties early in the assessment process to ensure that all appropriate issues are considered in the development of alternative proposed actions. In the case of the southern sea otter, FWS had a high level of participation from multiple interests seeking different objectives. Principal groups included fisherman, oil interests, and environmentalists.

Through the scoping process, FWS gained a considerable amount of valuable information that helped to shape the alternative actions. Additional information was gathered on economic impacts to commercial and sport fisheries, specific biological threats to the sea otters, potential changes that sea otters might produce in the nearshore community and ecosystem, and likely impacts that the sea otters might have on OCS oil and gas development. Recent monitoring indicates that despite the extensive interdisciplinary analysis, fewer than one-fourth of the first sixty-three otters translocated remained after eleven months (Booth, 1988).

The 1978 CEQ regulations that instituted the scoping process forced FWS to consider social and economic issues more explicitly along with additional policy alternatives. Caldwell et al. (1983) note similar experiences in other federal agencies. This expansion is desirable because more than scientific issues are involved in major federal actions. Through the scoping process, interested parties are given an opportunity to present their concerns, and the agency is permitted to determine whether the concerns merit further attention and analysis.

Other possible explanations for the change in methodological approaches and better integration are (1) agency personnel have become more familiar with the environmental impact assessment regulations and techniques for complying with the regulations, (2) private citizens and environmental conservation organizations like the NWF and the Natural Resources Defense Council act as watchdogs to force compliance with the regulations through the courts, (3) the FWS has developed internal documentation and training programs for agency personnel to ensure more effective compliance with CEQ requirements, and (4) over time the agency has acquired additional expertise in the behavioral sciences which has facilitated the consideration of economic and social viewpoints. Taylor (1984), Bartlett (1986a), and Caldwell et al. (1983) find similar results in other federal agencies.

DISCUSSION

Management implications of environmental impact assessment for federal wildlife policy are related primarily to policy formulation and implementation effectiveness. The EIA process in FWS has evolved considerably. A more effective consideration of a wider range of policy issues occurs. This has given the agency a more effective management tool to deal with complex, controversial management actions. Through the EIS process, a formal analytical requirement has been institutionalized in the FWS decision-making process. Whenever a potentially controversial and significant management decision has to be made, the service can initiate an environmental assessment to acquire the necessary information. The agency can contact affected or highly interested parties and elicit their comments on a proposed action. Through this process, interested parties are given access to the agency's decision-making process since available information shapes policy alternatives.

Furthermore, once the EIS is completed it poses a substantial body of information as a historical record of considerations taken in the process of making a formal decision. Such information could be used to initiate legal action against an agency or individual in the event that a particular decision contravenes the mandates of legislation or exceeds the legal bounds of bureaucratic discretion. That is, if a bad decision is made in spite of contravening evidence gathered in the EIA process, such information could be used in court to illustrate the in-adequacy of the decision-making process used by responsible agency officials.

Personal interviews with agency personnel suggest that some FWS managers, like their counterparts in other federal agencies, tend to make management decisions in a manner that they feel is most appropriate and then use the EIA procedures to support those decisions. Other agency managers feel that although agency decisions may not have changed, per se, implementation strategies do get changed. That is, once a decision has been made to do something, the agency proceeds to conduct that activity, but the EIA process may uncover a better, less environmentally degrading way of conducting the activity that is subsequently implemented. In the case of the southern sea otter, FWS biologists decided that it would be in the best interest of the species to translocate an experimental population. After the final EIS was completed, the agency translocated the ex-perimental population, but, through the EIA process, the FWS was forced to consider a substantially greater number of issues concerning other biological, economic, and social impacts and to develop mitigation strategies before initi-ating action.

RECOMMENDATIONS FOR WILDLIFE MANAGEMENT

If one accepts the truism that public policy is that which actually occurs, one could say that wildlife policy has been substantially altered by the EIA process requirements. Plans and projects are altered as a result of comments gathered during the EIA scoping process and the EIS drafting phases. Still, there is reason to conclude that the EIA process is less influential on wildlife policy than it could or should be due to a variety of institutional constraints.

Given the widespread dispersion of fish and wildlife management responsi-bilities at the federal level, it would be desirable for management agencies to combine their efforts and to formulate uniform guidance for wildlife-related impact assessment. This is especially true for the impacts associated with the increased presence of humans or the increased use of habitat by humans. On the basis of such guidance, greater emphasis could be given to the integration of EIA into the policy formulation process (i.e., "close the feedback loop" and provide greater reliance on EIA for policy management).

EIA could be an integrative device for planning future management actions. Unfortunately, agency personnel often fail to integrate adequately the scientific findings generated by the EIA process into their daily management actions. For example, recent FWS long-term planning efforts omitted any formal integration of EIA into service-wide planning documents. The service management plan, program management documents, and annual work plans almost totally avoided mention of EIA.

EIA has tremendous potential for improving agency management decisions with proper integration into planning. The information acquired through impact analyses could be used to formulate mitigation plans for action. These plans could be used to formulate budget proposals. Both plans and budget initiatives require information substantiating the severity of the problem at hand. Such information is necessary to develop effective management actions and to convince the agency, executive branch, and congressional decisionmakers of the need to fund such activities. At the very least, a formal process should be established to ensure that the information acquired through the EIA process is incorporated into annual work plans used to structure proposed work assignments and schedules.

The role of the NEPA coordinator or EIA coordinator (the person with the overall responsibility for the EIA process in an agency) should be enhanced in the management process in order to maximize effectiveness. The NEPA coordinator should be admitted to the highest management hierarchy in a bureau. As a result of his or her coordination responsibilities, the NEPA coordinator should have one of the most comprehensive management perspectives of any member of an agency over time. Consequently, the NEPA coordinator should not simply maintain a position that serves a procedural function. The NEPA coordinator could serve a substantive function of management integration. As a result of the potential problem identification aspect of the EIA process, this person would be in an ideal position to anticipate future problems within and across programs for strategic planning purposes and could advise other managers of the advisability of proposed actions. As a member of the management elite, the NEPA coordinator could promote efficiency and effectiveness across fish and wildlife and habitat resource bases. At a minimum, the necessity for EIA or EIS actions could be determined early in the policy process. For example, the NEPA coordinator could integrate information acquired through EIAs and EISs into discussions of proposed management actions among program managers. In the case of the southern sea otter, FWS could have avoided some of the delays in the implementation of the management action that occurred as a result of EIS requirements if the NEPA coordinator had been more effectively integrated into the management decision-making process.

Continuing with the idea of using the EIA process as an integrative management tool, managers at both the state and federal levels need to avail themselves of technological developments that can facilitate decision making. For example, a computerized information management system could be developed to

1. Establish a baseline inventory of fish and wildlife and their habitat for management purposes. As EIAs are developed, the information gathered could be incorporated into a computer database management system to serve as a baseline inventory.

2. Monitor key resources. The baseline inventory could be used for monitoring purposes to alert program managers to potential or imminent management problems. Resource managers could identify potential resource problem areas for periodic comparison with

the baseline data in order to make more accurate assessments of trends for selected key resources.

3. Conduct analysis of trends. This analysis could be used to establish budget and management priorities based on changes in natural resources.

4. Develop management strategies. Information gathered in the EIA process (especially for land acquisition actions) could be used for refuge, forest, and park managers to develop management strategies. Aside from the work of Caldwell et al. (1983) and Taylor (1984), little has been done to ascertain the degree to which managers do use EIAs in management, but it appears that most site managers seem to start de novo in the development of their management plans tending to ignore the vast information contained in EIAs and EISs or simply to manage in an ad hoc crisis-oriented management fashion in spite of the availability of such information.

Once such expert computer systems are developed they could be used for a variety of agency and interagency purposes to integrate management. Through the use of artificial intelligence techniques, such systems could be used for permit determinations and potentially to forecast likely consequences of management actions on selected key species and habitat types. Yet proper functioning of such computer systems may depend on the adequacy of quantified data in EIAs. A recent analysis of 150 U.S. environmental impact statements revealed that adequate quantified data proved to be available for only 53 percent of the 239 impacts identified; the most serious deficiency was associated with quantified data on biological impacts (Culhane, 1987).

The foregoing material illustrates the importance of the environmental impact assessment process in the development of wildlife policy and the conduct of management actions to conserve and enhance fish and wildlife populations and suitable habitat for fish and wildlife resources. On a broader scale, environmental quality, cultural, and social policy objectives are also facilitated through environmental impact assessment through explicit consideration of related values in interdisciplinary assessment teams. Strategies are identified in the EIA process, for example, for air and water quality enhancement, protection of environmentally sensitive areas, preservation of cultural resources, and minimization of negative social consequences. For a policy area in which scientific information necessarily *must* dominate the decision process—i.e., wildlife—it is even more crucial than for most policy areas that analysis (EIA) be institutionalized as a primary policy strategy.

PART II

IMPACT ASSESSMENT IN DEVELOPMENT PLANNING

7

Environmental Impact Assessment in the Philippines: A Case Study of the San Roque Water Resources Development Project

Ramon Abracosa and Leonard Ortolano

We use the San Roque Development Project to explore the way the Philippine environmental impact statement (EIS) system was designed and how it worked in place. We analyze a situation that was common in the Philippines and elsewhere: the simultaneous existence of two independent environmental impact assessment (EIA) processes, one following national laws and one responding to requirements imposed by international development assistance agencies.

We use the concept of "control" from organization theory to explain how the EIS system operated in the Philippines, as exemplified by the case of the San Roque project. Three forms of control are described: evaluative, instrumental, and professional.[1]

THE PHILIPPINE EIS SYSTEM

The Philippine EIS system was established in 1977 as a keystone in a comprehensive national environmental reform program. The EIS system, along with other landmark environmental laws, was promulgated by decree under the authoritarian regime of President Ferdinand Marcos.[2]

The most significant of the environmental laws was the National Environmental Policy, issued as a presidential decree in 1977. This law established a formal EIS system. Passage of this law was accompanied by the establishment of the

National Environmental Protection Council (NEPC), a multiagency environmental policy arm of the government.

The Philippine National Environmental Policy was modeled after the U.S. National Environmental Policy Act (NEPA) of 1969. As with NEPA, the core of the Philippine National Environmental Policy was a mandatory EIS system. The Philippine version was more comprehensive in that it initially covered all projects and undertakings by both public agencies and private corporations and entities. Later, in 1978, the coverage of the EIS system was reduced to those types of projects classified as "environmentally critical" and those located in specified "environmentally critical areas."

During the period in which the San Roque project feasibility study was being completed, the Philippine EIS system was designed to follow a centralized implementation strategy. Project proponents were required to submit a project description to the NEPC, and it was to be used by the council to determine whether an EIS was required. For small projects with minor impacts, the council would issue an environmental compliance certificate (ECC) based on the project description. For projects with significant impacts, an ECC would not be issued until the council was convinced that the EIS satisfied its rules and regulations.

Between 1977 and 1985, legal and technical loopholes in the EIS system's rules and regulations, combined with the general inability of the NEPC to force agencies to take the EIS system seriously, resulted in the outright disregard for the system by many agencies and private project proponents. These loopholes were created when the originally decentralized implementation scheme for the EIS system was abruptly changed to a centralized form in 1978 wherein the NEPC was mandated to evaluate and approve EISs prepared by agencies and private project proponents. This centralized scheme was resisted by the agencies who exploited loopholes in the enabling statutes as an excuse for noncompliance. NEPC, on the other hand, remained too politically weak and lacked the resources to be able to enforce the centralized EIS system.

Nevertheless, other control mechanisms, independent of the evaluative form of control set up for the EIS system, were at work to compel and influence the conduct of environmental assessments for proposed projects. The San Roque project provides an example.

THE SAN ROQUE MULTIPURPOSE PROJECT

One of the major Philippine energy plans of the late 1970s and early 1980s provided for the development of the Agno River on the main island of Luzon. A key part of this plan was the National Power Corporation's (NPC's) San Roque project involving construction of a multipurpose dam across the lower Agno River at San Manuel, north of Manila. The proposed San Roque dam is potentially among the biggest in Southeast Asia; the project was estimated in 1984 to cost $1.2 billion.

The Planning of the San Roque Project

In 1974, the NPC engaged an Italian consulting firm, ELC-Electroconsult (referred to hereinafter as ELC), to conduct a preliminary study of how the hydroelectric generation potential of the lower Agno River could be harnessed. The ELC study results, submitted in 1976, concluded that the most desirable way of utilizing the hydropower potential of the river is through a "two-drop" scheme, with one dam at Tabu and another downstream at San Roque. Of the two, the dam at San Roque was given higher priority (ELC, 1976).

A parallel study, also done by ELC, compared alternatives for solving water quality problems due to tailings produced by mines in the central Agno Valley. Chemical pollutants consisting of heavy metals and cyanide residues are present in the mine tailings. Although it analyzed two feasible alternatives, ELC recommended study of the possibility of impounding the tailings by means of a dam built across the Agno River.

In May 1977, ELC and a local consulting firm, the Engineering and Development Corporation of the Philippines (EDCOP), were authorized to conduct a feasibility study for a multipurpose dam at San Roque. A short time later, after the Philippine EIS system was established, NPC decided to prepare an EIS for the project. It wished to avoid project delays which could occur if the newly created NEPC decided to require NPC to secure an environmental compliance certificate. During this period, the significance of the EIS system was still unknown, and NPC did not want to test the council's ability to stop projects by withholding ECCs.

Toward the end of the feasibility study, it became apparent that the cost of the San Roque project would be high, and prospects of financial backing from the government and international funding agencies were uncertain. The project was deferred, and the EIA was called off because of the pointlessness of satisfying EIS requirements in the absence of a strong prospect that the project would be built. Notwithstanding these events, the NPC board authorized the project as part of NPC's power expansion program for 1981–1990, and the project was submitted for priority ranking and approval by the government.

The feasibility study, completed during March 1979, concluded that the San Roque project was both technically sound and economically feasible (ELC and EDCOP, 1979). It also indicated that the project, by trapping and diluting mine tailings, would significantly improve the water quality of the Agno River, and that there would be enough dead storage to impound all future mine tailings without shortening the useful life of the reservoir. The study mentioned adverse environmental impacts only in general terms.

Revival of the San Roque Project

On 22 June 1982, the government approved the ten-year power expansion program of NPC, which included the San Roque project as a major element.

With government backing assured, the NPC asked ELC to prepare detailed engineering specifications and bid documents based on the consultant's 1979 feasibility report.

As preparations for project implementation proceeded, the Environmental Management Office of NPC (which was elevated to departmental status in 1983) lobbied for funds for an EIA. It was not until May 1983, however, that the NPC board approved a contract for the assessment with Test Consultants, a local consulting firm. By then, "a firm signal to proceed with the project" had been made.[3] Since the bid documents had already been finalized and sent out at that time, the findings of the EIA could not influence those documents.

The most attractive bid, submitted by Japan's Marubeni, provided for Japanese government financing of the project through its Overseas Economic Cooperation Fund (OECF). After the Marubeni financing proposal received the president's approval early in 1983, the Philippine energy minister recommended that the project be financed by a combination of elements, the largest of which was an OECF "Yen loan." The package was modified soon thereafter to tie down a forthcoming "13th Yen credit" which would be available to the project only if it were committed quickly. Financing was a key factor influencing the timing of decisions. In fact, the NPC appeared bent on starting project implementation even before a formal EIA could be undertaken to examine the environmental impacts.[4]

Restudy of the San Roque Project

On 18 May 1983, NPC held a briefing on the San Roque project for OECF representatives and Japanese embassy officials. Subsequently, the Japanese government declared its intention to review the 1979 feasibility study. The review was to be carried out by Japan's International Cooperation Agency (JICA), the official agency responsible for Japan's overseas technical cooperation programs.

The Japanese inquired about an environmental impact statement for the project, noting that such a statement was not included in the feasibility study. They also raised other points, including the way water quality benefits had been treated in the feasibility report. In response, the NPC directed ELC to conduct a sensitivity analysis to determine whether the project would still be economically feasible without the water quality improvement benefits. This entailed removing the mine tailings impoundment function from among the project purposes. NPC saw this as a way of sidestepping questions about whether mine tailings might pollute the reservoir water and spread noxious substances to a vast area if the water were used for irrigation. Because of the need to obtain the 13th Yen credit quickly, NPC wanted to avoid a possible delay in project implementation.

The Environmental Management Department was directed by NPC to secure a letter from the executive director of the NEPC indicating that an EIS would not be required as a precondition to start project construction. By NPC's reckoning, the San Roque project was planned and authorized for implementation before the enforcement of the EIS system began.[5] NPC officials felt the EIS system started only in June 1982 when the system's rules and regulations were finally published in the *Philippine Official Gazette*. Even though it believed an EIS was not legally required, NPC declared its willingness to proceed with an assessment and to adopt any necessary mitigation measures. The environmental assessment appeared to be undertaken not so much for its own merits, but to avert potential legal obstacles to construction and to satisfy the Japanese government's concern over water quality issues.

A JICA technical mission arrived in Manila in July 1983 to discuss with the NPC some project-related concerns that had been raised by the Japanese government. The JICA team stressed the need to investigate further the water quality issues associated with mine tailings. On this count, the NPC informed the mission that it had already engaged the services of a local firm to carry out an EIA, and that the study was to include an investigation of water pollution associated with mine tailings. The EIA consultants, who were at the meeting, described the nature of their assessment. The JICA mission was not convinced that the EIA would be adequate to resolve potential water quality problems. They argued that the scope and objectives of NPC's environmental assessment were different from JICA's proposed restudy of the project. An ad hoc study *parallel* to the EIA would be undertaken by JICA, and it would focus on water quality.

Coordination between the EIA team and the JICA team was minimal, a situation fostered by a mutual impression that the restudy was to be an independent review of the project for use by the Japanese government, whereas the EIA was the NPC's own concern.[6] This separation diminished the chances that the EIA would be influential, since the JICA study would play the key role in the Japanese government's decision on whether to finance the project.

Based on the conclusions reached during the discussions between NPC and JICA, it was agreed that JICA would initiate an eighteen-month investigation (beginning in November 1983) of both the reservoir and irrigation water quality. That meant a delay in construction.

In an effort to disassociate the project from controversial water pollution issues and to hasten project implementation, the NPC argued that the water quality issues associated with mine tailings be addressed separately in the proposed JICA restudy, apparently believing that the project would remain feasible even without the water quality improvement benefit. NPC felt that mine tailings could be dealt with separately, thereby avoiding a delay in project implementation. Notwithstanding the project's apparent economic viability without the mine tailings storage benefit, the JICA mission argued that the proposed dam would be too large for its remaining functions and that, if mining tailings issues were omitted, a major redesign of the project would be required. JICA stressed the inseparability of the mine tailings problem (whether or not as part of the project) from *any* purposes of the reservoir because of unknown adverse effects the tailings might cause.

Consequently, the San Roque project had to be deferred until the JICA restudy could be completed. That meant that the project would not be scheduled to take advantage of the 13th Yen credit, which could be committed to the San Roque project only at the time the credit was available. Since the project remained under study at the end of the credit availability period, this funding opportunity was lost. Without the 13th Yen credit, the chances of the project's being implemented in the near term were greatly diminished. Following the Aquino assassination in 1984, a financial crisis struck the Philippines and reduced the ability of the government to raise the local currency counterpart required to negotiate loans with international development assistance organizations. These events doomed any chances for project implementation.

SAN ROQUE EIA EXPLAINED USING "CONTROL MECHANISMS"

Two different EIA exercises were conducted in planning the San Roque project, and the motivation for each can be explained using the concept of "control" from organization theory. In the context of EIA, control mechanisms consist of inter- and intraorganizational structures and processes intended to ensure that project proponents account for environmental impacts in their planning and decision making. (The definitions of the various control mechanisms used herein are taken from Ortolano, Jenkins, and Abracosa, 1987.)

The Philippine EIA system in effect during the planning of the San Roque project relied on an "evaluative" form of organizational control.[7] Evaluative controls include an explicit statement of the procedures to be followed in conducting an EIA, an organizational entity that appraises the acceptability of the EIA, and sanctions which that entity can impose if EIA requirements are not met. In the case of the Philippine EIS system, the NEPC promulgated EIS rules and regulations and was responsible for judging whether project proponents were in compliance. The NEPC's ability to sanction consisted of its power to withhold an environmental compliance certificate and thereby to stop projects that did not meet EIS requirements.

During 1978, when the San Roque feasibility study was ongoing, it was not clear to NPC whether the council would have the political power to exercise its ability to stop projects. At that time, it was largely to avoid any possibility of delay due to noncompliance with NEPC's requirements that the NPC decided to prepare an environmental impact statement for the San Roque project. Plans to complete the EIS were dropped soon after they were formulated since prospects for project funding were nil.

In 1983, when it looked as if the San Roque project would be implemented, the NPC revived the notion of conducting an EIA. This time, however, its motivation was not limited to the EIS system requirements. Indeed, by 1983, the NEPC had lost much of the political power it had once enjoyed, and the credibility of the EIS system had been seriously eroded as a result of long delays in the issuance of necessary support statutes such as presidential proclamations and letters of instruction to accompany the EIS rules and regulations (Abracosa, 1987).

The NPC's renewed interest in an EIA was based on its anticipation that Japan's OECF would probably require an environmental assessment as a precondition for funding. This phenomenon, in which an international development assistance organization uses material rewards as an incentive to obtain desired outputs, including environmental assessments, is termed "instrumental control."[8] Typically, the required assessments are ad hoc and are intended to address specific environmental issues relevant to the appraisal of a project as an investment.

Although international assistance organizations sometimes leave the conduct of environmental assessments in the hands of the project proponent, Japan's OECF chose not to proceed this way in the San Roque project. OECF insistence on conducting its own environmental assessment is an example of "professional control" (Hood, 1976; Jenkins, 1983). In the context of EIA, professional control is exerted when an assessment is motivated by internalized values of planners stemming from their training, experience, and professional beliefs. The Japanese technical specialists examining the proposed San Roque project saw the potential water pollution due to mine tailings as a major issue, and their call for an independent study was a professional judgment. They were not persuaded by the results of NPC's feasibility study and the early results of NPC's EIA, both of which indicated that water quality would not be a problem.

CONCLUSION

The case demonstrates the limitations of the NPC response to the Philippine EIS system—that of a regulatory hurdle to project implementation. This type of response results in EIAs undertaken after feasibility studies are completed and only when strong indications exist that a project will be implemented. The problem, of course, is that EIAs are undertaken too late to be of any real significance in planning and decision making.

Despite the absence of effective evaluative controls to institutionalize the Philippine EIS system, instrumental and professional control mechanisms exist for encouraging EIA within the Philippines. The latter mechanisms are outside the formal EIS system and result in ad hoc environmental assessments tailored to two main requirements: (1) ensuring the technical feasibility of proposed projects by preventing potential adverse effects that might endanger the long-term sustainability of project benefits and (2) meeting concerns of international development assistance organizations by thoroughly assessing environmental impacts that bear on a project's attractiveness as an investment. Not surprisingly, both these requirements are motivated by economic considerations.

From an individual agency's standpoint, ad hoc EIAs protect its independence. The agency is neither required to follow standardized procedures, nor forced to open itself up to outside scrutiny by a watchdog entity such as the NEPC. Agency planners are often able to retain control over what impacts are studied in depth and how assessment results are reported.

For projects requiring financing by international development assistance organizations, ad hoc EIAs are increasingly being viewed as a useful professional planning procedure.

NOTES

1. Data for the case study was obtained from memoranda and documents in the files of the National Power Corporation, the main agency responsible for planning electric power facilities in the Philippines. Additional information was gathered during in-depth interviews with agency planners and private consultants who worked on the project.

2. The institutional setting and political factors that explain the passage of the Philippine EIS system are described in Abracosa (1987).

3. Memorandum from the NPC Environmental Management Department to the NPC Contracts Committee, October 1982, Manila.

4. Separate contract negotiations for project preparatory work (e.g., site development and construction of access roads) had been initiated during February 1983. The contract for the EIA study was approved on 16 May 1983.

5. See NPC file memorandum, 7 July 1983. Subject: "Financing Activities for the San Roque Multipurpose Project—Guidance for Meeting with Japanese Government Mission Arriving July 27, 1983."

6. Personal interview with Mr. Okazaki, member of the JICA mission, 5 September 1984, Manila.

7. For additional information on evaluative controls, see Jenkins (1983), Ouchi (1977), and Pfeffer (1978). In the organization theory literature, terminology describing various control mechanisms is not standardized. For example, Ouchi (1978) uses "bureaucratic controls" for what are referred to herein as "evaluative controls."

8. This use of instrumental controls is an example of the resource dependency perspective detailed by Pfeffer and Salancik (1978). For additional details on the way development assistance organizations have used material incentives to encourage EIA, see Stein and Johnson (1979) and Horberry (1985).

8

Project Problems and Shortfalls: The Need for Social Impact Assessment in AID Projects

Kurt Finsterbusch
and Warren A. Van Wicklin III

A century and a half ago, Hegel wrote that "Peoples and governments never have learned anything from history, or acted on principles deduced from it" (*Philosophy of History*, 1832). Since that time, a policy science methodology called impact assessment, which examines the impacts of projects and programs for their lessons, has been developed. In this chapter, we examine sixty-four impact assessments of projects of the U.S. Agency for International Development (AID) and compare them to preproject design documents. Many development projects have disappointing results; poor design is one of the reasons. The lessons learned from impact assessments, however, can help improve project designs and, therefore, future results.

METHODOLOGY

The basic procedure that we have used for this study is a systematic comparison of preproject design documents with postproject impact assessment documents. We begin with the complete set of AID Project Impact Evaluation Reports (PIERs) produced for 1979 to 1986 by the Office of Evaluation. The set contains sixty-three reports from which we deleted five reports that covered food distribution or credit programs. The remaining fifty-eight reports describe and evaluate sixty-four clearly distinguished projects. For forty of these projects we also obtained preproject design documents. This data set is unique: both pre- and postproject impact assessments were available for the same set of projects, and both types of documents were written in a fairly standardized format, which facilitated systematic comparison. We developed three protocols to guide our review of the documents: one for the preproject design documents, one for the PIERs, and one for the comparison between the two (for information on this data set see Finsterbusch, 1984; Finsterbusch and Van Wicklin, 1987; 1989).

LESSONS FROM IMPACT ASSESSMENT FOR PROJECT PLANNING

Our analysis of over one hundred documents and reports leads us to five major findings:

1. Original objectives are seldom achieved
2. Project schedules are frequently revised
3. Project outputs are often not used as intended
4. Project outputs are often not adequately maintained or sustained
5. The main deficiencies of design documents are inadequate social analyses and false claims about host government commitment to maintenance and sustainability

These findings will not come as a surprise to anyone who is familair with AID projects; nevertheless, they do not seem to be remembered when new projects are designed. They are not merely negative; indeed, they offer a sound basis for revision of project planning.

Our first major finding is the frequent failure of projects to come close to reaching their goals. Our comparison of design documents with impact studies indicates that the stated output objectives and estimated developmental results greatly exceed actual results as demonstrated in Table 8.1. In fact, the quantifiable output shortfalls are shockingly large, and some of them rival the cost of overruns of notorious Pentagon projects.

We were able to compare the outputs predicted in the design documents with actual outputs for ten road projects. The actual outputs equaled the predicted in only two cases. In the other eight road projects, the actual road length on the average was only 36 percent of the predicted road length. The main reason performance fell so far short of goals was the much greater cost per kilometer than had been expected as indicated in the last column.

Table 8.1 indicates that severe output shortfalls were also found in irrigation and education projects, but the shortfalls were more modest in electrification and potable water projects. The shortfall was large in the one health program with appropriate quantifiable data, but this pattern does not seem to be replicated in the other health or nutrition programs we studied.

Altogether, the data in Table 8.1 document the poor record of achievement in AID projects. The reasons are numerous and will be discussed later for each type of project. Some general explanations, however, will be discussed here.

One explanation is that the design documents have a sales function of justifying the project to obtain funding. They are inclined, therefore, to be overly optimistic in estimating project outputs and the higher order benefits that result from the outputs. They also underestimate costs and time requirements. These errors result from many factors, but three main causes are an improper estimation of inflation, an insufficient adjustment for unforeseen circumstances, and faulty assumptions about user behavior. We will comment only on the last factor, which indicates a need for better social impact assessments. When the calculations of the document preparers indicate that the output will greatly benefit users, they are likely to assume that everyone who has the chance and need will use the outputs. Time and again, however, the impact assessment discovered that many potential users could not reap the benefits of or assume the risks for using the outputs. Feasibility studies in the design stage are needed to anticipate these problems and improve the estimation of impacts. The lesson is that *behavioral assumptions should be tested*.

The second major finding is that seldom are things done on time. The problems of delays and falling behind schedule, relatively common in Third World countries, often result in the squandering of resources. For example, workers are hired and put on the payroll, but they cannot work effectively because crucial equipment has not arrived, or it has broken down and replacement parts will take months to arrive. In millions of ways, events conspire to increase costs, which means cost overruns or less output. We have not discovered a solution to this problem except to suggest using conservative time estimates and more flexible management of projects to allow for adjustments to the unforeseen. In innovative projects, pilot studies might help determine some of the indeterminacies.

The third major finding is that project outputs are often not used as intended. When electricity is supplied to an area, AID hopes that many users will buy machinery and start producing more things. The users are delighted to have electricity to light their houses at night and run electrical appliances that make life more comfortable and enjoyable. Development agencies, however, are more concerned about economic development than the enjoyment of life so they are often disappointed when little of the electricity is used to drive water pumps to increase agricultural production or machinery for craft or manufacturing production. Likewise, some (but not many) rural roads do not increase agricultural production, some potable water is not drunk because of the chlorine taste but is used for vegetable gardens or bathing, and some education is used as a ticket to opportunities abroad instead of being used to fill important jobs at home. These outputs, however, should not come as surprising disappointments. If the beneficiaries had been studied beforehand, these outputs could have been anticipated. Better yet, if beneficiaries could participate in the design of the project, their benefits would most likely be greater (e.g., Dietz and Pfund, 1988).

Table 8.1
Expected Versus Actual Outcomes of Selected AID Projects

PIER #	Country	Expected Output	Actual Output	Time Delay	% Cost Overrun
RURAL ROAD PROJECTS					
1	Colombia	890 km	470 km	6 months	83%
6	Liberia/1	82 km	82 km	3-12 months	20%
	Liberia/2	167 km	142 km	> 4 years	30-50%
7	Sierra Leone/1	1,448 km	280 km	> 1.5 years	278%
	Sierra Leone/2	644 km	187 km	NA	145%
11	Jamaica	523 km	291 km	6 months	88%
17	Honduras/1	602 km	113 km	> 5 years	315%
	Honduras/2	304 km	304 km	> 18 months	NA
18	Philippines/1	750 km	406 km	NA	260%
	Philippines/2	650 km	388 km	NA	NA
RURAL ELECTRIFICATION PROJECTS					
16	Bolivia	53,000 users	42,000 users	> 2 years	NA
IRRIGATION PROJECTS					
12	Korea	66 projects	55 projects	NA	NA
29	Indonesia	550,000 ha	150,000 ha	> 2 years	60%
31	Sudan	310,000 fed	200,000 fed	> 3 years*	300%
35	Pakistan**	1,500 canals	1,300 canals	NA	61%
		425,000 acres	60,000 acres	(land levelled)	
54	Peru	27,900 ha	13,443 ha	NA	50%***
POTABLE WATER PROJECTS					
3	Thailand	250 systems	342 systems	0	0%
5	Kenya/1	NA	50% systems	> 2 years	95%
	Kenya/2	NA	< 50% systems	> 2 years	59%
	Kenya/CARE	30 systems	10 systems	> 1 year	107%
20	Korea	6 systems	5 systems	> 1 year	NA
24	Peru	20 systems	29 systems	> 1 year	-50%
			75 systems****		
32	Panama	500 systems	562 systems	0	NA
			645 systems****		
HEALTH					
9	Senegal	600 huts	< 200 huts	> 1 year	NA*
EDUCATION PROJECTS					
23	Nigeria	23 sets	12.5 sets	> 2 years	67%
25	Thailand	54 schools	45 schools	0	NA
46	Paraguay	59 schools	32 schools	> 2 years***	84%***

Table 8.1 (continued)

```
NA    No information available, not determinable
*     Project past deadline, not yet complete
**    Special circumstances explain much of the shortfall in this case.
      Two-thirds of AID funding was cancelled after Congress passed the
      Symington Amendment.
***   estimate
****  estimate for when project is completed
Source:  The data is derived from the set of Project Impact Evaluation
         Reports 1-63. Data is not listed for projects where such data was
         not obtainable.
```

The fourth major finding is the problem of inadequate maintenance and sustainability. Donor organizations are now paying much more attention to this issue, and our study does not capture much that is new. It does, however, support the following observations. First, maintenance and sustainability often require users fees or contributions of labor; these should be made an integral part of the project design. Second, users frequently have to become organized to fund or carry out maintenance tasks. Some projects, therefore, should involve community organizers. Third, the sustainability of a program or project usually needs national government support when the donor funding ends. This support must not be assumed but both earned and cultivated. Given the scarce resources of many Third World countries, only demonstrably successful projects that promise many future benefits should be sustained. Infrastructure projects, however, should be maintained so as not to lose the value of the original investment, assuming that maintenance costs are small compared to the investment.

Our last major finding concerns the deficiencies of the design documents. They are almost totally confined to technical and economic analyses and fail properly to plan projects for four reasons: they overestimate benefits, underestimate costs, underanalyze social factors, and overstate the government commitment to continue the project.

The explicit priority criteria for selecting or justifying most projects are the technical, economic, and financial soundness of the project. These three sets of analyses are proper and informative, but often they give unreliable estimates as pointed out in Table 8.1. Furthermore, all priceable benefits to users are included in the benefit-cost ratios, but costs seldom include the labor costs of users and many other nonproject costs that are necessary to achieve the benefits.

Some design documents include a modest social analysis which describes the intended beneficiaries and estimates some of the obvious consequences of the project on individuals and groups. Available studies of the target group may be cited, but original studies are not conducted. Much of the social analysis is background discussion and usually demonstrates a reasonable understanding of the target group. They are helpful for planning projects but usually are not adequate for anticipating how beneficiaries and others will respond to the project. More fieldwork is needed to give the designers more accurate estimates of user response and therefore more accurate benefit-cost ratios. In sum, feasibility studies are needed.

It appears that social impacts or social soundness are seldom used as major selection or justification criteria. The documents will often boast about how the project will benefit the poor and women, but it is not clear that these are critical factors used in choosing projects.

Finally, many design documents assert that the host government is willing and able to maintain the facilities produced by the project. The PIERs indicate that this claim was often untrue, and the long-term benefits were accordingly jeopardized.

LESSONS FOR SPECIFIC PROJECT SECTORS

Rural Roads

Rural roads probably do more than any other type of infrastructure to stimulate economic growth and development. By now all developing countries have considerable experience in planning, building, and maintaining rural roads. Designs for rural road projects, therefore, should be fairly competent and involve a reasonable assessment of impacts, but this is not what our study discovered, as demonstrated in Table 8.1. Higher than expected costs per kilometer invariably led to fewer kilometers constructed given a fixed budget. The largest errors in design documents' estimates, however, are not identified in Table 8.1. These are the predictions of the greatly increased economic activity that was to be stimulated by rural roads. Sometimes this error was due to poor choices of road location. As the Honduras Rural Roads I project (PIER 17) noted, "The roads lead from nowhere to nowhere." Another reason for a limited development impact was the failure of agricultural extension, credit, and other needed inputs to materialize to enable farmers to take advantage of the new market opportunities. The main reason for the inflated estimates, however, was that they were based on pure speculation and not on field studies.

On the other hand, some road projects did stimulate dramatic economic growth. In particular, new farmer market access (Honduras Rural Roads II [PIER 17]) or penetration roads (Colombia Small Farmer Market Access [PIER 1]) had much better cost-benefit ratios than upgrading feeder roads which collect traffic and feed into the arterial system. Constructing new roads where none existed previously greatly reduces transportation costs and increases travel.

In addition to the lessons about estimating benefits and costs, the twelve road projects for which we have impact assessments teach three important lessons: (1) beneficiary participation generally increases benefits and usually reduces costs, (2) funding agencies need a tough maintenance policy, and (3) roads substantially increase beneficiaries' quality of life in many tangible and intangible ways even though some negative effects were observed. Beneficiary participation in route selection and design improves the benefits of the road from their point of view and induces a commitment on their part to maintain the road when necessary. Community participation in the building of the road (which is especially large in "pick-and-shovel" roads) provides income for community residents and a greater sense of ownership, which also motivates maintenance. Finally, in a few cases with local participation, the beneficiaries became more active and effective politically.

Another finding in the impact assessment reports is the very poor maintenance found in eight of the twelve road projects reviewed. The other four projects had good maintenance on some roads and bad maintenance on others. In contrast, the design documents claimed that the provisions for maintenance were more than adequate. Some of these claims were inexcusable because the country already had a poor maintenance record on previous AID roads. Funding agencies must require effective maintenance on existing roads before funding the construction of new roads.

A very positive finding on the impact assessments is the generally enthusiastic attitude of beneficaries toward the road and its effects (see also Anderson et al., 1982). Their approval was especially strong where they participated in route selection and labor intensive construction. Some roads also had negative effects such as increased prices of land and the loss of land by some peasants who had no titles. Most effects, however, were positive. Moreover most of the negative effects could have been mitigated if they had been identified ahead of time in a more adequate social impact assessment.

In conclusion, the major lessons of impact assessment for future road project planning are fourfold. First, design documents should demonstrate, not just assume, that economic development is likely to result from the project. The results of similar past road projects can serve as the basis for projections, but some field testing of those projections is strongly recommended. Second, rural road projects should involve beneficiary participation in project design, implementation, and maintenance. Third, the project design should try to contain a realistic maintenance plan. Fourth, more analysis on possible negative consequences, such as land being taken away from peasants who lack documents of title, is necessary.

Rural Electrification

Electrification projects are attractive because they hold the promise of economic progress and they are a symbol of modernity. Furthermore, they should be able to pay for themselves over the long run from user fees. They have very expensive capital requirements, however, so developing countries often must seek assistance from donor agencies. In fact, AID invested $137 million in rural electrification between 1963 and 1980, host countries about the same, the Inter-

American Development Bank $400 million from 1969 to 1980, and the World Bank $676 million from 1976 to 1981.

In design documents, electrification projects are seen in mainly technical and financial terms. These documents included economic analyses that estimated the number of customers, but they were not based on empirical studies of demand for energy. Furthermore, the design documents clearly expected electrification to stimulate increased agricultural and industrial production but without any evidence to support their speculations. In fact, little economic development was stimulated by rural electrification in most cases, and often the development that did occur was not very rural but was really concentrated near cities and other market centers. The rural poor use the electricity for lighting and household appliances but not for producing goods. They greatly desire electrification and are willing to pay significant sums (by their standards) for service, so carefully selected electrification projects should quickly come to pay for recurring costs and become self-sustaining. Nevertheless the benefit-cost ratios in design documents should be based on low estimates of stimulated production according to the four impact assessments that we examined.

Irrigation

Expansion of irrigable land has been one of the greatest hopes for increasing agricultural production and the incomes of poor farmers. AID has invested hundreds of millions of dollars in irrigation, and the World Bank from $3 to $4 billion. Under the proper circumstances irrigation, combined with improved seeds and other inputs, can increase yields two or three times, or bring new land under cultivation. Yet irrigation projects are very complex, place severe demands on management structures, and require new social organizations and cooperative activities. They depend on the ability of beneficiaries to organize, utilize, and maintain irrigation systems. Preproject design documents rarely addressed these complexities or analyzed such complicating factors as the impacts of additional cropping and the work of irrigation on the microeconomics of individual farmers. As a result, they were overly optimistic. They often boasted of extremely high internal rates of return (for example 46 percent for the Indonesian project), which were not realized because of institutional and human factors.

As demonstrated in Table 8.1, the projections of irrigation project outputs exceeded the actual outputs. The shortfall, however, was usually not due to construction problems but to management, maintenance, and utilization problems. Most of the canals that were projected to be constructed or improved by the engineers were completed. Many of the canals projected to be completed by farmers were not, and many acres projected for irrigation were not irrigated. The engineers often succeeded but the projects failed. In part the project designers were at fault. Economic and engineering analysis dominated the designs and little attention was given to the institutional and social requirements for attaining maximum results. On the basis of the impact assessments, it is now clear that good engineering does not guarantee success. Good water management and the constant maintenance of the system are the keys to successful projects, and these factors require effective water user associations.

We conclude from our research that projects are more likely to succeed when beneficiaries participate in designing (and redesigning), implementing, and maintaining the project. In the Sederhana project (Indonesia [PIER 29]) farmers on Sumatra had little if any desire for the irrigation systems they were being given because the systems did not fit their conditions and cropping patterns. For example, the Risma Duma subproject provided irrigation to prosperous coffee growers who did not want to convert to irrigated rice growing. This should have been ascertained before the project started through consultation with the intended users and by bringing users into the planning decisions.

The major lesson from impact assessment for irrigation project planning is the need for feasibility studies, analyses of contingency behavior, maintenance plans, and user association development. Project planning would benefit from social analyses of the capacity of farmers to use irrigation and to organize effective user associations. Feasibility studies should also analyze how users adapt to unreliable water supplies and other contingencies. The design documents also need to develop realistic maintenance plans and programs for mobilizing users to participate in the design, implementation, and maintenance of irrigation systems.

Potable Water

Potable water has been a major funding priority but has not been very successful. In 1979 alone, AID spent $30 million, the World Bank $1 billion, the regional banks $400 million, the Organizaion for Economic Cooperation and Development $550 million, and other donors $430 million on potable water projects in developing countries. Despite these investments, the percentage of people without access to potable water was actually increasing at the turn of the decade because of population growth.

Potable water projects have lost favor among donors as a cost-effective means of improving health. The health effects tend to be fairly minor. Another justification of potable water projects according to preproject documents is the time saved from collecting and carrying water from other sources. These labor time savings projections were not empirically based; sometimes they grossly overstated the benefit-cost ratios. In general, potable water project plans were loosely sketched out and failed to specify clearly how the system would operate and be maintained.

Beneficiaries value water systems fairly highly and are willing to pay for their costs when the systems are designed to their specifications. Beneficiaries usually value water systems, however, for reasons different from those of the government agencies who provide them. Users want readily available water, and the government provides potable water systems to improve their health. The users may not drink the water because of its chlorine taste but use it in many other ways. The differences between the values of users and government planners makes it imperative to include community participation in design. Furthermore, systems last longer when the community operates, maintains, or pays for them. To facilitate community operation and maintenance the systems should be simple. Gravity-fed systems in Panama (PIER 32) and Peru (PIER 24) were sustained better physically and financially than diesel pump systems in Panama and Kenya (PIER 5). Finally, we find that ancillary components to potable water systems, such as latrines, health education, and so on, are usually unappreciated and contribute little.

Health and Nutrition

Basic health and nutrition services are badly needed in the rural areas because malnourishment and illness are widespread in many Third World countries. Usually neither the government nor the people can pay for health care or nutrition instruction in rural areas. Hospitals are provided in cities and clinics in good size market towns, but these services are not readily available to most rural peasants.

Because the need is so great, AID occasionally funds health and nutrition programs that are designed to reach the rural poor. These programs, which tend to be unique, are not standardized or well tested. The planning documents are more speculative than for infrastructure and other more standard projects. As a result, the projects tend to have more implementation problems. The four health projects in our sample were plagued by problems and failures which could have been anticipated in the design study but were not. Social and institutional assessments and pilot testing were needed but were missing. The lesson that we draw is that when health projects are relatively unique they should be tested in pilot projects before widespread implementation.

Education

Education is one of the most highly desired types of projects, and it is seen as a symbol of progress. Parents have a high demand for education as a means of social mobility for their children. In fact, education has often become an end in itself, rather than a means to economic growth, because of increasing credentialism.

Education projects, like those in health and nutrition, tend to be unique. Each needs a great deal of analysis that is specific to the situation. One common feature is that Third World governments are under severe budget constraints, and although they wish to meet the popular demand for education and to commit themselves to ambitious projects, their lofty ambitions are rarely achieved. Temporary expansions made possible with donor funding tend to diminish, if not cease immediately, once outside funding is removed.

One way that AID has been able to have a significant impact on education at relatively little expense is to focus on qualitative improvements such as curriculum development. These can have lasting effects without continuing investments. Our suggestions would be to continue in this direction, investing in low-cost high-impact projects. Preproject documents, however, need to be more realistic about finances, achievable outputs, the effects of political factors, the capacity of relevant institutions, and sustainability.

Agricultural Research

Agricultural research projects can have enormous or negligible benefits depending on experimental results and adoption rates. Their impact depends upon the increase in yields achieved, the importance of the crop, the area amenable to the new technology, the ability of farmers to utilize the technology, and the rates of diffusion. It is important to note that some of these factors are not within the control of the research project.

The two main reasons for the failure of some agricultural research projects were that they lacked beneficial innovations or that the innovations did not meet the needs of their target population. Many other factors sometimes severely limit the flow of benefits including the failure of the extension service, shortage of credit, the reasonable fear of the risks of innovations for small farmers, and unreliable supplies of seeds and other needed inputs. These concerns need to be addressed in design documents.

We have three suggestions for strengthening preproject documents. First, because these projects can have small to gigantic effects, they are difficult to assess with an impact assessment methodology. Preproject documents should mainly employ a socioeconomic feasibility methodology which identifies obstacles to adoption and diffusion of technologies and modifies the project design to circumvent these obstacles. Second, project design should pay more attention to dissemination. Third, project design must take into account the real world of the target farmers. Most preproject documents do describe the macro agricultural picture as background for the project. The micropicture of the small farmer should also be described and project planning built around it.

Agricultural Services

Agricultural service projects provide one or more critical inputs, such as fertilizer, seeds, or credit, that are needed to increase agricultural production. In general, the preproject design documents focused on the production of the input or service, but specified little about the means of delivering it. They also lacked feasibility studies of farmers' desire for and ability to use the input.

The PIERs indicate that the success or failure of agricultural service projects depends heavily on the performance of nonproject institutions and on environmental factors. The lessons for agricultural services projects are similar to the lessons learned from agricultural research projects. Much more attention must be paid to potential obstacles to dissemination and adoption of inputs and services. Also, the real world situation of small farmers needs to be better studied to determine the likelihood that farmers will be able to utilize such inputs and services profitably. Finally, the financial viability and the overall sustainability of the producing and delivery institutions must be planned to ensure project continuation at reasonable levels after the cessation of outside funding.

RECOMMENDATIONS

In summary we repeat that design documents are overly optimistic, do not anticipate schedule delays, assume widespread use of project outputs without an adequate rationale, and are unrealistic about maintenance. In other words, they do not adequately assess the feasibility of the implementation, maintenance, and use of the project and its outputs. Furthermore, they do not adequately assess potential negative impacts. In light of these shortcomings of current project planning processes, we offer the following recommendations for consideration and testing:

1. Planning documents for relatively standard projects such as rural roads should consider a designated list of issues which derive from a synthesis of evaluations, reports, and studies on that type of project. Not all issues should be studied because research costs must be carefully controlled, but they should be considered by a multidisciplinary team, and key issues should be selected for study.

2. We recognize that planning documents for nonstandard or innovative projects tend to be less reliable guides to successful project implementation. We therefore recommend the use of pilot projects and experiments to test, refine, and improve project design before widespread implementation.

3. Project impact evaluation reports and other evaluations have yielded many insights on projects. AID has already utilized the sixty-three PIERs for identifying issues and summarizing findings for several types of projects. These are good beginnings, but more systematic, detailed, and quantitative approaches to synthesizing findings and deriving lessons should be conducted. Donor agencies should develop data bases on various project types that synthesize and summarize the experience of past projects to guide the planning of new projects. The data base should identify problems and solutions, contingencies and adaptations, and model techniques, practices, and projects.

In sum, our recommendations suggest ways to learn from experience and to avoid the pitfalls of past mistakes. The key to this process of improving by learning is the impact assessment of completed projects (for another example, see Kottak, 1985). They determine the degree of success or failure of projects and identify the factors which help or hinder them. They provide the bases for policy changes and better project design. If postproject impact assessments continue to be conducted and analyzed for their program implications, the effectiveness of development projects should continually improve.

PART III

FUTURE POLICY DIRECTIONS IN IMPACT ASSESSMENT

9

Institutionalizing Science Impact Assessment Indicators into Public Policy

William N. Dunn, Andrea M. Hegedus, and Burkart Holzner

INTRODUCTION

The social utility of science recently has come to be viewed as an important science policy issue. While investments in the physical, biological, and social sciences continue to be seen as a contribution to the growth of knowledge, per se, there is an obvious growing concern that science policymakers and the public at large lack sufficient information to assess the social and economic impacts of science. In the absence of such information, policymakers cannot be expected to make decisions that yield advances in science, let alone gains in economic and social performance.

One response to this information deficit is the development of the field of science indicators (Elkana et al., 1978), a field that seeks to measure changes in various aspects of science. These changes, such as the growth in the number of natural science Ph.D.s or changes in federal dollars spent on scientific research and development (R&D), are then analyzed to monitor the structure and performance of science. Although the field of science indicators has continued to grow, recently attention has turned to ways in which science affects the structure

This chapter was prepared under Grant No. SRS–8519287 from the National Science Foundation, Science Resources Studies Division, Science Indicators Unit. Conclusions and interpretations stated in this chapter are those of the authors and do not necessarily represent the official position or policies of the National Science Foundation.

and performance of contemporary society (Holzner, Dunn, and Shahidullah, 1987; Dunn et al., 1987). Social impact of science (SIS) indicators have been developed by these authors in an attempt to supply policymakers with the information necessary to make informed decisions (Dunn, Hegedus, and Holzner, 1988). These indicators would provide the basic information for the practice of systematic and rigorous science impact assessment.

Policy-Relevant Science Impact Indicators

There has been a rising demand for science impact indicators that are policy relevant. This demand is a result of two recent developments (Kruytbosch and Burton, 1987). The Science Indicators Unit, within the Science Resources Studies Division of the National Science Board, has spearheaded successful attempts to monitor the achievement of science and technology through such refined measurements as bibliometric techniques, the analysis of patent and trade data, and the monitoring of science education and personnel. The National Science Board has just published its eighth volume of a biennial series that examines the roles played by science and engineering research and education in creating both new knowledge and new technical products and processes (National Science Board, 1987).

The second development that has increased the demand for policy-relevant science impact indicators is the advent of political initiatives that seek to improve the performance of science in addressing major social needs. Looking back to the 1960s, Congress required the National Science Foundation to include applied research in its program. In the 1970s, such initiatives as RANN, a university and industry cooperative program, were developed to strengthen the relationship between basic research and societal needs. The Engineering Research Centers is a more recent program that was specifically designed to link basic research to development and manufacturing capabilities of U.S. industry.

Knowledge Systems Accounting

A response to the demand for policy-relevant science impact indicators has been the attempt to develop knowledge systems accounting, a field that seeks to estimate the effects of science on society (Dunn and Holzner, 1987). In contrast to classical scientometrics (Price, 1963), which involves the quantitative study of the structure and performance of science, knowledge systems accounting involves the quantitative study of the effects of science on the structure and performance of social, political, and economic systems. The principal unit of measure in classical scientometrics is the science indicator, whereas the main unit of measure in knowledge systems accounting is the SIS indicator.

Knowledge systems accounting represents a special form of social impact assessment (Carley and Bustelo, 1984; Finsterbusch, Llewellyn, and Wolf, 1983). Other forms of social impact assessment include technology assessment, environmental assessment and impact analysis, benefits assessment, and cost-benefit analysis. Whereas social impact assessment is concerned with methods for the assessment of a wide variety of actual and potential effects in specific domains of interest—for example, cost-benefit analyses of health care issues or risk assessment of nuclear energy—knowledge systems accounting is guided by a different set of purposes, principles, and measures.

In knowledge systems accounting, the measures of interest are SIS indicators, or what MacRae (1985) calls policy indicators. SIS indicators are at once relational, causal, and normative. They are relational because they quantitatively represent linkages between science and society; they are causal because they are embedded in the logic of causal reasoning; and they are normative because they seek to identify those causal relations that facilitate and retard the achievement of social goals. The extent to which SIS indicators satisfy these three conditions determines their degree of policy relevance (MacRae, 1985; Peters, 1987).

THE DESIGN OF SIS INDICATORS

The task of designing SIS indicators is what Simon (1973) and others have characterized as an ill-structured or systemic problem. The designer of SIS indicators faces not one problem, but a system of problems which has one or more of the following characteristics (compare Harmon and King, 1985:28): (1) *competing design goals*, where the goals of the SIS indicators are not specific and the determination of which goals are to be included is part of the problem; (2) *indeterminate design states*, where it is not clear which states or steps must be included, and in what order, to obtain an acceptable solution; (3) *unspecified design rules*, where rules for the evaluation of SIS indicators are not clear; and (4) *unbounded design space*, where boundaries around the goals, states, and rules have not been established.

Confronted with a systemic problem, the designer of SIS indicators is not likely to succeed by employing methods appropriate for well-structured problems; for example, econometric measures designed to estimate the expected utility of information to single decisionmakers are not appropriate to evaluate more complex situations. These methods, while valuable for solving relatively well-structured problems, have been criticized on grounds that they ignore the systemic complexity of social processes in which multiple decisionmakers attach different values to the same information (Machlup, 1980). Ill-structured or systemic problems appear to exhibit a level of organized complexity that makes the application of many conventional analytic procedures inappropriate (Zadeh, 1972; Mitroff and Blankenship, 1973; Brewer and de Leon, 1983; Dunn, 1988).

Systemic problems thus require nonconventional methods. These methods have the following characteristics in common: a principal concern with improving the formation or structuring of a problem, as distinguished from its solution; the use of formal methods for discovering the structure of problems through inductive search procedures; and a reliance on external knowledge sources (distributed expertise) which bring alternative goals, rules, and informational sources to the task of problem structuring (Simon, 1973; Warfield, 1976; Saaty, 1980; Mason and Mitroff, 1981).

In this context, the design of SIS indicators is heavily dependent on our capacity to represent complex patterns of causation believed to govern the system of knowledge-related processes—mandating, production, structuring, storage, distribution, utilization—and their social impacts. The process of designing SIS indicators, when applied *in* as well as *to* knowledge systems, typically requires several principles. The process should incorporate multiple external perspectives and informational sources (externalization), apply publicly announced formal rules of assessing the causal and normative relevance of indicators (formalization), and utilize a measurement process that is readily understood and criticized by stakeholders in the social performance of society (simplification).

But the design of SIS indicators also must address social goals, since the social impacts that are of primary interest to policymakers and the public at large are closely related to socially valued states, such as health, education, welfare, security, and material well-being. When SIS indicators are related to social goals, it is more likely that such indicators will be responsive to the needs, values, and interests of policymakers and citizens; sensitive to unintended consequences, side effects, and spillovers of science; and open to the externally distributed knowledge required to adapt indicators to changing circumstances. In this manner, SIS indicators will be more likely to be used by policymakers to improve the social performance of science.

THE PROBLEM OF POLICY RELEVANCE

The policy relevance of SIS indicators is thus a function of their relationship to social goals. Strictly speaking, policy-relevant social impacts of science are effects whose occurrence or magnitude may be affected by public decisions to regulate or invest in science. Yet policy-relevant social impacts of science represent a subset of an enormous universe of social impacts, some of which are unrelated either to science or policy. Hence, not all social impacts are a consequence of science, and among those impacts that are due to science, not all are policy relevant. A good example of a nonpolicy-relevant indicator is the pattern of interregional migration. Controlling migration, but not through science policies, is on the agenda of most governments.

The process of measuring policy-relevant impacts of science, since it is embedded in the logic of causal reasoning, involves claims in the form: X causes Y. To make such causal claims, however, requires formal rules that permit distinctions among possible, plausible, and probable causes. While almost any aspect of science can be hypothesized as a possible cause of some social impact, the aim of design is to identify aspects of science that are plausible and probable causes of social performance. Plausible causes are causes with some known prior probability, and probable causes are established through inductive reasoning—

for example, the process of reasoning that X (as distinguished from some other factor) probably caused Y.

An SIS indicator thus measures a presumed social effect of science, which is its presumed cause. The logic of this causal relation may be expressed by the functional equation: $SIS = f(S) + error$, where SIS is one of the possible social impacts of science, S is science, and error is the proportion of variance in SIS that cannot be explained by S. For example, S might be represented by Waxman's discovery of streptomycin and SIS by the measured decline in reported cases of tuberculosis after 1945. The error accounts for the many factors other than S that are causally relevant to the SIS indicator.

Formal selection rules may be employed to reduce to manageable proportions the otherwise unmanageably huge pool of relational SIS indicators. These selection rules, based in part on Mill's canons (methods) of induction, have been developed and refined over the past fifty years (see Cook and Campbell, 1979). These rules require that any claim about a social impact of science meet six minimal conditions:

- *Plausibility*. There should be some known prior probability that a particular science output affects a given type of social performance.
- *Temporal precedence*. Measured science outputs should precede social impacts in time, and they should be examined longitudinally, not statically.
- *Active intervention*. Science outputs should be the product of active (deliberate) interventions designed to promote the achievement of given social goals.
- *Comparison*. Measured science outputs should produce similar measured social impacts in two or more contexts.
- *Contrast*. When science outputs are absent, social impacts observed in the presence of given science outputs also should be absent.
- *Covariation*. A measured science output should vary in the same direction (concomitantly) as a social impact.

These minimal conditions may be satisfied along a continuum of complexity. Simple and readily comprehensible visual profiles can be used to represent graphic displays of time series, while complex algorithms, comprehensible to specialists only, can be used to represent simultaneous equation systems. Given that SIS indicators must be utilized by diverse science policy stakeholders, simple alternatives are preferable to complex ones.

Typology of SIS Indicators

With these conditions in mind we can proceed to develop a typology of SIS indicators. In contrast with available classifications of social indicators, including those constructed by such authors as Duncan (1978) and by the U.S. Bureau of the Census, this typology is based on distinctions among types and levels of goals rather than lists of areas, such as health, education, income, and culture.

Table 9.1
Typology of SIS Indicators

Type of Social Goal	Level of Social Goal	
	Prime	Enabling
Aggregative Well-Being	Average Life Expectancy	Infant Mortality Rate
	Per Capita Income	Unemployment Rate
	Average Educational Achievement	School Dropouts Per Pupil
Distributive Well-Being	Average Life Expectancy of Poverty Population	Infant Mortality Rate of Poverty Population
	Per Capita Income of Rural Population	Unemployment Rate of Rural Population
	Average Educational Achievement of Minorities	School Dropouts Per Pupil Among Minorities
Subjective Well-Being	Evaluation of Importance of Good Health	Confidence in Medical Leaders
	Feelings About Present Life	Economic Expectations
	Satisfaction With Amount of Education	Evaluation of Spending on Education

Sources: U.S. Department of Commerce, Bureau of the Census, *Social Indicators III* (1980); and Duncan MacRae, Jr., *Policy Indicators* (1985).

This focus on types and levels of goals ensures that SIS indicators retain their policy-relevant and performance-related character. At the same time, this approach avoids the unnecessary and frequently unproductive practice of making sharp distinctions between "social" and "economic" indicators. The typology therefore includes "any useful measure of human conditions and related variables whether derived from economics, other social sciences, natural science, or sources outside basic disciplines" (MacRae, 1986:133).

One dimension of the typology of SIS indicators (see Table 9.1) distinguishes impacts associated with three types of societal well-being: aggregate, distributive, and subjective. These three aspects of societal well-being appear to capture in broad terms many of the most important social impacts of science. SIS indicators that focus on aggregative well-being—for example, average life expectancy, per capita income, or average educational achievement—measure states of societal well-being that are frequently discussed in terms of economic or social welfare, social welfare functions, or net economic benefits.

By contrast, SIS indicators that focus on distributive well-being measure variations in impacts among different segments of the community, for example, life expectancy, income, or educational achievement among persons above and below the poverty line. Distributive SIS indicators are closely related to concerns with societal equity and justice, including rival ethical hypotheses associated with Pareto (an optimal state is one where some gain without others losing) and Rawls (an optimal social state is one where those worst off gain).

Finally, SIS indicators that focus on subjective well-being measure impacts observed in the form of perceptions, expectations, or assessments of progress in the achievement of social goals. Attitudes toward science and technology; satisfaction with health, education, and employment; and economic expectations are examples of SIS indicators of subjective well-being.

The distinction between two levels of social goals (prime and enabling) is also important since it highlights impacts related to both ends and means. Yet these two levels also draw attention to types of impacts—that is, changes in the attitudes and behavior of target groups and beneficiaries—as distinguished from outputs that simply measure quantities per person (e.g., units of service). It is important to observe outputs of the knowledge system (e.g., science-based knowledge of proper nutrition), but prime and enabling impacts of science (e.g., life expectancy and nutritional intake, respectively) also must be observed. In short, by including in the typology two levels of social goals in each of the three areas of well-being, a focus on the social impacts of science rather than the outcomes of the knowledge system is retained.

In the typology of SIS indicators presented in Table 9.1, each cell displays an illustrative SIS indicator designed to measure impacts associated with the three types of societal well-being. Within each type of well-being, there are two levels of SIS indicators (prime and enabling) that express relationships between ends and means, or goals and objectives. Overall, the eighteen SIS indicators represent a cross-section of working hypotheses about possible impacts of science on selected aspects of social performance.

A system of SIS indicators can now be designed to attempt to represent the relational, causal, and normative linkages among the complex relationships at the science and society nexus. To ensure that the system is utilized by the policymakers and stakeholders involved, it must be developed to become an integral part of the decision-making process.

INSTITUTIONALIZATION OF SIS INDICATORS

A system of SIS indicators, as well as other forms of social impact assessment, not only can be viewed as a policy tool, but also can be utilized as a policy strategy (Caldwell, 1982; Taylor, 1984). Such a policy strategy would incorporate SIS indicators into the social plans and goals of the policymakers. This prospective approach to SIS indicators would seek to establish causal linkages between future policy outcomes and the science available for government intervention, as well as to broaden the range of evaluative criteria used to assess science (Peters, 1987).

In order to be applied as a policy strategy, the process of designing SIS indicators must be institutionalized as an integral feature of policy making. In this manner, SIS indicators would be more likely to be perceived as useful by stakeholders who affect and are affected by the process of science policy making.

Problems of Institutionalization

The design, development, and use of SIS indicators are complex social processes. As such, a system of SIS indicators must satisfy at least three conditions: the system must be responsive to external sources of new goals, rules, and information; it must supply minimal rule-based information about possible, plausible, and probable causes of observed impacts; and it must be useful, and perceived as such, by science policymakers and other stakeholders in the social performance of society. Although these conditions are not easily satisfied, the institutional arrangements for a system of policy impact assessment indicators proposed by MacRae (1985) provides a useful starting point.

Scientific, Technical, and Political Communities

Because the design of SIS indicators is a system problem, it is impossible to outline in advance a comprehensive and well-tested system of indicators that measures the social impacts of science. We can develop the broad contours of the types of indicators that appear to be required, but the specifications of particular indicators can be accomplished only through additional external search. Although publicly available rules of inductive inference assist in formalizing and simplifying the selection of indicators, the development of specific causal models requires continuous external search among key stakeholders in the social performance of science.

A workable classification of stakeholders is available in the form of the distinction between scientific and technical communities (MacRae, 1985:339). To these two groups we add a third, the political community. Whereas the political community is primarily concerned with issues of constituent representation and public accountability, the scientific community is chiefly concerned with the conduct of the research necessary to develop and test scientific theories. Technical communities, by contrast,

deal with laymen's practical problems, conduct related research, and subject both of these to mutual quality control. Such a group resembles a scientific community except that it is guided by practical rather than purely theoretical criteria of excellence; and concerned not only with internal standards but also with performing functions for, and thus interacting with, laymen (MacRae, 1987:434–35).

Technical communities, it should be noted, are responsible for most of the knowledge functions which mediate science and social performance.

Thus a system of SIS indicators would be institutionalized through specifically developed and supported relationships among scientific, technical, and political communities that represent the primary stakeholders in the social performance of society. For example, the design of a system of SIS indicators to monitor the impact of science on the judicial system might include representatives from Congress or the judicial branch (political communities), the National Institute of Justice (technical community), and the American Association for the Advancement of Science (scientific community).

Choice of SIS Indicators

The search for specific SIS indicators can be further expanded by institutionalizing the choice of indicators among members of scientific, technical, and political communities. These three communities constitute a rich source of plausible rival hypotheses that would be used not only to broaden the range of candidate indicators, but also to account for the discovery of unrecognized and unintended side effects, sleeper effects, and spillovers of science.

In addition, the relationships among these communities provide a means of interaction in the development, testing, and use of SIS indicators. The major steps in the development and use of SIS indicators include choice of policy-relevent SIS indicators; preparation and dissemination of SIS indicator statistics; public definition of problems arising from science, including unrealized social goals as well as unintended negative consequences of science; and science policy choices that affect relationships between science and social performance (MacRae, 1985).

The development of commonsense and scientific (causal) policy models is essential to establish the plausibility of relational indicators. Equally important, these models depend on prior information supplied by political communities (e.g., the National Science Board or Congress), technical communities (e.g., the Office of Technology Assessment), and scientific communities (e.g., the American Society of Chemists or the American Psychological Association).

Summary

By involving scientific, technical, and political communities in the design of SIS indicators we may increase the likelihood that a system of indicators will be used by policymakers to improve the social performance of science. The extent to which a system of SIS indicators is actually used to inform or guide science policy making depends on its degrees of institutionalization so that it can be maximally responsive to the goals, values, and informational sources supplied by the scientific, technical, and political communities. The institutional arrangements outlined above provide a preliminary sketch of ways to make SIS indicators an integral feature of science policy making in a democratic society.

CONCLUSION

To achieve a desired social impact, the outputs of science are typically transformed in accordance with practical demands of the social context in which
science is applied (Mulkay, 1971:71). To observe and measure that transformation, a system of relational SIS indicators must be developed—one that has
the capacity to discern the effects of knowledge-related activities by which
science outputs are synthesized, organized, distributed, and utilized.

The design of SIS indicators is a systemic problem involving ambiguous design
goals, indeterminate design states, unspecified design rules, and an unmanageably huge design space. These characteristics are not solely or even primarily a
product of the imperfections of measurement; they result from the complexity
of the social arrangements that govern knowledge-related activities in contemporary society. As such, the design of SIS indicators should proceed on the basis
of principles appropriate for solving systemic problems. These principles include
externalization, formalization, and simplification.

The design of SIS indicators also should address social goals, since the social
impacts of science are of primary interest to policymakers. When SIS indicators
are related to social goals, it is more likely that such indicators will be responsible
to the needs, values, and interests of policymakers and citizens; sensitive to
unintended consequences, side effects, and spillovers of science; and open to
the externally distributed knowledge required to adapt indicators to changing
circumstances. In this manner, SIS indicators will be more likely to be used by
policymakers to improve the social performance of science.

A typology of SIS indicators can be designed to ensure that indicators retain
their policy-relevant and performance-related nature. The design of such a system
would focus on an institutionalized network of technical, scientific, and political
communities that would develop, and eventually utilize, the SIS indicators. The
indicators would be associated with three types of societal well-being—aggregate, distributive, and subjective—and would distinguish between two levels of
social goals—prime and enabling. In this manner, a system of SIS indicators
could be adapted as a policy strategy and more easily integrated into the decision-
making process. In the final analysis, the causal relevance of science to social
performance depends on our capacity to link the complex knowledge system of
modern science to the achievement of social goals.

10

Judicial Impact Analysis: Missing from the Gene Pool of Policy Influence

William W. Nicholls, Jr.

The whole machinery of our intelligence, our general ideas and laws, fixed and external objects, principles, persons, and gods, are so many symbolic, algebraic expressions. They stand for experiences; experience which we are incapable of retaining and surveying in its multitudinous immediacy. We should flounder hopelessly, like the animals, did not we keep ourselves afloat and direct our course by these intellectual devices. Theory helps us to bear our ignorance of fact.

—Santayana, 1896

Judicial impact assessment (JIA) has been a hybrid in the barnyard of policy impact studies. Whereas traditional policy impact studies have been the product of public policy scholars and public policymakers (both elected officials and bureaucrats), JIAs have been born of a conjugation of species only partially compatible and without substantial commonality of interests—lawyers and political scientists.

Traditional policy impact studies—environmental impact assessment (EIA), technology assessment, social impact assessment (SIA), and cost-benefit analysis—have contributed to the building of theoretical explanations of the policy process as well as to the generation and fine-tuning of public policies. JIAs have been more like the mule—a creature capable of hard work, likely to be contrary, often abused, frequently misunderstood, and almost always sterile.

Traditional policy impact studies have become institutionalized in many nations and at various levels of government. The elected branches of American national government both have subunits dedicated to assessing impacts of extant and potential policies, and impact analysis is an imbedded part of the policy process. But JIAs have remained largely irrelevant.

JUDICIAL IMPACT ASSESSMENT: A SOLID BASE AND GOOD INTENTIONS

JIA is grounded in solid and respectable research traditions. It arose in the 1960s as a part of the flourishing of policy impact studies across a broad array of policy areas. Largely the province of public law specialists in political science departments, JIA applied the research traditions of the larger field to the decisions of the judicial branch, most commonly to those of the U.S. Supreme Court. The decisions chosen for impact assessment tended to fall into the public law field, such as school desegregation and criminal justice cases.[1]

Judicial impact assessors, like other scholars of policy impact, took a political process view of impact. That is, a judicial decision was (and is) viewed as that part of a policy model that transformed inputs of various types into an output (the decision), which is translated by other policy participants into results (outcomes) for various policy-consuming populations, who in turn react in various ways producing inputs leading to future court output (Goldman and Jahnige, 1971).

The political process of conceptualization replaced the narrow "legalistic" view of judicial decisions. The legalistic approach focused on defining the law in light of judicial decisions rather than on placing these decisions within the context of public policy (Sheldon, 1974:200–226). Judicial impact assessors sought to fill this void.

Similar to impact studies of nonjudicial policies, JIAs have identified and defined the relationships of populations having direct or indirect connections to judicial decisions: how transmitting, receiving, and consuming populations shape ultimate decision impacts has been described in detail. There has also been recognition that decisions have both unintended and intended consequences (Johnson, 1977). Models of the impact process specifying the relationships of these groups have become accepted as descriptions of the place of the judiciary in the political process (Johnson and Canon, 1984).

Twenty years of impact studies and model building have produced a consensus that courts make policy decisions and that these policy decisions have impacts.[2] Yet such solid if unsurprising achievements, well rooted in accepted research traditions, have been insufficient to transcend inherent bars to direct policy influence.

BARS TO JIA POLICY INFLUENCE

JIA as a policy strategy has been almost completely sterile. The sterility is striking when compared with the fecundity of, say, EIAs. Barriers to the policy influence of JIAs are several.

JIAs must account for multiple constituent groups including advocates, recipients, opponents, implementors, monitors, and those indirectly affected. These must be identified with specificity regarding their relationship to the decision at issue while taking into account how their interrelationships shape impact. In addition, the intrusion of intervening events may help shape decision impacts and must be considered. For example, a JIA of the *Miranda* v. *Arizona* decision would consider the requirements of that decision for change in police behavior, if the police implement the required changes in a meaningful manner, if the consuming population of suspects avails itself of the offered right to counsel or protected right to refuse to answer questions, if police compliance is consistent across suspects or groups of suspects, if consistent monitoring programs exist, and if these reveal changes in the number and content of confessions obtained during apprehension. Additionally, the analysis should consider how state courts apply the U.S. Supreme Court's decision within the context of state law. That is, do the state court systems enforce the *Miranda* rules or do they force appeals to the federal courts to bring about compliance?[3]

Further, court decisions must be evaluated in light of subsequent decisions and state or federal statutory changes. The greater the temporal distance from *Miranda* to time of JIA, the more likely that subsequent decisions or statutes will have an impact. Also, changes in police personnel over time may bring in officials with greater or lesser commitments to decision implementation.

As is readily apparent, the above requirements for a complete JIA necessitates massive investment of resources. The assessor must also gain access to police activities or suspects; both of these groups may have motives to deny access or to conceal their actual behaviors. The assessor must be able to collect and analyze sufficient data to make scientifically acceptable inferences within a short enough period of time so that intervening events do not confound the results.

Resource demands and the technical difficulties associated with properly done JIAs are tangible challenges. Less tangible but no less real bars to institutionalization of JIA are the legal mind set and the political sensitivity of the judiciary.

Law school training tends to emphasize attention to the case at hand as a discrete event or situation and not as a member of a class or group of like events or situations. Lawyers and consequently judges, for example, look for probable cause to justify a warrant to search a specific person or place suspected of having evidence of a specific criminal act. Concepts such as proximate cause and last clear chance are also indicative of the individual and event specific nature of legal training.[4]

The U.S. Supreme Court has emphasized the requirement of individualized specificity in many decisions. A recent example is *Booth* v. *Maryland*, 96

L.Ed.2d 440 (1987), in which the Court, Justice Lewis F. Powell delivering the opinion, found that the inclusion of victim impact statements (VISs) as part of the sentencing process in death penalty cases was impermissible. The Court reasoned that an unacceptable risk is created that the jury may impose the death penalty in an arbitrary and capricious manner because the focus of the VIS is not on the defendant but on the character and reputation of the victim (at p. 441). The Court went further to hold that presentation of the VIS at sentencing "can serve no other purpose than to inflame the jury and divert it from deciding the case on the relevant evidence concerning the crime and the defendant" (at p. 441).

The *Booth* decision is of particular relevance here because it addresses an attempt at a form of JIA institutionalization. The VIS is designed, among other things, to better enable the sentencing judge or jury to assess the impact of a crime on its victim(s) and, presumably, thereby facilitate the rendering of a more appropriate sentence. An important goal of programs of this type is to improve community confidence in the criminal justice system.[5] The Supreme Court in *Booth* required that these desired impacts be accomplished by maintenance of a specific focus on the crime and defendant and by avoidance of factors not relevant thereto.

The political sensitivity of the judiciary has also been indicated in many U.S. Supreme Court decisions. One such decision is *Stone* v. *Powell*, 427 U.S. 465 (1975), which presents a detailed discussion of JIA research on exclusionary rule cases. In *Stone* v. *Powell*, the Court, Justice Powell again writing the majority opinion, restricted the authority of lower federal courts to grant habeas corpus relief when the state has afforded an opportunity for full and fair litigation of Fourth Amendment violation claims. Justice Powell devoted over eight pages of his opinion to scholarly JIAs which had assessed the impact of the exclusionary rule—as created and imposed by the Supreme Court—on public respect for law and on police behavior and effectiveness.

Justice Powell noted the mixed conclusions reached by the authors of the several JIAs cited. This lack of consensus failed to assist the Court in resolving the conundrum of protecting Fourth Amendment rights against unreasonable search and seizure without hamstringing legitimate law enforcement efforts (at p. 494). Yet reading Justice Powell's opinion in *Stone* makes clear his concern about the impact on society of Court decisions.

Although concerned with decision impact, the Court as a general policy has long sought to avoid usurping or appearing to usurp the policy-making prerogatives of the elected branches. Court-driven JIA would be an obvious reversal of this practice and would strip the Court and lower courts as well of their veil of legal objectivity. Among other things, the monetary bottom line for policy making and the lack of budgetary authority for the judicial branch keep it in a dependent position. Efforts to institutionalize JIA will not alter this dependency and bear genuine risks to the myth of judicial objectivity.

Some of these risks may be highlighted by analyzing other proposed institutionalizations of JIA. Daniel E. Koshland, Jr., editor of *Science*, provides an example in a March 1988 editorial. Koshland expresses discontent at what he perceives as court-created delays due to "minor legal technicalities" obstructing the implementation of scientific advances such as genetic engineering. In this and other areas, these unspecified minor legal technicalities are, according to Koshland, enabling judges to substitute their personal preferences for the professional judgments of experts. As an example, Koshland states, "In a more recent example a judge who was against capital punishment found technical errors in 90 different trials, in each case invalidating a death penalty decision" (Koshland, 1988:1225). Yet if we do not insist on error-free imposition of the death penalty, regardless of who finds the errors, what standard of decision do we require in less profound matters? Stated another way, how much deference do we expect of courts toward experts and impact assessments?

Koshland laments that our society is becoming a nation of men and not of laws. But his prescription would tend to hasten that demise, not remedy it. Imposition of JIAs prior to court decisions risks institutionalizing deference to experts in preference to law, minor technicalities included.

The thrust of Koshland's editorial, and some other JIA proposals, is not toward an institutionalized JIA system but toward the creation of a "science" court modeled on the Court of Patent Appeals.[6] The Court of Patent Appeals was created because of the increasingly complex and technical nature of patent cases and the lack of technical training of most judges of courts of general jurisdiction. Science courts could be established by Congress and qualifications of scientific training set for those appointed as judges. They would presumably have the skills to knowledgeably evaluate the decisions of bureaucratic experts and those who challenge them.

Koshland does recognize the conceptual similarity of JIA and EIA, although he refers to project consequences as if these will be mutually perceived and understood by all scientific evaluators. In fact, the multiplicity of considerations and potentially confounding intervening factors which occur for both EIA and JIA suggest that scientific evaluators probably will reach differing, if not conflicting, conclusions about impact as was the case for ex post facto JIA of the exclusionary rule decisions. If impact cannot be agreed upon after the fact of a court decision, can we expect agreement before one is made?

THE PROJECTIVE AND INSTITUTIONALIZATION CONTRASTS

The contrast of policy influence potential between JIA and other types of impact assessment may best be highlighted by focusing on projectivity and institutionalization. EIA, technology assessment, SIA, and cost-benefit analysis all tend to be both projective and institutionalized; JIA tends to be ex post facto and noninstitutionalized. Although being ex post facto does not improve the chances for JIA policy influence, neither is it a preventive. Some JIA scholars have argued that accurate impact assessment requires the passage of several years (Canon, 1974). Courts, especially the U.S. Supreme Court as illustrated by *Stone v. Powell*, can and do reassess past decisions in the context of current cases. Likewise, ex post facto assessments of the impacts of technology inspired the drafters of the National Environmental Policy Act (NEPA) and the Technology Assessment Act, and these continue to provide guidance for those conducting projective impact assessments (e.g., Darling and Milton, 1966).

Projectivity, though important, is not as significant a distinction between JIA and other impact assessment systems as is institutionalization. JIA is not, as previously noted, institutionalized. EIA, technology assessment, SIA, and cost-benefit analysis in varying degrees are.

For the United States, NEPA and its implications provide both a common set of processes and goals for EIA and an authoritative mandate that these be employed by the executive branch of the national government. The policy potential of EIA is thereby preordained, though its precise extent is not guaranteed (Bartlett, 1986a:109–10). NEPA is a product of political rationality, but it does not preclude political irrationality in environmental policy making. It does, however, impose ecological rationality as the means through which environmental-policy-relevant data are compiled and processed.

In contrast, JIAs enjoy no such commonality of heritage. JIAs are speculation, except after a court decision has occurred. Goals of judicial decisionmakers may be as numerous as the judges themselves. Indeed, the collegial nature of most appellate courts imposes often competing group goals upon those of individual members. The principles that judges seek to actualize by their decisions include ideological views regarding public policy and about the role of courts. Justice Felix Frankfurter was a prime example of a public policy liberal who often voted with public policy conservatives because of his concept of the Supreme Court's proper role. Frankfurter felt that the Court should exercise restraint vis-à-vis the policies of the elected branches. Some members of the present Court face a similar dilemma from the conservative public policy perspective. Other judges are less ideologically driven, responding to other influences on a case-by-case basis and sometimes forming a balance of power of collegial courts controlled by neither liberals nor conservatives (Pritchett, 1948; Schubert, 1965).

Decisions are not made discreetly without an awareness of prior and future decisions, of other judges with whom and against whom one is voting, of the potential content of a decision, and by whom the Court's opinion will be written. Some judges are majority prone; they will vote with the majority once it has become apparent. Former Chief Justice Warren Burger has been accused of voting with the majority and against his own ideological views so that he could assign the opinion writing task and thereby ameliorate the resulting decision. The small group context of decision making mitigates against dissent and toward presenting a united front to the outside. The *Brown* decision has been examined as an example of justices burying their disagreement with the majority for the sake of the Court (Ulmer, 1971a).

Furthermore, changes may occur from case to case in both guiding principles and intragroup relations. A judge may be guided by his feelings for the "intent of the Framers" in a case of one type and refer to the "plain meaning of the words" in another. Direct evidence of these ebbs and flows may appear in opinions or may await memoirs. Both of these sources appear after the decision and often have multiple purposes. Opinions, unless solitary, necessarily represent the views of more judges than the author alone and serve not only to state the decision but also to justify it, to hold together the majority group by honoring necessary rationales, and to sell the decision to a variety of groups from the public at large to elected officeholders to lower court judges. Memoirs may go beyond strict history to embellish the role played by the author and his friends and to undercut their opponents (Ulmer, 1971b).

The difficulty of the foregoing for JIA is that each case is fraught with multiple guiding principles and influencing factors, at least some of which cannot be identified with certainty. In contrast to EIA, JIA shares no general goal more specific than societal continuation. Institutionalization of JIA as a projective tool would be burdened with the ideological values of those pushing the enabling legislation. If the hurdle of an unconstitutional violation of separation of powers could be leapt, which is doubtful, there exists no consensus as to the intent or goal of institutionalizing JIA as exists for EIA expressed in NEPA.

CONCLUSION

Sterile hybrids doing useful work have a place in the world but are prevented by nature from contributing to the genetic future. So it is with JIA. JIA is impractical prior to court decisions because of the competing and often conflicting factors that shape these decisions. Predecision JIA would merely add to the conflict rather than shape and channel it. Ideological disagreements over such subjects as the death penalty would override the informative value of JIA even if problems of constitutionality were overcome. Indeed, cases with major ideological quarrels already tend to bring forth great volumes of a partisan form of JIA, the amicus curiae brief. All interested parties may submit briefs to the court which purport to offer objective indicators of the correct decision and warn of the dire consequences of a mistake.

Appellate courts decide cases in such a way that the nature of what a JIA would study is not known until the decision is made. That is, appellate courts are not required merely to pick one side or the other as in criminal trials. They may do so or they may go beyond the case at hand to prescribe a general course of action as was done by the *Miranda* v. *Arizona*, 384 U.S. 436 (1966), decision. Or they may decide the case and enunciate a compromise between competing ideologies as has occurred in several post-*Miranda* decisions that narrowed the scope of *Miranda* without overturning that decision. A JIA assessing the impact of keeping or doing away with *Miranda* might be irrelevant to a decision which does some of both. Thus, the ideologically based nature of the decision process suggests that JIAs should not be institutionalized and are likely to remain historical.

The JIA need seen by *Science* editor Koshland and others, with the aforementioned limitations, suggests the creation of a special science court whose judges would be required to have scientific as well as legal training and whose jurisdiction would include appeals from regulatory agencies overseeing such fields as genetic engineering, pharmaceuticals, and the handling and dispatch of toxic chemicals, as specified by Congress. Such a court would be competent to evaluate the various scientific evidence presented by the contending parties and to apply the requirements of law. Presumably the contending parties would be motivated to present scientific evidence of the highest possible quality in support of their contentions.

The more ideologically laden civil liberties and rights of accused cases, among others, would be left to ex post facto JIA and the hope of each person that future judges will correct past decisions with which they disagree. An imposed institutionalization of an ideologically limiting set of goals, perhaps necessary for long-term society survival in the case of EIA, would be indicative of the demise of the diversity necessary to our political survival in the case of JIA.

In the United States a general policy strategy is likely to be successful when broad policy consensus exists and ideological disagreement is minimal. When policies move from the abstract to the concrete, impact assessment is a means by which they are defined. Ideological differences over policy adoption will resurface at the impact assessment stage. Consensus building thus must have success before impact assessment can become institutionalized.

Noninstitutionalized impact assessment may contribute to consensus development as happened with NEPA, but the JIA experience shows that good science does not guarantee a consensus. When ideological disputes rage, my "science" is better than your "science." A consensus is required for impact assessment to be assured of a major role in a successful general policy strategy and for the "science" to become ours.

NOTES

I thank the editor and an anonymous reviewer for their comments and guidance. The deficiencies of course are mine, not theirs.

1. There are dozens of articles that assess the impact of the rights of the accused and school desegregation decisions of the U.S. Supreme Court. Examples are Canon (1974) and Wasby (1970). Other topics receiving a lot of attention from impact analysts include the school prayer and reapportionment cases. Examples of this research are Beaney and Beiser (1964) and Landau (1965).

2. The continued popularity of works of this vein is indicative of acceptance into the political science mainstream. For example, Goldman and Jahnige, *The Federal Courts as a Political System* is in its third edition. The first edition was published in 1971 and the third in 1985.

3. For an assessment and additional references on this subject, see Nicholls and Smith (1982).

4. Obviously, class actions are an exception, but even here the wrong alleged must be specified and the alleged wrongdoer identified.

5. I obtained federal grant funding for and oversee a victim's advocate program in Pitt County, North Carolina, which has as a duty the preparation and presentation in court of victim impact statements. It should be noted that programs of this type have intermedicate goals of political benefit for those elected officials associated with their operation.

6. For a detailed discussion and assessment of the science court concept, see Martin (1977).

11

Developing Local Cultural Resource Policy through Environmental Impact Assessments

Robert M. Sanford, Thomas W. Neumann, and James F. Palmer

INTRODUCTION

Enviromental resource policy at all levels can be influenced by impact assessments. One area in which the contribution from assessments is particularly needed is cultural resource management. The regional diversity of cultural resources requires locally specific knowledge gained through research. Policy that is to be responsive to the resource must also be made at the local level because it is at this level that the resources are most likely to be known, identified, and controlled. Environmental laws favor the review of impact assessments. Such assessments tend to be very site specific and, for cultural resources, require a high degree of knowledge specific to a particular locality.

There are some problems regarding organization, funding, evaluative criteria, and definitions faced in cultural resource assessments. In order to understand these problems, key terms and the legal basis for assessments must first be understood.

Cultural resources are environmental resources that reflect some aspect of human culture. As such, these resources range from archaeological sites and historic structures to landscapes and indigenous subcultures. Like other environmental resources, cultural resources are physical, pollutable, and often nonrenewable. Cultural resource management (CRM) is an activity that includes cultural resource assessment, but also involves the application of management skills to preserve cultural heritage (Fowler, 1982). Cultural resource assessment is the primary stage of CRM called upon in the environmental assessment process. This stage generally involves the use of archaeological and historical research methods to document quantity and quality of the cultural resources of a proposed project area in accordance with legal mandates. An evaluation is made of the importance of the resource. Only "significant" cultural resources receive protection through state or federal law.

THE LEGAL BASIS FOR CULTURAL RESOURCE ASSESSMENT AND POLICY

Cultural resource policy began in the late nineteenth century with the establishment of Yellowstone Park, the preservation of Indian ruins, and the appropriation of Civil War battlefields (Rosenberg, 1981). Federal responsibility toward cultural resources on federal land was first acknowledged by the Antiquities Act of 1906 and amplified by the Historic Sites Act of 1935. Archaeological survey and evaluation became part of the federal response to the impacts of reservoirs and dams through enactment of the Reservoir Salvage Act of 1960. The National Historic Preservation Act of 1966 marked a move by the federal government to encourage states to conserve and evaluate cultural resources.

The National Environmental Policy Act of 1969 (NEPA) set up a review process for environmental impact evaluation that included aesthetics and cultural resources. This act, along with the Archaeological Resources Protection Act of 1979 and other acts tied to specific activities and environments, increased the span of cultural resource assessments by linking them to federal permit processes. Many states have enacted similar legislation with regard to state permits and review processes.

In New York, for example, the State Environmental Quality Review Act (SEQR) of 1978 requires that cultural resource impacts be evaluated in environmental assessments that are similar to those required by NEPA. New York also has other laws that require state agencies to assess and mitigate the impacts of their activities on cultural resources, but it is SEQR that primarily affects the business community and local government policy.

In addition to SEQR assessments, many local government agencies and commissions require cultural resource evaluation for projects in known sensitive areas. Local bodies tie this review into their permit process as part of a required determination that a project poses no harmful threats. The bases for their determinations are borrowed from state and federal law, environmental criteria, and the results of previous local assessments. These determinations establish the foundation for policy even though a review process rather than the application of specific standards is involved.

NEPA, SEQR, and laws in other states, such as Act 250 in Vermont, clearly establish the context of cultural resources in environmental impact assessment.

This context serves as an example for local mandates for assessments. It should be noted that it does not necessarily imply management inasmuch as most states do not use the concept of continuing supervision over permitted activities (Rosenberg, 1981). In order to illustrate aspects of how cultural resource assessment, environmental review, and local policy interact, we first look at some general issues and then present a case study.

DIFFERENCES IN PERCEPTION

Review processes are generally evidentiary and are often adversarial, particularly where the quantification of qualitative factors is involved. Even without litigation, assessments can be controversial when differing perceptions arise on how to define, quantify, evaluate, and manage cultural resources. Differences in cultural resource perceptions result in a disjointed approach to these nonrenewable resources. This approach is complicated by the demands of the business community. It also confuses local government attempts at policy.

The archaeological profession recognizes certain issues, including controversial definitions of resources, levels of analysis, and evaluation procedures, as being at the forefront of cultural resource assessments. These issues arise out of differing understandings of the obligations of the archaeological profession, legal requirements, and the needs of those who require archaeological assessments as part of environmental review processes.

Examining the relationship between the field of archaeology (defined academically) and the requirements of environmental law shows that there are basically three groups involved. The first is the public sector agencies, boards, and commissions. This group has, at the state and federal levels, a set of procedures underscored by legislation that dictates what should be examined. Those procedures were, in part, set forth by the academic archaeological community in the 1970s. Although these procedures do have structure and rational organization, they are nonexpansive, reactive, and applicable only to public lands, publicly funded projects, or publicly declared sensitive areas. This creates some difficulties for the local level where no state lands are involved and often no local guidance exists.

The second group consists of private sector concerns—generally, developers, construction contractors, and engineering firms. These take their lead from the public sector, directly fund whatever environmental impact assessment is done, and are reactive in the permitting process but active in the land-alteration process.

The last group is the academic archaeological community. This group, which seldom deals directly with the first two constituencies, perceives the consulting process needed to assess cultural resources impact as sullying, in much the same way that Edwardian society drew the division between "pure" athletics (amateur and unpaid) and "corrupted" athletics (professional and paid). Archaeologists are further hampered by training that prepared them for extensive, slow, and cautious excavation of archaeological sites—procedures for which routine funding is rare and, in the arena of cultural resource assessments, is thereby not practical.

Complications emerge from the above structure. Public agency personnel administer policy derived from formulated laws and are required to determine whether a pending action does or does not fit into existing regulations. Assessments, however, are done by academically trained and, often, academically employed archaeologists, whose understanding of the status of the cultural resource base is ahead of what the laws and policies were designed to protect, but whose training in data recovery is on a grander temporal scale than review processes can typically accommodate. In addition to the pressure from their colleagues to adhere to scientific norms and "appropriate" behavior, such archaeologists can, as subcontractors, have their potential conflict of interest reinforced by difficult requirements.

The business community usually has physical control over cultural resources and, although an environmentally sound project may be desired, its members are more concerned with financial matters. Their financial concerns come from two directions: project delays caused by the review process and the direct cost of the necessary cultural resource assessments. To be blunt, it makes good business sense for a developer to "accidentally" obliterate an unrecorded archaeological site; the interest on the bank loan, per day, generally exceeds the cost of hiring an archaeologist for a month to salvage whatever cultural resources were there.

It is in the interest of society that a solution be found to this counterproductive situation. Differences in perceptions among the public, academic, and private sector groups need to be assessed and responded to in environmental policy. To explore these differences, in 1983 a survey was made of the three groups in the State of New York most affected by cultural resources policy: state and federal agency offices that could potentially be involved in some aspect of cultural resource regulation or management, archaeologists, and the business community. The purpose of the survey was to determine how the three groups perceived cultural resources, the significance of those resources, and the preparation their training provided in this area. Government agencies (including specific departments) were taken from the New York Department of Environmental Conservation (DEC) statewide *River Conservation Directory* (1981). Archaeologists were taken from the American Anthropological Association's *1982–1983 Guide to Anthropology Departments*. All firms who had applied for permits for land-alteration projects from the DEC during a one-year period constituted the business group (for more detail on the survey administration and results, see Sanford, 1984).

Questionnaires were mailed with stamped return envelopes to seventy-three government offices (thirty-eight were returned, twenty-four fully completed), to ninety-six academic and nine professional archaeologists (thirty-three and three returned, twenty-three and three fully completed), and to sixty-eight businesses

Table 11.1

Knowledge and Attitudes toward Cultural Resource Assessments of the Three Affected Groups

Questions	Percentage											
	Gov't Agencies				Archaeologists				Businesses			
	A	N	D	U	A	N	D	U	A	N	D	U
1. New York laws adequately define significant.	6	17	17	61	7	41	22	30	0	28	20	52
2. 'Significance' needs a clearer definition.	42	27	6	27	33	26	26	15	17	33	0	50
3. 'Significance' varies by government agency.	42	39	0	19	39	27	4	31	28	22	6	44
4. Need to improve cooperation among gov't agencies.	83	11	6	0	60	28	12	0	57	14	29	0
5. Need to improve education of public.	72	22	6	0	85	15	0	0	14	43	43	0
6. Need to improve education of gov't agencies.	63	32	0	5	62	39	0	0	57	29	14	0
7. Need to improve agreement among archeologists.	67	7	27	0	54	38	8	0	57	29	14	0
8. Need to improve state policy.	85	8	8	0	91	4	4	0	83	8	8	0
9. Prehistoric sites are part of the natural environment.	42	46	13	0	52	39	9	0	36	36	29	0
10. Colonial sites are part of the natural environment.	25	36	39	0	54	23	23	0	20	40	33	7
11. Sites are not just cultural resources but also natural res.	50	35	15	0	63	25	13	0	33	17	40	0
12. sites should be protected regardless of the cost.	23	50	27	0	35	50	15	0	7	21	71	0

Note: Percentages may not sum to 100 due to rounding error.
   A = agree; N = neutral; D = disagree; U = unknown.

(twenty-one fully completed). Results of the survey as they bear upon the issue here are given in Table 11.1.

The twelve questions itemized in Table 11.1 deal with three basic issues. Questions 1 through 3 treat a knowledge of how to apply "significance" to cultural resources and consider how well understood that important concept is. The management of cultural resources hinges entirely upon that concept; all policy decisions are premised upon it. Questions 4 through 8 deal with possible deficiencies in training, in the basic CRM concepts, in applying those concepts, and in the sharing of information. The last questions, 9 through 12, cover both attitude and knowledge of New York's SEQR.

The results of the survey reflect an absence of exposure to CRM during professional training, even for archaeologists. Although vague definitions may not be in violation of state administrative acts, they can make impact assessment difficult. The first three questions show that agency personnel are not comfortable with "significance" as they have been exposed to the term. Almost two-thirds have no idea if "significance" is clearly defined. The principal decisionmakers in this category, the professional archaeologists, either do not know (29 percent) or feel that the issue is murky. This has a clear effect on the business community, the group that has to act after expert-based government decisions have been made.

No one surveyed in the private sector thought that significance was adequately defined; no one argued against the need for a clearer definition. Actually, significance is rather clearly defined in both state and federal law (e.g., see 36 CFR 60). Where the problems emerge is in the confusion among archaeologists regarding the roles of the academic expert and the cultural resource manager. Persons in these roles approach the question of significance differently. Any area being researched by an academic is automatically highly significant by his or her definition, yet to the public manager, significance often can only be based on how a resource compares with lists of previously determined significant resources. Definitions are not consistently employed. This contributes to a confusion that is exacerbated by the deference that government agency personnel give to the expert (Butler, 1987). The result is a reaction, not a policy. Left without clear guidance, even though they are expected to pay the cost for the indecision, are the private-sector developers.

The private-sector developer is concerned ultimately with getting the necessary clearance to continue work and with what is or is not allowed. Questions 4 through 8 indicate that contradictions exist in the entire review process, such that developers would like *both* the archaeologists *and* the government agencies to act together (questions 6 through 8). The developer is required to underwrite data collection for the permitting process and reasonably expects clear determination. Unlike, say, a soil percolation test, the cultural resource survey rarely yields tangible results that bear directly upon the success of the business venture. The difference of opinion shown in question 5 underscores this situation.

Archaeologists and government personnel feel strongly that the "public" (which in this situation means the third group, the private sector) needs to know more; that the problem is somehow somebody else's. The private sector believes that the problem lies with a confused policy, a confusion that it must then underwrite (questions 5 and 8).

The confusion does exist. Even government personnel feel that definitions vary by agency (42 percent in question 3). According to NEPA, SEQR, and other environmental laws, cultural resources are a subset of natural resources.

It is disconcerting to find that 50 percent of the agency personnel and 37 percent of the archaeologists appear not to agree (question 11).

The survey clarifies the structure of managerial confusion. The archaeological community is often trained in cultural resource assessment or research but not in management, and it frequently tries to apply a purely academic approach to a much broader issue. In making "not significant but avoid it" statements about sites, archaeologists obviously do not understand the CRM process. At best, they are attempting to hedge their bets (Butler, 1987:822).

Archaeologists constitute a partisan community that is professionally accountable for errors in empirical evaluation of the presence and potential of a resource. Government employees are taught to make decisions, but only within the framework of procedure established through precedent. "Precedent" is largely controlled by the archaeological community. Both communities wish that the other would somehow clarify what each should be doing. The developers, who are paying for the cultural resource evaluation, are left waiting.

CASE STUDY: CENTRAL NEW YORK

Environmental laws set up definitions and processes for cultural resource evaluation. When such laws are not locally based or do not tie assessments into local policy and practice, there is a greater likelihood that a "cookbook" approach will occur, neglecting some contingencies. Standard procedures to revise earlier definitions are too slow. They are structured in "academic/agency time" and not in the timeframe for local development decisions and review processes. The procedures are not tied into a local feedback system between policy, practice, law, and the resource base.

The New York SEQR review process, for example, requires that cultural resources be assessed prior to any land-alteration project if (1) public funds are involved, (2) public lands are involved, (3) cultural resources previously listed as eligible for the National Register of Historic Places are on or adjacent to the land, or (4) environmentally sensitive areas are involved. In all four cases, the lead agency is the Department of Environmental Conservation.

What happens when the land-alteration project is private in funding and ownership, there are no register eligible sites nearby, and the area is not considered environmentally sensitive? The lead agency defaults to the local level. SEQR is based on the assumptions that there is time to act and the broad outline of cultural resource variability is known.

An example is provided by the Syracuse metropolitan area, which had the highest unemployment rate in New York from 1986 to 1987. Paradoxically, it also had the third highest increase in real estate value (behind Boston and New York) in the nation over that same time. This development has been a welcomed boon to the neighboring rural townships, since it helps mitigate the out-migration of their tax base. This is particularly true in those areas on the Heiderberg-Onondaga Escarpment just south of Syracuse, an area where the views are spectacular. The escarpment has a second feature of note: it has a high concentration of prehistoric and early historic archaeological sites.

In 1987 a local developer went before one such town board to request permits for a sixty-acre development. The fourteen houses to be built would represent an increase of $58,750 per year in property taxes. The town relied on SEQR guidelines and had no cultural resource review or management policies of its own to augment its local permit process.

During the public hearings, it was learned that an extensive early historic Iroquois cemetery and village had existed on the property. The town, eager to comply with SEQR but not to imperil its own revenue interest, negotiated with the developer to have ground clearance monitored for all but two lots. On the remaining two lots (where the Iroquois site was known to be) he was to conduct a detailed site examination. The developer would have to fund the necessary evaluations.

A problem emerged. The developer had received his bank loans prior to the imposition of the town's requirement. His costs would now include the archaeologists' fees as well as finance charges. Two burials were exposed on the first lot examined. Instead of the anticipated two-hour delay in land clearance to comply with town requirements, there was a three-day delay as the burials were salvaged. While the burials were being removed, he had his equipment dig out the cellar hole on the adjacent lot. Subsequently, he did this on half of the remaining lots, thereby destroying any archaeological data that may have existed.

The archaeologists found that the Iroquois village had extended over more of the property than had been suspected. The town, in setting the permit guidelines, had unintentionally allowed for the destruction of this part of the site. The developer had no legal obligation to do more than what he was doing. The importance of the site became clear with the completion of the archaeological assessment when the last two lots were developed. The site was the location of a previously unknown Iroquois refugee camp, where the entire Onondagon Nation collected between August 1696 and September 1697. It was the first evidence of continued stone tool use by the Iroquois that long after European contact. It was also, because of town agreements with the developer and the default mechanism in SEQR, unsalvageable beyond what was originally anticipated.

OBSERVATIONS AND SOLUTIONS

SEQR, in regard to cultural resources, shows aspects of "hindsight management" by not proceeding beyond the assessment stage. It attempts to provide for resolution of problems that have already occurred; it only poorly anticipates. In situations like the above, it is sound financial management to sacrifice the cultural resource base. In addition, the process establishes a conflict of interest for the archaeologist who is subcontracted by the developer. At its best, the client-oriented approach to contract archaeology is merely a technical service, not a science (Raab et al., 1980).

Four partial solutions can be offered that apply to this case study as well as to the general problems identified in the survey. First, there is a need for greater recognition that environmentally sensitive areas can include cultural resources, and for more effective use of any existing legal provisions for recognizing this. The Heiderberg-Onondaga Escarpment above Syracuse, for example, should have required automatic cultural resource reconnaissance surveys. This would have prevented many of the problems that emerged.

Second, there is a need to reduce the financial burden on the private developer. Most cultural resources are held in private hands; most cultural resource assessments done in these cases have the archaeologist as a subcontractor. The archaeologist's role is easier to fill when there is less pressure to compromise.

An emergency salvage fund would help situations like this, allocated by the state on a county-by-county basis, in proportion to the number of sites known per unit area, land remaining undeveloped, and rate of development. These three sets of statistics, it might be noted, are already compiled, computerized, and available in New York to the Department of Environmental Conservation as well as the Department of Parks, Recreation, and Historic Preservation and the Education Department (Office of the State Archaeologist).

The fund itself could be structured and managed like an insurance policy, with funds generated from building permit surcharges that, should funding not be needed for the particular project, be partially refundable when it is adequately determined that no resources requiring mitigation are present. Something like this is already done by insurance companies for small businesses, where surcharges are levied on businesses in high-risk areas to cover additional costs. The fund would help protect the developer from excessive losses due to construction delays while helping to defray the costs for the salvage of the cultural resources. Public funds would, where appropriate, cover preservation, artifact curation, and documentation or publication.

Third, there is a need for improved training. Part of the variation seen among archaeologists in the survey is a consequence of differences in the time when professional training was received. CRM was not an issue until the mid–1970s. The difference between cultural resource management and cultural resource assessment needs to be understood so that the benefits of assessment alone are not overemphasized. The gap between contract archaeologists and academicians requires reduction.

In addition, there is a greater need for environmental professionals to be exposed to cultural resource management prior to the start of their professional lives. Most engineering programs now include a course in general environmental law, but seldom are cultural resources addressed. Aside from considerations of historic preservation (e.g., standing historic structures), it is rare for planners, architects, or landscape architects to have any such preparation. The importance of cultural resources to the businesses in which these individuals eventually work may be gauged from the single engineering firm of Louis Berger and Associates: over $5 million of gross annual revenue comes from cultural resource activity alone (*Engineering Review*, 1985).

It is our experience that educational institutions have been reluctant to set up such training, primarily because it has never been needed before. University administrators tend to react, not anticipate. A sound curriculum program is needed to prepare environmental professionals, particularly those involved with land alteration, in the management of cultural resources.

A fourth step is to provide more guidance for local agencies and planning commissions. Usually such guidance is triggered only by a state-regulated activity. Local policy needs the contribution of state-level regulatory expertise in order to put together a cohesive policy system. This does not mean borrowing and applying a state-level policy. It means developing local policies that are locally responsive to the resource base as well as to local development and management needs. This will promote effective, locally regulated activity managed by a local policy when state or federal regulations are insufficient with respect to cost or to the preservation of the resource base.

CONCLUSION

Environmental impact assessments are necessary in developing sound CRM policy. Assessments reveal specific resources, issues, and potential solutions associated with a particular location. CRM policy needs to be locally based in order to be responsive to the community, to the participants in environmental change, and to the resource base. Cultural resources in particular require a local approach because they are very specific to location, and they are newly integrated into processes typically seen as involving only natural resources. Assessments can provide a rapid input to local administrative processes and should be used in providing feedback to shape CRM policy. Assessments themselves are specific applications of science to an evaluative process.

NEPA, SEQR, and environmental impact assessments have gone a long way toward creating federal (and state) policies that bring science into the process of making decisions that will affect the environment (Bartlett, 1986a; Caldwell, 1982). Caldwell has broadly characterized ''science'' as

(1) method (in fact, a body of methodology) for creating and testing knowledge. It is developed and used as (2) an occupation by 'scientists' who seek to establish a body of (3) knowledge (i.e., tested fact and theory), which is often referred to as 'science.' Finally, as previously noted, a distinction is sometimes drawn between so called 'pure' science or basic science and its (4) application to human needs and purposes. And so it is knowledge, derived by professional scientists through methods believed to be scientific and applied to public affairs, with which we are primarily concerned (Caldwell, 1982:18).

When defined in this way, the assessment and management of cultural resources relies upon the application of science, just as surely as the assessment of biological or geological resources does. In fact, Caldwell (1982:41) recognizes the inclusion of historic and cultural preservation as a necessary component in the convergence of knowledge into a coherent environmental science.

Nevertheless, the science associated with cultural resources has not received the same recognition and stature as has, for instance, ecology. Even though laws and regulations exist to establish state and federal policies toward cultural resources, there is sufficient confusion among government employees, developers, and practitioners to stymie their implementation at the local level.

If a truly integrated environmental science is to evolve and contribute to making environmentally related decisions, there must be a greater awareness of its lesser recognized components. Because cultural resources tend to be site specific, the awareness of them and their scientific investigation must address the problems encountered at the local level.

PART IV

CRITICAL PERSPECTIVES

12

Impact Assessment and Regulating Technological Change: Why the Philosophy of Technology Is a Political Problem

W. D. Kay

It is ironic that the bulk of technology assessment literature is itself technological, i.e., it is concerned primarily with practical issues of methodology and policy formation. Ironic, perhaps, but not surprising. Given that all forms of impact assessment have become important policy-making tools, it is only to be expected that practitioners would devote a great deal of attention to perfecting their craft.

At the same time, however, a tool is only as good as the a priori knowledge that underlies its use, and there are serious reasons to question the general level of theoretical knowledge that technology assessment proponents bring to their tasks. Even though research in the philosophy of technology and the idea of technology assessment began at roughly the same time, the two have rarely intersected (Mitcham, 1985). Nevertheless, such a joining is important. Far from being distant, "abstract" issues, philosophical questions have a direct impact upon the design and implementation of technology regulatory policy. I hope to illustrate this by reviewing some of the major conceptual issues surrounding technology and technological development and by pointing out their policy implications.

EPISTEMOLOGICAL ISSUES

As is so often the case with philosophical concepts, the most basic questions are in fact the most difficult.[1] Whereas at first glance the task of defining "technology''—differentiating between technology and nontechnology—would seem to be clear enough, it has turned out to be a particularly complex problem.

In the popular mind, technology is usually linked to science or mechanics. Even the terms "science" and "technology" are often used interchangeably. Clearly, however, technology may not necessarily refer to anything mechanical. Indeed, as the example of computer software illustrates, it need not have physical form at all.

Furthermore, science and technology constitute two very distinct, albeit related, modes of thought. In one of the early discussions of the issue, Henryk Skolimowski points out that science seeks to "know what," whereas technology seeks to "know how" (Skolimowski, 1972). Thus, while science values knowledge for its own sake, technology values knowledge for its utility. Their connection comes in the translation of one type of knowledge into the other, as when the discovery of the physical relationship between electricity and magnetism led to the development of television and radar. It is this translation that gives rise to the notion of technology as applied science.

This view, however, has been criticized as being overly simplistic (Pinch and Bijker, 1987). To begin with, there are many sources of knowledge that are not scientific (as narrowly defined). Should actions based upon such knowledge be considered technologies? Economic policies, for example, are a clear attempt to utilize knowledge of cause and effect (e.g., the relationship between interest rates, the money supply, investment, and economic growth) to achieve some desired end. From psychoanalysis to marketing, there are literally thousands of cases of these "social technologies," many of which are even incorporated into "traditional" ones. The creation and design of automobile air bags, for instance, was influenced by the knowledge that many drivers were not voluntarily wearing seat belts and were unlikely to be persuaded to do so. In short, since it is intended for use by human beings, technology must make use of knowledge concerning human behavior, as well as that relating to hardware alone.

Having said this, however, it is difficult to know where to stop. Astrologers claim to make use of presumed relationships among celestial objects to predict the future. Could not this activity be considered an application of knowledge? What of alchemy, faith healing, magic, and witchcraft? In other words, how are technologies to be distinguished from other, nontechnological, goal-directed behavior? This is an especially tricky issue for policymakers, since an essential part of policy formation involves defining the relevant policy domain (i.e., determining what things are to be regulated). It is important that the defining criteria be consistent and that distinctions not be made arbitrarily. On the other hand, the policy must remain within reasonable bounds.

Some would exclude from any definition of technology those practices whose factual premises are held to be untrue,[2] but this approach is clearly inadequate. In the first place, such a definition would eliminate many scientific applications. As our knowledge of the world changes, old ideas are often discarded, yet their applications are still regarded as technologies. Even today, ancient calendars from many parts of the world are admired for their accuracy, despite the fact that they are based upon outmoded ideas of celestial mechanics. Human beings have been utilizing techniques for centuries with little or no idea of the factual principles involved. Obviously, the label "technology" cannot be reserved solely for those applications whose underlying principles are known to be absolutely correct. Otherwise, there would be very few technologies in the world.

Moreover, even if such a distinction were theoretically acceptable, it would be of little use to policymakers. If the goal of technology policy is to guard against potentially harmful applications, it makes little sense to exempt those based upon bogus factual claims. In fact, historically, the opposite has been the case: regulation of drugs and medical practices, for example, began as a response to the wide marketing of so-called quack remedies.

Still, the question remains: how does government set effective boundaries for its regulatory policies? Suppose, for the sake of argument, that policymakers have settled upon the traditional definition of technology-as-hardware. Such an approach would still face difficult definitional problems. James K. Feibleman has argued that simply saying "application of knowledge" (even scientific knowledge) makes the term "technology" much too broad. Instead, he argues, the definition should include only those "applications" that have come into common use. In other words, Feibleman sees technology as the *routinization* of applied knowledge (Feibleman, 1972; see also Braun, 1984).

This has some attractive features. First of all, it eliminates from consideration the thousands (if not millions) of inventions developed every year that, for one reason or another (usually failure in the marketplace), turn out to be short lived. Second, because it takes account of more than just hardware, this definition incorporates many of the social aspects of technological development (as in the air bags discussed above).

On the other hand, this view also has some serious drawbacks, particularly when seen as a guide to policy. To begin with, this approach delays government action until some activity has become routine, a strategy which runs counter to the original idea behind technology assessment. Second, it mistakenly (from a policy standpoint) equates routinization with importance or seriousness, suggesting that harm comes only from those innovations that see wide use. This is clearly untrue. Many short-lived techniques, such as the attempts at crossbreeding that produced gypsy moths (another example of incorrect factual premises, incidentally), have had serious environmental, social, and economic impacts (Lawless, 1977). Such applications are obviously reasonable candidates for regulatory action.

Actually, this time question arises before an innovation even has a chance to become routine. Research and development (R&D) is a lengthy process, often requiring many years in the case of large-scale technologies. This process is generally seen as consisting of separate steps—basic research, applied research, technological development, product development, production, and usage (Pinch and Bijker, 1987:21–23). At what point, however, does something cease to be research and become technology? The problem is further complicated by the fact that not all technologies follow the same development paths. Some—such as those based upon relatively unexplored scientific principles—do in fact demand long periods of gestation; others emerge fairly quickly, perhaps skipping one or more of these steps. Moreover, it is hard to see how any demarcation between pretechnology and technology could be operationalized. As U.S.–Soviet debates over the Strategic Defense Initiative (SDI) illustrate, it is not always clear when an object moves from the research stage to the development stage.

Once again, this presents a problem to policymakers. In addition to defining a policy domain, any type of regulatory policy must have a clear sense of when the regulations ought to begin. Put another way, at what point does the R&D process enter government jurisdiction? When blueprints are being drawn up? When the first prototype is built? When full-scale production actually begins? This decision is made all the more difficult by the fact that technologies (or pretechnologies) can produce significant side effects even in the early stages of their development. The SDI case mentioned above provides a clear example of a technology influencing events before it even exists. At this time, no scientist, engineer, or government official has any idea what the system will look like, yet it has already had a profound impact on foreign and defense policies, as well as arms control negotiations with the Soviet Union.

Since the logic of this argument suggests that effective regulatory policies may require some controls over basic research, policymakers must approach the issue carefully. How can a democratic government justify restrictions on freedom of inquiry? Furthermore, since the potential dangers of any innovation cannot be precisely known in its early stages, how can government officials be able to weigh the presumed benefits of such an intrusion against its costs?

In short, policymakers have yet to develop a clear idea of what it is that they are attempting to regulate. In the absence of a conceptually sound definition of technology,[3] development of a coherent and consistent strategy for dealing with its impacts becomes extremely difficult.

ONTOLOGICAL ISSUES

By far, the vast majority of research in the philosophy of technology has been devoted to the relationship between technology and human beings. This literature is much too extensive to review here. The following discussion is thus limited to topics that ought to be of immediate concern to policymakers.

In the discussion of routinization presented earlier, I suggested that techno-logical development is best considered a social phenomenon in that it is subject to a number of nontechnical influences. Put another way, it would appear that the effects of technological change are only partly due to changes in hardware. Equally important ingredients include the manner in which society adopts new technologies and the uses to which they are put—decisions which are often guided by nontechnological criteria (see, for example, the historical discussions in White, 1974; Burke, 1978; Rybczynski, 1983).

The implications of this are intriguing. To begin with, it means that identical technologies may produce completely dissimilar outcomes when introduced into different cultural settings. Rybczynski (1983:209–10), for example, tells of significant differences between the American and Mexican uses of passenger buses. In the United States and Canada, the onboard atmosphere of a bus is formalized and impersonal. The driver is placed in the role of a uniformed chauffeur or pilot. In contrast, Mexican buses are far more "humanized." The buses frequently have names, and the drivers (who usually do not wear uniforms) interact freely with the passengers.

Moreover, this social aspect of technology would seem to suggest that, over time, technological change can take place even if the technology itself remains unchanged. This can be most clearly illustrated by what might be called intergenerational technology transfer. It is not at all unusual to see a succeeding generation using a technique differently than the generation in which it was first introduced. The washing machine, for example, was initially seen (or at least advertised) as a convenience that would allow women to devote more time to other domestic duties like tending children and shopping for food. Years later, however, that same device has become one means by which women (and now men) can engage in pursuits other than housework (Cowan, 1974). In short, the generation that pioneers a particular innovation will not necessarily view it in the same way as one which has never known a time without it.

Not only does this feature of technological development create problems for forecasting, but also it raises the other end of the time question discussed earlier: when should regulations end? If it is possible for social changes to produce completely different (and probably unexpected) impacts with the same technology, it could be argued that some—and it would be, practically speaking, impossible to know in advance which ones—would have to be regulated (or at least monitored) indefinitely.

Up to this point, I have made repeated references to something called the effects of technological change. As with the other concepts described here, defining the nature of technological impacts appears simple. After all, the changes resulting from new technologies are fairly obvious. Such appearances, however, are deceptive. Although it is true that the actual physical manifestations of innovation are reasonably clear, interpreting their deeper significance is an entirely different matter.

Consider, for example, advances in communications. It is fairly easy to list the development of telephones, television, and satellites and to describe how each device makes it possible to send and receive messages almost anywhere on earth. What these changes have actually *meant*, however, is a matter of some dispute. Not long ago it was fashionable to speak of a "global village," a world brought together by electronic media, where all linguistic, cultural, and even political differences would melt away before its unifying influences. Recent developments, on the other hand, point to precisely the opposite effect. Some new communications technologies have actually led people into greater isolation, as can be seen by the growing use of "walkman" private radios and tape players. The fact that two very different, although plausible, conclusions can be drawn from the same technology would seem to indicate that, despite its wide use in the assessment literature, the concept of "total impact" is not all that well understood.

Of course, the degree of understanding varies from one area to another. Among the best understood technological impacts are those relating to other technologies. Engineers are able to predict, sometimes with great accuracy, what second-, third-, and even fourth-generation technologies will emerge from those already in existence or under development. It was this ability, for example, that allowed the planners at the National Aeronautics and Space Administration to state confidently in 1960 that hardware for a manned moon mission would be available within ten years (Logsdon, 1970). In addition, knowledge of technical effects is reasonably well developed in the life sciences (Lowrance, 1976) and economics (Sahal, 1981). Although certainly far from perfect, this knowledge base is sufficient to allow for reasonably effective regulation.

Aside from these three areas, however, very little is known about the overall *social* nature of technological change. The best that can be said at this time is that some ethical, psychological, and political impacts are known to occur. It is known, for example, that new technologies (particularly in the field of medicine) place strains on existing ethical, social, and legal systems by creating new opportunities for action, e.g., organ transplantation and new techniques involving human reproduction and life extension (Mesthene, 1970; Lawless, 1977; Scott, 1981; Grant, 1986). It is known that the introduction of increasingly complex technologies can establish new social relationships, as well as undermine those already in existence (Mesthene, 1970; Grant, 1986; for an anthropological perspective, see Pelto, 1973). It is known that enhanced abilities to detect objects that are very small or very far away has changed human perceptions of the world, particularly with respect to risks (Lowrance, 1976; Slovic, Fischhoff, and Lichtenstein, 1980). The specific implications and ramifications of these generally known impacts, however, are merely speculative. Very little empirical research has been done on these types of questions, with the result that the overall relationship between technological and social change remains largely unknown.

For policymakers, this presents two problems. First of all, it is very difficult, if not impossible, to regulate the effects of technological change without a clear understanding of what these changes actually are. In other words, what are regulators looking out for? What are they regulating against? Second, this lack of knowledge once again raises the familiar problem of policy domain. If, as the examples described above would seem to indicate, the overall consequences of technological development are essentially open-ended, what guidelines can regulators employ in setting boundaries for their policies? Put another way, how extensive or wide-ranging are these regulations to be?

CONCLUSION: PHILOSOPHICAL QUESTIONS, POLICY ISSUES

Technological development is usually held to be a well-defined, precise undertaking. Governmental policies regulating it have been in existence for many years. Despite these facts, the questions raised here suggest that the study of technology as a social subsystem is still in its infancy. In other (blunt) words, those responsible for regulating technological change *cannot really have any idea about what they are doing.*[4]

The need here is twofold. First, continuing inquiry into the basic concepts of technology and technological development must be encouraged and expanded. Second, those involved in the regulation of technology (including those engaged in technology assessment) must become more sensitive to these questions, as well as to those who are seeking answers. As matters presently stand, many scientists, engineers, and assessment practitioners are too quick to dismiss the philosophical literature as abstract or irrelevant. Unless this changes, technology assessment, for all of its presumed sophistication and precision, will remain conceptually underdeveloped.

The phrase "philosophy of technology" may at first appear to be an oxymoron (the speculative combined with the practical), but this chapter has, I hope, shown that the latter actually has great need of the former. Technology is based upon knowledge, but, as the philosophical literature illustrates, most of the knowledge utilized up to this point is limited and narrowly drawn. Thus, what practitioners clearly require is a little more "love of wisdom."

NOTES

1. This designation of epistemological issues follows that used in Vig (1988).

2. Richter (1982:85), for example, uses this line of reasoning in declaring that Hopi Indian rain dances do not constitute a technology.

3. There are a number of epistemological issues that I have elected not to discuss. These include the question of whether technology simply represents an extension of existing human abilities or something altogether new (Rapp, 1981; Vig, 1988), as well as the ideas of "autonomous technology" (Ellul, 1964; Winner, 1977), and the growing feminist literature (Griffin, 1978; Gray, 1979; Rothschild, 1983). Although these issues are certainly important, their relevance to policy making is less immediate.

4. Some supporting evidence for this claim can be found in current federal technology policy. In the last few years, the U.S. Congress Office of Technology Assessment, for example, has been ordered to conduct assessments on a few topics—notably federal coal-leasing policies and strategies for cost reductions in Medicare—that more closely resemble traditional policy analysis than technology assessments. Apparently, Congress is as confused over the definition of technology as everyone else.

13

Policy through Assessment of Type II Statistical Risks

Kristin Shrader-Frechette

The gas company and city government in Oxnard, California, recently prepared separate environmental impact assessments to determine the effects of siting a liquefied natural gas (LNG) facility near the small coastal town. On at least one issue, the controversial assessments were radically at odds. The two respective risk estimates of the average annual probability that someone in Oxnard would die from an LNG accident, if the facility were built, differed by a factor of 300 (Kunreuther et al., 1987:261). Even worse, a comparison of ten studies, produced in West Germany, the Netherlands, the United Kingdom, and the United States, found that expert estimates of risks to people living near LNG terminals varied by a factor of 100 million (Otway and Peltu, 1985:12). Similar uncertainties plague analyses of a variety of technological and environmental impacts. They suggest that perhaps no question about assessment is more controversial than how to evaluate the likelihood of allegedly low-probability, high-consequence events like an Oxnard LNG explosion or a Chernobyl nuclear core melt.

Part of the controversy surrounding potentially catastrophic impacts is caused by the fact that experience with new technologies, like nuclear fission and liquefied gas, is so limited that the frequency of low-probability, high-consequence accidents is uncertain. For example, before the Browns Ferry nuclear accident occurred, government experts said that it had the same probability as that of a large meteor striking the earth; yet it, and no meteor strike, has taken place.

Assessors likewise called the Chernobyl accident "highly improbable" before it happened (Raloff and Silberner, 1986:292). In the face of similar uncertainties and the potentially catastrophic impacts of particular technologies—a nuclear core melt could kill 150,000 people (Mulvihill et al., 1965)—people are often disinclined to believe any expert who tells them that the likelihood of a given high-consequence impact is acceptably low.

In response to citizens' allegations that certain risks are greater than estimated by experts, many impact assessors typically discount the opinions of the public. In so doing, they pursue a strategy that I shall call "dismissing the layperson." The purpose of this chapter is to show (1) that such a strategy is often misguided, (2) that it originates, in part, in erroneous tendencies to reject producer, rather than consumer, risk and (3) that there are prima facie grounds for minimizing consumer risk when analyzing technological and environmental impacts.

THE FALLACY OF DISMISSING THE LAYPERSON

Those who assess technological risks and environmental impacts distinguish between actual or objective risk judgments of experts, as opposed to perceived or subjective risk evaluations of laypeople. They typically point out that there is often a wide divergence between expert and lay opinion regarding the probabilities associated with particular impacts, particularly in the area of low-probability hazards like nuclear power. Hence assessors frequently conclude that the risk judgments of laypersons, regarding how great or grave a risk is, cannot be trusted (Cohen and Lee, 1979:707; Häfele, 1979:139; Starr, 1972:26–27; Lave, 1979:484). M. Maxey (1979:410–17), for example, claims that the public is a group of paranoid neo-Luddites; N. Rasmussen (1975:37) charges that laypeople are "inconsistent" in their risk attitudes; C. Starr (1972:26–27), D. Okrent (1980:372), M. Maxey (1979:410–17), and B. Cohen and I. Lee (1979:720) maintain that the public is ignorant and inconsistent in fearing statistically less significant hazards, like nuclear accidents, more than accidents with a higher probability, e.g., those in automobiles. They say laypeople are too concerned with "imaginary" catastrophes (Starr, 1972:26–27), and that they rely on intuition, not scientific judgment, in making their risk evaluations (Starr and Whipple, 1980:1116–17).

Impact assessors explain the divergent risk evaluations of laypeople by claiming that ordinary citizens do not know the relevent accident probabilities (Starr and Whipple, 1980:1117); experts claim that, because of systematic biases, like the availability heuristic (Kahneman and Tversky, 1982:201ff.), the public tends to overestimate the incidence of events like the Challenger explosions, or the Bhopal toxic leak. They likewise maintain that, if the public knew the relevant probabilities, then laypersons' evaluations of risks would be consistent with those of experts.

Apart from whether risk and impact assessors are right to dismiss lay opinions, it is important to know why assessors might be wrong in their judgments. I shall focus on the two main reasons why the expert views appear questionable. *First*, experts' dismissing public fears as irrational runs contrary to the norms of many contemporary research traditions. Social scientists, in aiming at the ideal of objectivity, are supposed to look at the facts, at people's behavior, and not merely to impose their own subjective models of rationality on the world. Even in ethics, moral philosophers aim at this sort of objectivity. We construct ethical theories which we test by means of whether they fit with our most basic beliefs, arguments, and intuitions about right and wrong. (Substantiating these claims about scientific and philosophical research would take us too far afield; however, see Hospers, 1980:87–103; Frank, 1980:210–19; Hart, 1979:20ff.; and Feinberg, 1979:80ff. for support of these points.) If a theory in social science did not describe the actual behavior of the persons studied, or if a theory in moral philosophy did not fit the beliefs of most thoughtful humans, then it would be extraordinarily difficult to prove that either theory was correct. (Admittedly, however, some scholars nevertheless employ ideological, rather than empirically warranted, theories.) Hence it is paradoxical that, instead of claiming that their risk theories are wrong, when they are inconsistent with widespread lay perceptions of the risk, assessors typically allege that the public is irrational.

Second, experts often discount public opinion about risk by making two gratuitous, reductionistic assumptions: that citizens' aversion to potentially catastrophic risks is a result of their ignorance of probabilities and that any risk analysis not based solely on probability of fatality is irrational. Both assumptions can be shown to be wrong. Since there are obviously many other factors (than probability of fatality) relevant to rational risk evaluation (Shrader-Frechette, 1985:55–196), one response to these assumptions is that laypersons typically use more complex valuation schemes to assess risks. The schemes include a variety of parameters, such as how equitably the risk will be distributed, whether it might cause violations of rights and civil liberties or threats to individual autonomy and economic welfare, whether the risk is unknown, and whether it is imposed involuntarily (see Lowrance, 1976:87). Moreover, laypeople claim that one might take a high probability risk if the *benefits* were very great, but one might reject even a low-probability risk if the benefits were questionable or the consequences too serious (Fischhoff et al., 1980:192).

For example, citizens might realize that even the government admits that a commercial nuclear catastrophe could wipe out an area the size of Pennsylvania, and that victims would be prevented, by law (Price-Anderson Act), from being compensated for more than 1 or 2 percent of their total losses (Shrader-Frechette, 1983:73ff). The same consumers might also realize that there are other ways than fission to create energy. Hence, rather than describe their nuclear risk merely in terms of probability of fatality, these laypersons might evaluate nuclear impacts at least in part in terms of ethical parameters, e.g., whether a risk can be compensated or distributed equitably. B. Fischhoff et al. (1978:141–42) and other psychometric researchers claim, in fact, that the public correlates risk acceptability more closely with equity than with many other factors. But if so, then there could be rational grounds for society's aversion to high-consequence, low-probability risks like nuclear accidents.

This point is clear if one considers a rational response to the invitation to play Russian roulette. Suppose the probability that a bullet is in a chamber when the trigger is pulled is one in 17,000—the same likelihood, per reactor-year, as a nuclear core melt, according to the U.S. Nuclear Regulatory Commission (Rasmussen, 1975). Even with such a small probability, a person could still be quite rational in her refusal to play the game. A reasonable person could even maintain that the probability in question is irrelevant. Any probability of fatality might be too high, if the benefits of taking the risk were not great enough.

When Fischhoff et al. (1978:148–49) studied public perception of risk, they discovered, consistent with the Russian roulette example, that perceived risk could be predicted almost completely accurately on the basis of one variable, the "severity of consequences." But if so, then Starr and Whipple (1980:1116), as well as other assessors, could be wrong in claiming that "the bulk of disagreement over nuclear power is about accident probability" and in dismissing the risk judgments of laypeople. (For discussion of these points, see Shrader-Frechette, 1985:157–196.)

TYPE I (PRODUCER) RISKS AND TYPE II (CONSUMER) RISKS

If assessors are often wrong in dismissing lay opinions on risk, why do they do so? At least one of the reasons may be that they typically prefer Type II, over Type I, risks, whereas consumers tend to prefer Type I, over Type II, risks. Statisticians tell us that when a decision is made about a hypothesis, at least two different types of error may occur. Errors of Type I occur when one rejects a hypothesis that is true; errors of Type II occur when one accepts a hypothesis that is false. Statistical procedure dictates that we make assumptions about the size of each of these types of error that can be tolerated, and on this basis we choose a testing pattern for our hypothesis. The concept of *significance*, for example, is often defined in terms of a Type I risk of error of either .01 or .05, where there is not more than a 1 in 100 or a 5 in 100 chance of committing the error of rejecting a true hypothesis.

Determining significance, however, is not a sufficient basis for answering an important question. Which is the more serious error, Type I or Type II? An analogous issue arises in law. Is it a more serious error to acquit a guilty person or to convict an innocent person? In assessing technological impacts, ought one to minimize the Type I risk, which C.W. Churchman terms the "producer risk," or ought one to minimize the Type II risk, which he calls the "consumer risk"? That is, ought one to run the risk of rejecting a true hypothesis, of not using a technology that is really acceptable or safe, or ought one to run the risk of accepting a false hypothesis, of using a technology that is really unacceptable or unsafe? To decrease producer risk might hurt the consumers; to decrease consumer risk might hurt the producers (Churchman, 1947; see Axinn, 1966).

Most experts probably prefer to minimize the Type I risk. Their preference might arise in part from the fact that many impact assessments (e.g., U.S. Nuclear Regulatory Commission, 1975) are performed by those who are closely associated with the technology being evaluated and who are therefore sympathetic to it and to those who implement it. Such assessors typically underestimate the risk probabilities (Cooke, 1982), at least in part because it is difficult to identify all risks and also because unidentified risks are typically assumed to be zero. Preferences for minimizing producer risk also probably arise as a consequence of the fact that technical experts almost always use widely accepted Bayesian decision rules based on expected utility and subjective probabilities, rather than the maximin decision rule that requires one to choose the option whose worst outcome is better than the worst outcome of all the other options (Harsanyi, 1975:594). This means that, even when everyone agrees that the probability of a high-consequence impact is low, using a Bayesian decision rule typically generates a choice in favor of the potentially catastrophic technology or environmental impact, whereas using a maximin decision rule probably produces a verdict against the technology or environmental impact (Cooke, 1982:341–42). In other words, different norms for rational decisionmaking under uncertainty produce conflicting evaluations about the acceptability of the impact. Contrary to most assessors, I shall argue that there are prima facie grounds for minimizing consumer, rather than producer, risk—for minimizing Type II risks.

THE PRIMA FACIE CASE FOR MINIMIZING CONSUMER RISK

In arguing that there are prima facie grounds for reducing consumer risk, I mean that, all things being equal, one ought to take this approach (see Shrader-Frechette, 1985:84ff., 117ff.). Obviously the decision to minimize consumer or producer risk must be decided in part on a case-by-case basis, e.g., in terms of the particular benefits at stake. Arguing that there are prima facie grounds for reducing consumer risk therefore amounts to arguing that the burden of proof (regarding risk acceptability) should be placed on the person wishing to reduce producer, rather than consumer, risk. This means that, in the absence of evidence to the contrary, one has grounds for assuming that consumer risk ought to be minimized.

There are at least ten different reasons for holding that assessors' prima facie duty is to minimize the chance that an unsafe technology is implemented, that is, to minimize consumer risk. The first seven of these arguments focus on minimizing the risk faced by consumers, as the *kind* of risk most deserving of reduction. The last three arguments focus on the public as the *locus* of decison-making regarding risk, since it is typically laypeople who argue for reducing consumer risk. (In addition to these ten arguments, a great many other considerations could be brought to bear in favor of minimizing consumer, rather than producer, risk, although there is neither time nor space to sketch them here. Some of these arguments, for example, reiterate the famous debate between Rawls [1971:152ff.] and Harsanyi [1975] over choosing a minimax, rather than a Bayesian expected-utility decision rule.)

First, one justification for minimizing consumer risk is that this procedure appears more to be consistent with scientific practice. Hypothesis testing in science operates on the basis of limiting false positives, limiting incorrect rejections of the null hypothesis. Scientists design studies to guard against the influence of all possible confounding variables, and they demand replication of study results before accepting them as supporting a particular hypothesis. They apply tests of statistical significance which reject results whose probability of being due to chance, whose p value, is greater than, for example, 5 percent. Moreover, it is difficult to see how the scientific enterprise could function without such rigorous reluctance to accept positive results. As Abraham Kaplan (1964:253) put it: "The scientist usually attaches a greater loss to accepting a falsehood than to failing to acknowledge a truth. As a result, there is a certain conservatism or inertia in the scientific enterprise, often rationalized as the healthy skepticism characteristic of the scientific temper."

Second, the preference for Type I risks, for producer risks, and for minimizing consumer risk, or Type II risks, is also plausible in societal decisionmaking under uncertainty because it appears to be consistent with the standards of proof required in criminal cases, as opposed to cases in torts. Our law requires the jury in a criminal case to be sure beyond a reasonable doubt that a defendant is guilty before deciding against him; standards of proof in criminal cases thus also reveal a preference for Type I error, a preference for rejecting a true hypothesis, a preference for the risk of acquitting a guilty person. Our law requires the jury in a case in torts to believe no more than that it is more probable than not that the defendant is guilty; standards of proof in civil cases thus apparently reveal no preference for either Type I or Type II error.

What that suggests, as Judith Jarvis Thomson points out, is that "our society takes the view that in a criminal case, the society's potential mistake-loss is very much greater than the society's potential omission loss" (Thomson, 1986:158). Presumably this difference in the standards for proof in civil and criminal law stems at least in part from four facts. One is that consequences to the defendant in the criminal case are more likely to lead to grave harms, e.g., death or life imprisonment, than are consequences to society. Grave harms, for both plaintiffs and defendants, also are likely to be greater in the criminal case, hence the tougher standard of proof. Likewise, there appears to be a greater potential for abuse in criminal law than in civil or tort law, since all crimes are potentially political crimes, especially in a tyrannical society. This may arise from the fact that criminal law enforces the power of the state, whereas civil or tort law merely enforces the power of the legal individual. Finally, the state needs to protect its moral legitimacy by minimizing Type II risks in criminal cases. If it fails to convict the guilty, the state commits wrong in a more passive (and hence less reprehensible) sense than if it errs by convicting the innocent. If standards of proof in cases of consumer risk ought to be analogous to those in criminal cases, since both involve grave harms, then this analogy provides a good reason for minimizing consumer, rather than producer, risk.

Third, minimizing false positives, judgments that an unsafe technology is acceptable, is also prima facie reasonable on ethical grounds. Most political theorists, regardless of their persuasion, would probably agree that it is more important to protect the public from harm than to provide, in some positive sense, for welfare. This is at least in part because protecting from harm seems to be a necessary condition for enjoying other freedoms (see, for example, Shue, 1981; Lichtenberg, 1981).

Jeremy Bentham (1962a:301), for instance, in discussing an important part of liberalism, argued that the sole object of government ought to be the greatest happiness of the greatest possible number of the community, and that happiness consists in maximum enjoyment and minimum suffering. However, he cautioned, much as others might, that "the care of providing for his enjoyments ought to be left almost entirely to each individual; the principal function of government being to protect him from sufferings." In other words, Bentham established protection from harm as more basic than provision of enjoyments.

Admittedly it is difficult to draw the line between what constitutes positive and negative laws. Nevertheless, just as there is a basic distinction between negative rights and welfare rights (see, for example, Becker, 1984:76), so also there is a basic distinction between protective laws (prohibiting infringements) and welfare laws (providing some good). Moral philosophers continue to honor distinctions not only between protective laws and welfare-enhancing laws, but also between closely related concepts, such as killing and letting die, and between acts of commission and acts of omission (see, for example, Bentham, 1962b:36; Feinberg, 1973:29, 59; Rachels, 1980:38; Shrader-Frechette, 1985:77–78).

A *fourth* reason for minimizing consumer risk is that producers and implementers of technology, not consumers, receive the bulk of benefits from it. Because they receive most of the benefits, they ought to bear most of the risks and costs. For one set of persons (consumers) to carry most of the risks of a technology, while another set (producers and shareholders) receives most of the benefits, is unfair. It is asymmetrical, in an ethical sense, and it amounts to a gerrymandering of the concepts of justice and property (see Hoffman and Fisher, 1984:211–20).

Of course, it might be objected that assessors have a duty, for the good of the economy (which allegedly maximizes overall welfare) to minimize producer, rather than consumer, risk. Harsanyi (1975) uses this argument. To defend this point, however, the objector would have to show that his position does not amount to violating a basic ethical rule—prohibiting the use of persons, consumers, as means to the ends of other persons, producers and society as a whole— a rule presupposed both by tort law and by the legal guarantees of the Fifth and Fourteenth Amendments to the Constitution (Shrader-Frechette, 1985:71–72; 1983, 33–35). Such a defense should be difficult since it would require justifying the violation of a right to security (see Frankena, 1962:10, 14; Shue, 1981; Lichtenberg, 1981). The objector would also have to show that, contrary to what conflicting assessments suggest, risk probabilities as calculated by experts provide an objective basis from which to pursue societal welfare. If D. Kahneman, A. Tversky, and others (Eddy, 1982:267; Oskamp, 1982:292; Slovic et al., 1982:475) are right, this point should also be difficult to prove, since there is strong evidence that experts have as many heuristic biases, e.g., overconfidence, in estimating probabilities as do laypeople. And if so, then expert arguments (that minimizing producer, rather than consumer, risk maximizes overall welfare) might fail. If they do, then the fourth reason for minimizing consumer risk stands.

Fifth, there are prima facie grounds for limiting consumer, rather than producer, risk because consumers typically need more risk protection than do producers. They need more protection both because they usually have fewer financial resources and less information to deal with the societal hazards that affect them and because they are often faced with bureaucratic denials of public danger.

Laypersons' vulnerability in this regard is well established in a number of cases in environmental risk. When the toxic polybrominated biphenyl (PBB) was accidentally used in cattle feed in Michigan, for example, it was the most widespread, least reported chemical disaster ever to happen in the western world. There was strong evidence of contamination in September 1973, but detailed articles on the problem did not appear, even in the local papers, for two more years. Larger newspapers, like the *Detroit Free Press* and the *Detroit News*, did not examine the crisis until four years after it became evident. The reason for ignoring the problem for so long was that the local bureaucrats denied the claims made by the farmers. What typically happened was that, after a reporter interviewed the owner of a contaminated farm, he or she checked with the Michigan Farm Bureau and the Michigan Department of Agriculture who told the reporter that the PBB contamination was under control and that the farmer's allegations were false. Because of all this bureaucratic denial, PBB led to the deaths of tens of thousands of farm animals and to the contamination of nine million people who ate contaminated meat (Peltu, 1985:132).

The mercury poisoning in Japan likewise is a good example of a typical failure to protect against consumer risk because of bureaucratic denials, industry indifference, and the isolation of the afflicted. In Japan, the dangers of mercury poisoning were identified in 1940, deaths were reported in 1948, and the Minimata poisoning occurred in 1953. Only in the 1960s, however, did public awareness of the problem cause officials to take action against mercury contamination. Because of these and similar instances of whistle-swallowing (rather than whistle-blowing) in cases such as asbestos, biotechnology, and chemical dumps, there is a strong possibility that new consumer risks will be ignored. Hence there is reason to believe that the public, rather than industry, has a greater need for protection (Peltu, 1985:132–36).

A *sixth* reason for minimizing consumer risk, especially in cases of uncertainty, is that the public ought to be accorded rights to protection against industrial decisions that could threaten their health or physical security. These rights arise out of the consideration that everyone has an obligation to compensate those whom he harms. If so, then those victimized have a right to compensation.

The problem of protecting the consumer against the extended effects of industrial decisions typically addresses three general kinds of protection: namely, prevention, transferral of loss, and retention of the risk. When consumers protect themselves against losses due to the decisions of others by maintaining enough assets to sustain damages caused by those decisions, they protect themselves by *retention* of the risk. When they use mechanisms like insurance and legal liability to *transfer* the risk or loss, people protect themselves against harm resulting from other persons' (industry's) decisions by transferring the majority of the loss to someone else, namely the insurer or the liable party. The practical advantage of risk transfer over retention is that it does not require one to retain as many assets, idle and unproductive, as a way of guarding against damages. The moral advantage is that, if the harm itself is caused by another legal/moral "person," an industry, then that person is liable, not the individual harmed. And if the person causing the damage is liable, then there are practical grounds for using this moral responsibility as a basis for the individual or his insurer to remove the financial responsibility from the victim. Insurance is probably a better vehicle for risk transfer than is liability, for the reasons already given (Denenberg et al., 1964).

Prevention, of course, is the most thorough way for members of recipient populations to protect themselves against losses resulting from the decisions of others. By eliminating the sources of the risk, the potential victim has more to gain, practically speaking, than by using insurance and retention as means of protection. This occurs because prevention does not tie up any of the potential victim's assets. The moral grounds for prevention are that, in cases where those responsible or liable cannot redress the harm done to others by their faulty decisions, risk should be eliminated. In other words, if everyone has rights to redress harm done to him, and if those who make faulty industrial decisions cannot make good on the injury that they have caused to persons or property, they ought not be allowed to put others in jeopardy. They ought not place themselves in a position where they have any responsibility for societal or industrial decisions. To do so, when they cannot meet claims against them, is to deny in-principle rights of victims to compensation or redress of damages.

But if risk prevention is justified in cases in which industrial decisionmakers cannot adequately compensate or insure their potential victims, then this suggests a *seventh* reason for minimizing consumer risk: incompensable risks ought not be imposed on those who fail to give free, informed consent to them. The public has a right to protection against incompensable harms caused by others.

If we consider Judith Jarvis Thomson's notion of "incompensable harms,"

harms so serious that no amount of money could possibly compensate the victim, then it appears that death, at least, is an obviously incompensable harm; there is no way to compensate a dead person. As Thomson puts it, speaking of another case, "however fair and efficient the judicial system may be, . . . [those] who cause incompensable harms by their negligence cannot square accounts with their victims" (Thomson, 1986:158). This means that anyone who imposes a significant risk of death on another, without his free, informed consent, is imposing an incompensable, and therefore morally unjustifiable, harm.

This raises the question of when someone is imposing a significant risk of death on another, without his free, informed consent. Although the boundary cases would be difficult to decide, potentially catastrophic technologies like nuclear power do appear to impose a significant risk of death on another. Even the government admits both that a nuclear accident could kill 150,000 people and that the core melt probability, for all existing and planned U.S. commercial reactors, is 1 in 4 during their collective thirty-year lifetime (Shrader-Frechette, 1983:85ff.). To the degree that this hazard is imposed on citizens without their free, informed consent, to that extent is the risk both unjustified and incompensable. Moreover, U.S. citizens are prohibited by law from obtaining full compensation from the negligent utility in the event of a commercial nuclear catastrophe (Shrader-Frechette, 1985:74–78). Hence there are strong grounds for believing that the nuclear risk is incompensable and therefore unjustifiable.

Other cases of incompensable harm seem to arise most often in connection with potentially catastrophic, involuntarily imposed technologies whose risks are uncertain, e.g., specific lethal pesticides or LNG facilities. Precisely because these technologies are catastrophic, and because they have the potential to cause incompensable and involuntarily imposed harm, one might argue that the risks they impose are unjustifiable. This is all the more true if the probability of harm is uncertain, because the person imposing the risk is in principle unable to know how grave a danger he is imposing. And if there is uncertainty about the level and nature of the harm, then it also would be difficult (if not impossible) to prove that imposing such a risk would lead to a greater good for all.

Someone might object, of course, that assessors have a duty, for the good of the economy (which allegedly maximizes overall welfare) to minimize producer, rather than consumer, risk (Harsanyi, 1975). I responded to this objection earlier, in connection with the *fourth* reason for minimizing consumer risk. If the earlier response is correct—some experts who allege that minimizing producer risk maximizes general welfare are wrong—there is a *seventh* reason for minimizing consumer risk: to protect the public's rights to free, informed consent, especially in matters concerning bodily security and especially when expert opinion on risk may err.

Moreover, one ought not discriminate against someone solely for reasons of economic efficiency. This means that one ought not jeopardize consumers' rights to security in the name of economic welfare, even if a conservative stance regarding consumer or public risk could set back the economy or could cripple a particular technology.

MAXIMIZING CONSUMER RISK COULD HURT THE ECONOMY

Obviously, however, no one is eager either to cripple technology or to set back the economy in order to minimize consumer risk. For this reason, it is important to point out that many dangerous technologies have at least the potential to set back the economy. Nuclear technology, for example, has set back the economy in the sense that it could not have survived without protection from normal market mechanisms. If there were no government-guaranteed liability limit for catastrophic accidents involving commercial nuclear fission, no major U.S. atomic interests would ever have gone into the generation of electricity. Even the major pronuclear lobby, the Atomic Industrial Forum, admits this (Shrader-Frechette, 1983:ch. 1). The upshot is that, although nuclear utilities have been relieved of the burden of competing in an open market, including the liability market, they nevertheless have the potential to cripple the economy with a dangerous accident that could (on the government's own estimates) wipe out an area the size of Pennsylvania. In other words, because of the liability limit, the producer risk is minimized, while the consumer risk from nuclear power is maximized, a maximization that could easily contribute to economic harm (Shrader-Frechette, 1983:ch. 4).

Hazardous technologies could also set back the economy in the sense that many of the most dangerous industries (in terms of high consumer risk and high consumer risk aversion) are also among the most capital intensive. Because they are so capital intensive, they threaten the flow of available money for other societal projects and hence jeopardize the economic well-being of society. This is particularly the case with nuclear technology (see, for example, Lovins and Price, 1975).

If the two previous argument sketches are at least partially correct, they suggest that insistence on the operation of the free market (free from regulations to minimize consumer risk and free from liability limits to minimize producer risks) might be just as threatening to dangerous technologies as to consumers who are risk averse. They also suggest the proponents of maximizing consumer risk and minimizing producer risk are inconsistent; often they wish to interfere with the market to protect themselves, the producers, but they complain when risk regulation interferes with the same market, in order to protect consumers. Given this inconsistency, it is unclear why uncompensatable risks should be borne only by their victims, rather than also by their perpetrators, as in the case of the Price-Anderson Act (see Cooke, 1982:345–47).

ECONOMIC ARGUMENTS CAN PRESUPPOSE USING HUMANS AS MEANS

There are other problems, however, with the basic argument that one ought not mandate high levels of consumer safety because this would hurt the economy, technology, or progress. This line of reasoning sounds vaguely like several others, for example: "We can't abolish slavery because this would destroy the economy of the South"; or "We can't pass the ERA, because women won't stay home and take care of their children, and this would hurt the family." What is peculiar about all three of these arguments is that they all pit important values, like family and economic well-being, against moral values, like citizen safety or abolishing racism and sexism. The arguments are troubling because they force us to choose between two goods.

Judith Jarvis Thomson's response to such arguments, e.g., those that force us to choose between risking our lives and starving, for example, is simple. "It is morally indecent that anyone in a moderately well-off society should be faced with such a choice" (Thomson, 1986:172), a choice between safety and economic well-being or between women's autonomy and family welfare.

What is troublesome about these three arguments—technology, slavery, and women's rights—is that they all propose using humans—whether citizens who are at risk from technology, blacks who are victims of slavery, or women who are disadvantaged by sexism—as a *means* to some economic or social *end*. Yet if Immanuel Kant was correct, humans ought never be used as means to some end of other persons, especially not if all humans have equal rights and equal dignity. It is true that we do often have to weigh the interests of one group in society over those of another, and we do often discriminate. Yet the only grounds justifying discrimination, the failure to treat one person as equal to another, as W. Frankena has pointed out, is that the discrimination will work to the advantage of everyone, including those discriminated against. Any other attempt to justify discrimination fails because it would amount to sanctioning the use of some humans as means to the ends of other humans.

Applying this insight about justified discrimination to the case of technology assessment and Type I and Type II risks means that a necessary condition for discriminating against consumers and citizens who prefer conservative health and safety standards would be to prove that rejecting conservative standards would work to the advantage of everyone, including all consumers. In other words, the burden of proof is on the producer attempting to put the consumer at risk. The prima facie desirable position is to minimize consumer risk for the seven reasons already stated.

MINIMIZING CONSUMER RISK BY GIVING CONSUMERS DECISION-MAKING POWER

Eighth, there are also strong economic grounds for minimizing consumer risk whenever this minimization is consistent with consumer preferences. It makes sense to let consumers decide the fate of technologies (and therefore to minimize consumer risk, if they wish), since consumer sovereignty is not justified merely by reference to the alleged unseen hand controlling economic events, but by democratic process and procedural rationality. (For analyses of collective strategies whereby consumers might exercise their sovereignty, see Shrader-Frechette, 1984:286–312; for a discussion of procedural rationality, see Bartlett, 1986b:223ff.) This justification is a revered one: "no taxation without representation" (Schelling, 1984:145–46). One likewise could argue that there ought to be no imposition of risk without the free, informed consent of those who must bear it. This dictum holds true in medical experimentation, and it could easily be shown to have an analogue in risk management (Shrader-Frechette, 1985:107ff.). Welfare economics establishes the convenience and efficiency of consumer sovereignty, and citizens themselves have safeguarded it by means of "arms, martyrdom, boycott, or some principles held to be self-evident. . . . [I]t includes the inalienable right of the consumer to make his own mistakes" (Schelling, 1984:145–46).

Ninth, minimizing consumer risk, in the name of consumer self-determination, is also consistent with most ethical theories about situations in which paternalism is or is not justified. In his classic discussion of liberty, John Stuart Mill (1986) makes it clear that it is acceptable to override individual decisionmaking only to protect others or to protect someone from selling himself into slavery. Any other justification for a limitation on individual freedom, claims Mill, would amount to a dangerous infringement on individual autonomy. But if Mill is correct (and I shall not repeat his arguments here), there are no paternalistic grounds for overriding consumers' hesitancies about accepting a particular technological risk. In other words, paternalism appears acceptable only to protect from slavery the person whose judgment is overridden or to protect others from being harmed by the person whose judgment is overridden. But notice what is happening with the "dismissing the layperson" argument and with attempts to minimize producer risk: experts are arguing that citizens are overprotective of themselves. The assessors want to provide the consumer with less, not more, protection, and largely for the benefit of the producer. Hence their paternalism is suspect.

At this point, producers might object that consumers want the benefits associated with technological risks and, therefore, those who argue for reducing consumer risk must bear the charge of behaving paternalistically toward those who do not want consumer risk minimized. There are at least two responses to this objection. For one thing, there is substantial social-scientific and philosophical evidence that those bearing high levels of consumer risk have not given free, informed consent to the imposition of the risks (Emmett et al., 1978:367–74; Egerton, 1981:43–45; Shrader-Frechette, 1985:97–122). Moreover, economists have long recognized that risk imposition represents a diminution in welfare for those on whom it is imposed (Starr, 1976:16). Since producers impose risks on consumers, the producers ought to bear the burden of proof in justifying the imposition, particularly since consumers typically have not given free, informed consent.

Finally, *tenth*, minimizing consumer risk might be less likely to lead to social disruption and political unrest than minimizing producer risk. Although developing this point is not the goal of this chapter, there might be pragmatic and political, as well as ethical and economic, grounds for following consumer preferences to minimize consumer risk. This is because effective hazard management, as many risk assessors have pointed out, requires the cooperation of a large body of laypeople; otherwise, accidents, costly publicity, and civil disobedience may result.

The long controversy over the Seabrook, New Hampshire, nuclear facility illustrates the fact that hazard management at a nuclear reactor, for example, cannot be begun or the plant opened without cooperation between producers and consumers. Moreover, expert control is no substitute for this cooperation. Both producers and consumers must agree to do without some things and to accept substitutes for others. They must vote sensibly, act reasonably, and engage in much give-and-take over regulations and standards. They must obey safety rules, and they must use the legal system sensibly. If they do not, a hazardous technology could be crippled. In other words, "even if the experts were much better judges of risk than laypeople, giving experts an exclusive franchise for hazard management would mean substituting short-term efficiency for the long-term effort needed to create an informed citizenry" (Slovic et al., 1982:488). This is close to a point made by Thomas Jefferson: the only safe locus of power in a democracy is the people. Minimizing consumer risk, when the public demands more safety, is one way to locate power with the people. It is also one way to make assessment both more democratic and more sensitive to the ethical dimensions of environmental impacts.

NOTE

I thank Robert Bartlett and anonymous referees for constructive criticism. Whatever errors remain are my responsibility.

14

Bureaucracy or Analysis: Implications of Impact Assessment for Public Administration

Robert V. Bartlett and Walter F. Baber

Public administration, as a profession, seems always to be in a state of becoming. Bureaucracy may have a broad reputation for unresponsiveness, but public administrators spend much effort considering their relationship to changing social circumstances. This is largely because public administration is, primarily, something people do; it is not a self-contained academic discipline (Waldo, 1955). Public administration as action is the practice of governing, the making of decisions in bureaucracies, the administrative part of the policy process. Bureaucratic agencies are, in Dwight Waldo's words, "government's central instrument for dealing with social problems" (Waldo, 1972: 222). And people in those agencies are affected by whatever "forces and turbulence" exist in society as they attempt to increase or decrease the rate of social change or alter its direction. This explains the profession's extensive efforts to envision its role in the future; a chapter to that effect enters prominently into most public administration textbooks, and articles on the subject occur with regularity in the profession's literature (Baber, 1983).

In the midst of this turmoil, three central challenges arise. First, public administrators as professionals seek means to improve the *effectiveness* of government policies and programs. Second, in a large and complex system, characterized by divided and overlapping functions carried out at multiple levels of government, an essential component of effective action is *coordination*. Third, bureaucratic power in a democracy is always derivative of some representive process, which poses the issue of *legitimacy* whenever administrative action advances the interest of some at the expense of others. These problems seem universal in modern democratic government. They are endlessly vexing and, as we shall see, interrelated. And they emerge and reemerge with a regularity that is at once reassuring and troubling.

These problems give coherence to the theoretical line of inquiry and historical development of public administration as a field of study, but their persistence casts doubt on its ability to progress as a profession. And in no other area are these issues more evident than in the development of impact assessment as a tool for the conduct of public policy. In its efforts to manage the effects of technologically driven change on our natural and social environment, public administration confronts its future directly and inescapably. In ways that are only gradually being recognized, building impact assessment procedures and strategies into the fabric of government provides novel responses to each of these challenges, offering us a glimpse of new avenues for promoting effectiveness, coordination, and legitimacy in public administration.

THREE CHALLENGES, THREE RESPONSES

Effectiveness is a relatively new and often elusive term for an administrative concern of long standing. In considering the intention of the founders of the American republic, we are generally drawn to their evident desire to prevent dangerous accumulations of political power in any branch or level of government. We often overlook the concern expressed in the debates at the Constitutional Convention and in many places in the Federalist Papers (especially numbers 68 and 69) for the development of a vigorous executive. Effectiveness in this classical formulation simply means energy and dispatch in the pursuit of the clear mandates of an elected legislature (Karl, 1987; Yates, 1982). This view of executive power was echoed a century later by Woodrow Wilson who argued that administration should exercise "large powers and unhampered discretion" (Wilson, 1887). His assumption was that, given the opportunity to display administrative energy and to exercise administrative discretion, bureaucratic officials would perform in a competent, professional, and politically neutral manner. This would serve the public interest and advance the fortunes of those politicians, regardless of party, who brought effective professionals into government and empowered them to act. Their effectiveness would, thereby, justify the confidence placed in them by elected officials and legitimize their influence over public affairs.

In another era, this concern for effectiveness would manifest itself in a growing interest in program evaluation—the rigorous use of measures and comparisons to provide information on the results of public programs (Wholey, 1976). Such retrospective analysis provides data that are useful in designing managerial and policy changes that could provide more effective future performance. Having recognized the utility of feedback mechanisms for improving effectiveness, public administrators also have been a willing market for any "feedforward" planning technique that could be developed. This is precisely the appeal of impact assessment. A foremost example is, of course, the assessment required by the National Environmental Policy Act (NEPA). Forcing government to undertake impact analysis is an attempt to establish feedforward processes, that is, prospective analyses, to inform a particular category of policy decisions (Dryzek, 1983b; Bartlett, 1986a). The development of such techniques—others include risk assessment, cost-benefit analysis, and technology assessment—allows public administrators, at least in theory, to break the analytical bonds that have made their search for greater effectiveness largely reactive. It also allows the administrator to project his growing concern for substantive policy outcomes into the future and to extend the promise of effectiveness beyond mere identification and correction of errors already made.[1]

Coordination is another persistent problem confronted by public administrators. A number of definitions of coordination could be offered (Seidman, 1980). At its most basic level, coordination involves the management of functional interdependencies among individuals. More simply, coordination exists when people who depend upon one another to accomplish their work enjoy cooperative relationships. This is, of course, much more easily stated than achieved (Schick, 1981; Molnar and Rogers, 1982). Coordination can be difficult to achieve because people and organizations have different analytical and managerial capacities, employ different operating procedures, possess unequal resources, and hold different policy priorities.

Coordinative arrangements designed to overcome these difficulties tend to fall into two categories. Some coordinative techniques depend, at base, on "central coordination" through authoritative coercion. The second category of coordinative techniques consists of consultative behaviors, information sharing, and negotiation among equals: "mutual adjustment" (Lindblom, 1965, Lindblom, 1977; Braybrooke and Lindblom, 1963; Sundquist, 1969). Obviously, the two approaches described here are not mutually exclusive. They constitute two tracks toward coordinated action that can be followed simultaneously. Experience with the coordination of federal grants-in-aid is a useful example. On one hand, the federal requirement for a "single state agency" to administer grants in broad policy areas was an obvious attempt to create an administrative mechanism capable of exerting central coordination. On the other hand, Office of Management and Budget circulars A-85, A-95, and A-98 were significant examples of consultative and information-sharing procedures.

But a note of caution is in order. The coordinative potential of any mechanism or activity may be strictly limited by more powerful political concerns (see, e.g., Johnson, 1985). And mutual adjustment mechanisms are often less than fully voluntary systems, depending in many instances on coercion from above or outside to ensure participation by all relevant parties.

As an example of the coordinative potential of impact assessment, the envi-

ronmental impact statement requirement in NEPA is instructive. Whereas the
act exhibits its drafters' obvious interest in producing policy outcomes that would
be more environmentally sound, its internal mechanisms are not obviously coercive. Impact statement and public hearing procedures do not dictate outcomes;
they create new political processes through which citizens, politicians, and other
expert bureaucrats might reasonably be expected to press their legitimate demands
for more environmental sensitivity in national policy making (Friesema and
Culhane, 1976). The objective is not to force bureaucracies into specific actions,
but to reshape the dynamics of the policy process (Bartlett, 1986a). In Serge
Taylor's evocative phrase, the impact assessment process established by NEPA
is designed to make bureaucracies think (Taylor, 1984; Bartlett, 1986b).

Although no one will object to thinking as such, impact assessment of this
sort can still be more coercive than it first appears. For example, it would seem
that the American national government has no authority, constitutionally, to
impose impact asssessment requirements on the states against their will. But it
can, and often has, set such standards as conditions for new or continued grant-
in-aid assistance upon which state governments are heavily dependent (Kettl,
1983). Still, the coordinative influences which result from the establishment of
regular analytical procedures prior to the initiation of major government projects
is clear enough. And, at least in the view of Congress, the benefits of that
coordination justify any loss of state and local discretion that may be involved.

Finally, *legitimacy* is an issue that has confronted public administration at
least since its inception as a self-conscious field of endeavor.[2] The issue is most
pressing when bureaucrats wield coercive authority on behalf of the state (Rohr,
1985, 1986). But in a democracy there must be an answer to the broader question,
how is it legitimate for unelected officials to do anything at all? The traditional
answer to this question refers back to elected officials. To fully understand this
answer and the reasons it has become problematic, a brief historical digression
is necessary.

At one time in U.S. history, Congress had so extended its control over bureaucratic detail that Woodrow Wilson was moved to complain that the national
legislature had assumed virtually all of the substantive powers of government.
From this historical distance, it is difficult to imagine that there was ever any
concern that Congress might exercise any of its mandated functions too ener-
getically. But Allen Schick (1976) reminds us that the administrative reform
movements that gave rise to public administration as a distinct field were a
reaction to the results of just this kind of legislative domination. In attempting
to shake off the intrusive influence of legislatures, public administration was
building a paradox into its very foundation. If public administration had to be
freed from detailed legislative control to be effective, how could it then claim
to exercise its power legitimately (Yates, 1982)?

In the absence of direct legislative supervision of the sort that distressed
Wilson, what accountability mechanism can be used to justify bureaucratic

power? A potential answer exists in the growing influence of the modern American presidency. Throughout virtually all of the twentieth century, presidential power seems to have been in a constant state of growth. Two world wars, numerous economic crises, and a series of cold war confrontations have led a succession of presidents, both Republican and Democratic, to expand the powers of the office. These new-found capacities, together with the historical powers to appoint and remove administrative employees, to reorganize the executive branch, and to appeal directly to public opinion for political support, ought to combine to give the president solid control over bureaucratic agencies. That presidents, in fact, enjoy surprisingly little control over the bureaucracy can be traced to their dependence on bureaucratic expertise to supply much of the content of public policy and to the capacity of bureaucracies to coopt those sent by the president to bend them to his will (Rourke, 1984; Weinberg, 1977).

An alternate source of bureaucratic legitimacy has been sought through citizen participation. The central assumption of citizen participation is that the public knows what it wants and, if given the opportunity, will make its wishes clear directly to bureaucratic policymakers in a way that elections generally cannot (ACIR, 1979). Citizen participation is a broad and varied phenomenon. Methods of participation include attendance at public hearings, use of initiatives and referenda, service on program advisory boards, and membership on governing boards that actually direct program operations. Policy areas where these techniques are used vary just as broadly, including human services delivery, public works and zoning, education, and environmental protection. Enabling legislation is almost as diverse. From the Model Cities and Community Action Act to a variety of "open meetings" laws in states and localities, citizens have been invited into the halls of government during the past twenty-five years as never before in history, notwithstanding the lack of enthusiasm of the Reagan administration for such extensive participation (DeSario and Langton, 1987; Neuse, 1983). The purpose of this intricate dance of participation has been, among other things, to enhance public acceptance of governmental undertakings by reducing citizen alienation from a government that has become increasingly bureaucratic (ACIR, 1979). But as a tool for legitimizing bureaucratic power, citizen participation is limited in a number of ways.

First, it is not clear that participation in public programs is particularly representative. Participants generally represent organized interests (including other government agencies), come from only a limited range of those likely to be affected by the program in question, and are often unrepresentative in socioeconomic terms (Nagel, 1987; Rosenbaum, 1976). Because conventional participation is frequently found wanting, reformers and analysts are often inspired to propose more innovative forms of citizen participation (Arterton, 1988). Second, there is an obvious and ever present danger that bureaucratic agencies may turn techniques for citizen participation into tools for citizen co-optation (Riedel, 1972). Agencies sometimes "orchestrate" citizen participation. Third, although there is empirical evidence that citizen participation sometimes does result in greater bureaucratic responsiveness, there is also evidence that the impact commonly is grudging, minimal, and symbolic. Citizens often lack the time, expertise, and political staying power to have a significant effect on bureaucratic operations (Kweit and Kweit, 1982). But if citizen participation is inadequate as a legitimizing influence on bureaucracy and if control by elected officials is no longer credible, how does one justify the enormous power of government agencies? The answer, at least from the bureaucratic point of view, is obvious.

In the modern administrative state the legitimacy of administrative action derives primarily from three facts: (1) things that citizens have come to think must be done by government can be accomplished only by the bureaucracy; (2) by achieving a high degree of effectiveness, bureaucrats bring a technical expertise to government that it would not otherwise command; (3) by striving for greater coordination in government operations and policy, bureaucrats introduce whatever uniformity and reliability that government enjoys. Without this substantive and managerial expertise, and without the standardization of policy according to written rules and procedures, modern government would be torn apart by its many inherent centrifugal forces. Gone would be the ability of big government even to approximate achievement of its professed goal of horizontal equity (equal treatment for equals). And gone would be any chance of controlling the impacts of growth and technology on our natural and social environment. In this admittedly bureaucratic perspective on legitimacy, the effectiveness and coordination achieved by bureaucracy are its ultimate justifications.

This doctrine seems especially well suited to a discussion of impact assessment as a source of bureaucratic legitimacy. Legislation such as NEPA allows Congress to establish a national policy statement and to mandate procedural reforms calculated to advance its policy goals without excessive tinkering with day-to-day government operations. The uniformity and clarity of NEPA's procedural requirements allow those in the executive branch to focus appropriate analytical efforts on concrete environmental issues, holding specific individuals accountable for adequate planning and acceptable outcomes. And the creation of the environmental impact statement document allows citizen groups more effectively to focus their limited resources and to sustain their participation in policy planning through judicial or legislative challenges if they find bureaucratic responses to be inadequate or misleading.

IMPACT ASSESSMENT AND THE THREE CHALLENGES

So, at least in theory, impact assessment of the sort mandated by NEPA provides potential partial answers to some of the most vexing problems faced by public administrators as a group and public administration as a profession. But theory is not enough. It is important that we begin to examine empirically the effects of impact assessment processes on decision making within organizations. Unfortunately, this is far more easily said than done. When we witness environmentally sound decision making, for example, how much credit should we grant to NEPA, to other environmental legislation, and to preexisting environmental sensitivity in government having nothing to do with any legislation? Given the time required to effect change in bureaucratic decision making, should we judge whatever progress that is attributable to impact assessment legislation to have been rapid or slow? If we wish to quantify the impact of impact assessment, how do we count and weigh changes in proposals as a consequence of the impact assesssment process? And, how do we handle proposals that were amended or abandoned prior to the formal environmental impact statement stage in anticipation of NEPA requirements (Caldwell, 1982)?

Although these difficulties may not be insurmountable, solutions to them are not readily apparent. For that reason, it may be more desirable to judge the impact of impact assessment on bureaucratic decision making by examining the attitudes and opinions of those immediately responsible. For example, a 1981 survey of employees of the Corps of Engineers, U.S. Forest Service, Bureau of Land Management, and Soil Conservation Service offers some indicative data. Employees who were engaged in implementing environmental impact assessment in field offices of these four agencies were asked several questions about the effects of the environmental impact statement (EIS) requirement of NEPA on the decision-making process within their agency.[3] Although the survey was designed for other purposes, the responses to several items allow us to construct an intelligible, although not definitive, account of how one impact assessment process relates to the issues of bureaucratic effectiveness, coordination, and legitimacy. The evidence is illustrative and suggestive only; in particulars our arguments might be only partially relevant (or perhaps even more incisive) with respect to other differently institutionalized impact assessment systems.

Impact assessment personnel were asked whether "NEPA with its EIS requirement has had a beneficial effect on the communication of scientific and technical information *between* your agency and the scientific community." The 416 respondents to the survey agreed with this notion in considerable numbers (53.3 percent); fewer than one-fifth disagreed (18.5 percent); the rest were uncertain. This reflects a high level of borrowing of information by bureaucracy directly from the scientific community. This "transfusion" of expertise from outside of government suggests one reason why bureaucracy seems able to maintain its effectiveness in the policy process. Elected decision makers often have to maintain their power despite scientific and technological advances; bureaucrats remain powerful because of them.

Respondents were also asked whether "NEPA with its EIS requirement has had a beneficial effect on the communication of scientific and technical information *within* your agency." The responses to this item reveal an unmistakable endorsement of impact assessment. A substantial majority of the respondents (78.7 percent) agreed that impact assessment had improved their internal use of scientific and technical information. The results are equally impressive when they are broken down by agency.

If impact assessment can enhance the effectiveness of bureaucratic action by improving the scientific content of agency decision making, what evidence can be found of its coordinative influence? Such evidence might be found in at least three places. Regional coordination might be evidenced in the capacity of agency headquarters staff to control the activities of regional offices or in the enhanced ability of state and local governments to interact in federal decision making. Coordination within the agency might result if the environmental impact assessment (EIA) requirement strengthened the hands of planning staffs in agency decision processes by making long-term thinking more influential in agency activity. This would naturally tend to exert a coordinative influence over the actions of individual bureaucrats, to the extent that agencies can affect individual behavior. Finally, impact assessment might improve coordination by encouraging more "mutual adjustment"—more consultation, more information sharing, and more negotiation (Sundquist, 1969). In all three of these areas, empirical evidence is available from the survey of impact assessment personnel in the four federal agencies.

During the first decade of NEPA's implementation, EIA was seldom an integral part of the decision-making process; rather, EIA was often undertaken merely to comply formally with what was seen as a procedural legal requirement. Obviously, a strategy with some appeal to agency headquarters was to centralize the EIS preparation function (Bardach and Pugliaresi, 1977). Not only could new expertise thus be "efficiently" used and the rest of the agency kept "uncontaminated" by multidisciplinary influences, but the new procedural requirements could be worked to exert greater control over field employees. Calls by reformers and policy scholars for integration of EIA into basic project planning (e.g., Friesema and Culhane, 1976; Caldwell, 1976, 1978) were followed in the late 1970s by NEPA implementing regulations that formally endorsed and required such integration. This was the context in which respondents to the survey were asked whether their "agency's central staff has used the science requirements of NEPA to strengthen its control over regional and field offices." The results cast doubt on this particular coordinative influence of impact assessment, at least by 1981. Only 27.1 percent thought that the central staff had thus increased control. Although there was a relatively high level of uncertainty on this issue (26.8 percent), most respondents with an opinion felt that NEPA had not contributed to greater control over field operations (46.1 percent).

Respondents were also asked to what extent state and local agencies had proven to be useful sources of information about the potential environmental impacts of proposed actions. In this respect, regional coordination as a consequence of the EIA process seems to gain empirical support. Over four-fifths of those responding found state and local agencies to be at least moderately useful as sources of information on potential environmental impacts (84.1 percent). Of the twelve other sources of information specified in survey questions, only the three available within the agency itself (the expertise of in-house personnel, library materials, and previous studies by the agency) were found to be more useful. Clearly, state and local governments have a significant opportunity to influence the course of environmental decision making. In this respect, at least, the potential for greater intergovernmental coordination as a result of NEPA is clear.

If the evidence for greater regional coordination as a result of NEPA is mixed, what of coordination within the agency resulting from greater influence exercised by planning staffs? The available data make a strong case for this proposition. Overall, 68.1 percent of the respondents agreed that science required by NEPA had been used by the planning staffs within their agencies to strengthen their position in the agency's decision process. Responses in each of the separate agencies were consistent. The capacity of impact assessment to strengthen the coordination of an agency's decision process by enhancing the planning function is clear enough from these results. Greater coordination may occur because of a greater reliance by the agency on expertise, particularly multidisciplinary expertise, as a basis for legally justifying its planning and decision making in the face of the impact assessment requirements by NEPA. Planning staffs are strengthened at the expense of hands-on decision making by traditional line and political employees.

With regard to coordination through mutual adjustment, evidence of the facilitation of expert consultation and information sharing between government and the scientific community and within agencies has already been presented. NEPA and the logic of EIA require such consultation prior to the completion of an EIS. NEPA also requires, prior to reaching a final decision on any proposal, that the EIS be made public and available to the president, to citizens, to other bureaucracies, to Congress, and to the courts. The result is a forced opportunity for much greater coordination with agency outsiders through whatever political or legal mechanisms are available (Taylor, 1984). Evidence of this process at work between bureaucratic agencies is evident in response to a question whether "NEPA with its EIS requirement has had a beneficial effect on the communication of scientific and technical information *among* various government agencies." A clear majority of respondents (58.6 percent) agreed that NEPA had improved the sharing of scientific and technical information among federal agencies. Agreement ranged from 77.3 percent for the Corps of Engineers to 43.7 percent for the Forest Service. Information sharing of this sort is an essential foundation of coordination through mutual adjustment. Impact assessment forces government agencies to engage in a greater sharing of the scientific and technical information upon which their claims to expertise are founded.

Finally, do the improved effectiveness and coordination that seem to result from the impact assessment requirement of NEPA in any way enhance the legitimacy of agency decision making? It is difficult to imagine what a direct measure of legitimacy in a survey of agency personnel would look like. Nevertheless, some inferences are possible. Although they are indirect, as are the other inferences drawn so far, they may be quite useful in illustrating the role impact assessment seems destined to play in the future of bureaucratic decision making.

Survey respondents were asked whether strengthening their agency's science capabilities because of NEPA had enabled the agency to be less dependent on information supplied by sponsors or economic interests. A plurality of the respondents (42.6 percent) believe that NEPA has had just such an effect. There are, however, variations among the agencies. Nearly two-thirds of the respondents in the Corps of Engineers (65.4 percent) reported greater independence from nongovernmental sources of information; however, in the Soil Conservation Service, barely one-quarter of the respondents (25.8 percent) held a similar view. One is tempted to conclude that impact assessment helps agencies to resist outside pressures to whatever extent they are able and motivated to do so. In fact, this line of reasoning is consistent with the findings of Jeanne Clarke and Daniel McCool, in their comparative analysis of seven agencies, that already rich and powerful agencies such as the Corps usually are able to take advantage of opportunities to become more powerful (Clarke and McCool, 1985). This hypothesis finds support elsewhere in the data. When asked about the usefulness of information provided by groups outside of government, Corps of Engineers respondents consistently rated these sources as less useful than did respondents from other agencies. So, to the extent that independence can be taken as a reflection of an internal sense of agency legitimacy, these data lend support to the idea that the effectiveness and coordination enjoyed by agencies as a result of the EIA requirement of NEPA lead to an enhanced sense of agency legitimacy.

OLD PROBLEMS, NEW PROBLEMS

Our argument has been that impact assessment can serve as an answer to three recurring problems of public administration. By enhancing bureaucratic expertise in dealing with complex and interdependent policy issues (such as environmental protection), impact assessment provides one method for improving government effectiveness. By strengthening the role of planning staffs in agency decision making and by forcing opportunities for mutual adjustment with other agencies and with other interested outsiders, impact assessment can also have a coordinating effect on government operations. And by improving both bureaucratic effectiveness and coordination, impact assessment supports one of the remaining theories that can justify the extent of bureaucratic power in the policy process.

A note of caution is in order here. Impact assessment does not automatically answer, resolve, or eliminate the major philosophical or political challenges to modern public administration. And it poses at least one vexing new problem: impact assessment is itself an activity that demands nontraditional organization and management by public administrators (Bartlett and Baber, 1987).

Moreover, if impact assessment can improve bureaucratic expertise, it might also increase the tendency toward elitism in the policy process. If impact assessment can have a coordinative influence on government, it might also threaten the decentralization of power. And, if impact assessment can increase bureaucracy's ability to resist the influence of interests outside of government, it might constitute a latent threat to the value of popular sovereignty enshrined in our political rhetoric for over two hundred years. These issues are clearly beyond the scope of this analysis, but their potential seriousness should be sufficient to justify further examination of the generally unquestioned assumptions underlying our growing use of impact assessment as part of the strategy of modern public administration (Baber, 1988).

NOTES

We thank William R. Mangun, Lynton K. Caldwell, Robert C. Paehlke, and especially Michael E. Kraft for valuable criticisms of an earlier draft. Parts of this chapter are based upon work supported by the National Science Foundation under grant PRA–79–10014. Any opinions, findings, conclusions, or recommendations expressed are those of the authors and do not necessarily reflect the views of the National Science Foundation.

1. For example, no better formulation of the effectiveness imperative could be offered than John H. Baldwin's: "The challenge of the next decades involves the recognition of entropy and its origins and the management of entropy to change these inevitable detrimental impacts into forms less damaging to human and natural systems" (Baldwin, 1985:9).

2. There is considerable disagreement on how the term legitimacy should be used. Here, we use it in a minimal sense. Legitimacy is the likelihood that authoritative decisions will be accepted by those toward whom they are directed. As such, legitimacy implies more than merely being legal (Rohr, 1985, 1986).

3. The questionnaire, methodology, and results for each question are reported in Bartlett and Caldwell (1983). The survey, which focused on the science dimensions of environmental impact assessment, was conducted in the summer of 1981 with the cooperation of the four agencies. Questionnaires were sent to two persons in each field office of each agency—one person with an environmental analyst perspective and one with an agency planner or manager perspective. Potential respondents were instructed to complete the questionnaire only if their office had been significantly involved with a project requiring an environmental impact statement in the previous three years. A total of 532 forms were distributed. The response rates exceeded 92 percent for each agency. Deducting forms returned but uncompleted because of lack of impact assessment activity still left a response rate greater than 73 percent for each agency, for a total of 416 usable responses.

15

Environmental Impact Assessment, Entrepreneurship, and Policy Change

Geoffrey Wandesforde-Smith

Administrative entrepreneurship needs to be added to the family of concepts with which we try to fashion plausible interpretations of environmental impact assessment (EIA) policy and practice. In this chapter I want to comment particularly on the big questions it has seemed appropriate to ask about EIA over the past twenty years and on the vision of EIA as a self-regulating and self-sustaining learning process that, through analysis, adapts policy to a changing world.

THE BIG QUESTIONS ABOUT EIA

New questions about the meaning of the EIA process have always run ahead of the availability of definitive answers to earlier questions about how the process works and why it works the way it does. By the term EIA process I refer to the entire set of procedures in the United States structured pursuant to the National Environmental Policy Act (NEPA) of 1969, which includes but is not limited to the preparation and review of environmental impact statements (EISs). At the state level, specific names may include the environmental impact reporting (EIR) process, or simply the environmental assessment process. In other countries, EIA is often practiced but not under any firm legal mandate with its own special terminology. Describing any or all of these as EIA processes helps keep things simple.

Once upon a time, in the United States, NEPA was just one gleam in the eyes of those who dreamed of many ways of making federal agencies stewards of the environment (Caldwell, 1970; Wandesforde-Smith, 1970, 1971; Sax, 1973). After the federal courts showed interest in the statute, it seemed important to know how litigation might turn a vague form of words about report writing into a strictly enforceable requirement for the preparation and review of EISs (Anderson, 1973). The qualities of the evidence bearing on this question were still being debated when the initial focus on the courts shifted.

There followed a period in which interest in the differential impact of EIA as a policy instrument arose from the differences in the way various federal agencies were organized to implement a law the courts had taken seriously (Andrews, 1976; Liroff, 1976; Mazmanian and Nienaber, 1979). An alternate but related line of inquiry stemmed from criticism about the form and content of EISs. It asked whether the impact of the statute was better explained by the scientific quality of the descriptions and analysis impact statements contained than by organizational variables (Caldwell, 1982; Caldwell et al., 1983).

More recently, as the U.S. Supreme Court has appeared to drain much of the substantive promise out of NEPA (Goldsmith and Banks, 1983; Schoenbaum, 1985; but see also Coggins and Wilkinson, 1987:355–56) and as the Reagan administration has minimized interest in using EIA as a policy tool, the big question is whether the success of EIA can be guaranteed despite large sea changes in the political context for statutory implementation and enforcement. Such collapses of active political support for EIA policy at the highest levels of government are not confined to the United States (Formby, 1987).

For some, the answer seems to lie in the formal structure of an EIA process (Ortolano, Jenkins, and Abracosa, 1987) and in the opportunities this provides for widespread participation in assessments (Sproul, 1986). For others, the answer depends on whether formal structures can tap the powerful, informal incentives that operate inside every administrative agency, and which link it to the external world, so as to produce agencies that continuously and progressively think about environmental values (Taylor, 1984; Sagoff, 1987).

If, by whatever combination of formal and informal mechanisms, EIA can be made an adaptive, bureaucratic learning process, then, clearly, it has great value. If, in addition, it can be shown to be a process wherein adaptive learning occurs largely independent of prevailing political circumstances, then EIA might reasonably be described not only as valuable but also as a process for problem solving and decision making with much the same power and generality as partisan mutual adjustment—the intelligence of democracy (Lindblom, 1965)—with which, indeed, impact assessment as a policy strategy has recently and sometimes favorably been compared (Taylor, 1984; Dryzek, 1987; see Chapter 14 in this book).

There is the possibility, thus, that impact assessment has a strong comparative advantage over other environmental policy strategies (Sproul, 1986; Sagoff, 1987). Indeed, the prospect may be so bright that EIA can remain viable in the face of unfavorable or hostile political regimes (Elkin, 1980; Stone, 1987). Certainly, the question implied by the title of the present book and outlined in Chapter 1 is a good one: Can the successful institutionalization of the particular form of analysis—let's call it ecological rationality (Dryzek, 1983a; Bartlett, 1986b)—demanded by EIA produce such a significant and, perhaps even more important, dependable, long-term strategy for pursuing environmental policy goals that it has to be ranked as one of the major policy innovations of the past quarter century?

This, clearly, is the conclusion to which Serge Taylor (1984) was drawn in *Making Bureaucracies Think* and to which he has now drawn others. The acceptability of this historical interpretation of what we have learned about EIA depends very heavily, however, on there being a close alignment between conceptualizations of the EIA process, on the one hand, and of basic processes of policy change, on the other hand. Was Taylor's account convincing on this point?

In some respects, Taylor produced a straightforward continuation of previous contingency approaches to understanding EIA policy and practice. That is, he tried to identify and assess the full range of factors, internal and external to the implementing agencies, on which the success of EIA might depend. In the end, however, as I have argued elsewhere (Wandesforde-Smith and Kerbavaz, 1988), the contingent nature of Taylor's vision gave way to a different, more intriguing, but more troublesome formulation. It is worth restating briefly my understanding of Taylor's argument because, as we shall see, it raises questions about policy change that lie at the heart of much contemporary political theorizing.

POLICY CHANGE IN A SELF-REGULATING ORDER

Taylor wanted to understand how analytical competition of the kind promoted by an EIA system improved the ability of public organizations to adapt to complex and changing problems (Taylor, 1984:325). Under what conditions, in other words, was EIA likely not only to change policy but also to change it for the better?

One of these circumstances, Taylor decided, was a high degree of structural fragmentation in the polity, the existence of a large and diverse "system of organizations" (Taylor, 1984:24). Another was the prevalence of vague goals, uncertain means, and diverse situations, circumstances that required a case-by-case contextual balancing analysis of all the factors relevant to a decision problem before an outcome could be specified. A third circumstance stemmed from institutional interdependence and reflected the unacceptability of giving one public agency strong formal powers over others (Taylor, 1984:301). If there were no more than this to Taylor's thesis, it would be quite unremarkable.

Beyond this, however, Taylor concluded that EIA coped with circumstances of political fragmentation, took into consideration uncertain and ambiguous decision criteria, and dispersed power "without any conscious maximizing calculations on the part of a coordinated set of actors'' (Taylor, 1984:162). Indeed, to underscore the self-regulating and self-sustaining character of EIA, Taylor argued that it worked largely independently not only of tactical and strategic initiatives generated by individual actors but also of assumptions about institutions and beliefs shared by groups, coalitions, and broad social movements (Taylor, 1984:306–7). These conclusions rested on the theory that EIA tapped two of the most powerful dynamics inherent in the structure of pluralist political systems—dynamics that arguably make such systems marvelous, incrementally progressive, and, above all, self-regulating engines of social and political change.

One was the natural tendency for actors who must settle their differences by bargaining in the shadow of the law (Mnookin and Kornhauser, 1979) to seek stability in their continuing relationships (Taylor, 1984:ch. 12; see more generally, Macaulay, 1963, 1985; Stewart, 1985; Yngvesson, 1985). This is the glue that holds together the internal architecture (Taylor, 1984:37) of an EIA process.

This dynamic motivates people inside and outside public agencies to develop information about environmental impacts, for example, by exploiting the legitimacy and credibility of their respective knowledge bases. It causes outsiders to demand analysis and to fuel the fires of analytical competition among multiple and redundant critics of agency initiatives. It makes managers worry about what the courts might do to agency reputations in EIA litigation and, thus, it undergirds the willingness of all involved in the EIA process to heed and abide by an oversight agency's rules of the game.

Clearly, the natural desire to maintain continuing relations is portrayed here as a very strong, albeit informal, source of behavioral cues for those using EIA to change policy. It is this incentive for stability that makes judgments about the form and content of EISs the product of political interaction, *not* scientific and technical debate (Taylor, 1984:255). It is what makes the process "hill climb" toward successful institutionalization of environmental values, even though "individual outcomes are influenced by an unpredictable collection of contextual factors" (Taylor, 1984:163).

It is less clear, however, how far Taylor thinks this political interaction within the EIS process extends to other political judgments important to overall EIA success, such as how to allocate resources among a variety of agency missions. The range of political judgments made by the people he studied in the Corps of Engineers and the Forest Service, thus, appears unrealistically confined to the EIA process in isolation.

The other dynamic Taylor saw at work in EIA stemmed from what he vaguely called the "natural forces" in society "which are too strong to transform or to fight directly" (Taylor, 1984:325). These forces seem to arise from a tension between procedural and substantive rationality, on the one hand, and from the conflict between the power and generality of social decision rules, on the other hand.

These large forces act as limiting factors that keep society's characteristic modes of decision making from arriving at extreme solutions. They are important because, together with the internal architecture of an EIA system, they explain what drives the politics of EIA. In addition, they explain why the limits of what EIA (and presumably other policy strategies) can accomplish always push the system toward a new political equilibrium.

For example, sometimes society has solved its problems by relying very little on powerful substantive rules firmly grounded in rational analysis. It has relied, instead, on political judgments reflecting an unusual degree of homogeneity in the beliefs people hold about what their problems are and what needs to be done about them (cf. Barber, 1988; Sagoff, 1988). A wide and deep consensus for such judgments developed from the greatly increased public concern about environmental issues of the late 1960s and early 1970s. Policy was then changed through "the informal coordination provided by the ideological premises of a widespread social movement" (Taylor, 1984:329). At other times, science, working within clear and narrow limits to the problems to be addressed, has guided policy change through "an unforced consensus based on logic and empirical evidence" (Taylor, 1984:329). And "when neither scientific nor conventional consensus is strong enough, politics [such as may be promoted by the internal architecture of an EIA process] is called upon to fill the spaces left by incomplete knowledge" (Taylor, 1984:329).

There is nothing in this account, however, about how society shifts from science to politics to ideology, or back again, as ways of solving problems. Nor is any attention given to human agency as a cause of policy changes associated with these shifts in styles of conflict resolution. The unexplored implication is simply that the process is one of natural evolution "in a world in which science cannot provide unequivocal answers to all important questions" (Taylor 1984:329).

Taylor has two hypotheses, then, about the self-sustaining and self-regulating properties of EIA, and both of them rest on natural attributes of American pluralist democracy. The first, a continuing relations thesis, holds that the evolution of EIA is guided by a powerful but informal incentive. It comes from the natural inclination individuals have to seek stable relationships as a framework for bargaining and negotiation in a changing and uncertain world. The second, an equilibrium thesis, argues that EIA is one of several processes automatically kicked into play by the natural limits of scientific and ideological consensus as bases for social problem solving. It converges, like other forms of pluralist politics, on solutions that promote a new political equilibrium in the wake of social upheavals like the environmental movement of the late 1960s.

ENTREPRENEURS AND POLICY CHANGE: A FRESH VISION

This conception of policy change resounds with premises used by many contemporary political theorists in the United States—S. Beer, W.D. Burnham, R. Dahl, S. Huntington, C. Lindblom, S. M. Lipset, T. Lowi, G. Pomper, and A. Wildavsky, for example, all of whom, as Dean Mann (1986) so deftly shows, are obsessed with the structural fragmentation of the American polity. They see different meanings in the fact of fragmentation, although in most cases it is the power of the system to shape the people and politics within it that is stressed, rather than the reverse. The idea that the system is part of the problem rather than part of the solution, that it paralyzes, blocks, or displays other disabilities that get in the way of effective social problem solving, is especially prominent.

Thus, the American political system "is a self-regulating political order that has evolved in response to major change in the economic system and social order, but has retained its capability to protect basic political rights and to impose restraints on other political actors within the social and economic system over which it has sovereignty" (Mann, 1986: 28). Mann compares this self-regulating order to an ecosystem:

Its function is not automatic, of course, not governed by some fixed principles of biology or chemistry; rather it is the result of human will and human values within the context of the evolving physical framework. *But these human values and volitions are themselves shaped and transformed by the traditions, understandings, and experiences of a society that has had centuries to develop its basic orientation toward problem-solving mechanisms. And those mechanisms constitute the governing framework of the . . . system* almost as surely as the interaction of sunlight, atmosphere, soil, water, or rock. (Mann, 1986:28. Emphasis added)

I take this to mean that all explanations of the pace and direction of policy change are ultimately reducible to structural variables. I take it to mean more particularly that the influence of human volition is discernible but that it is bound, in the long run and the larger scheme of things, to seem both short lived and limited. And I take it to mean quite precisely that, at the most basic level and in the most parsimonious model, causation in an explanation of how and why a policy instrument like EIA works must run from structure to volition, rather than vice versa.

This strikes me as an incongruous vision; certainly, it is a vision that, to use Mann's own words, I do not share. I say this particularly because Taylor (1984) and even more so Mann (1986, after Ingram and Ullery, 1980) expressly credit individual and group initiative with the adoption of NEPA and many other environmental policies of the last twenty years.

If, as Mann (1986:18–20) insists at some length, political entrepreneurs can take advantage of fragmentation to cause policies to be adopted, the same human agency of causation ought to be at work in policy change during implementation and enforcement—indeed, in all phases of the policy cycle where fragmentation and its disabilities are fundamental facts of political life but also provide opportunities for people to initiate change (Browning, Marshall, and Tabb, 1984;

MacIntyre, 1985a, 1985b). I can see no logical or theoretical reason to assume otherwise. Given this, I want to argue that EIA survives and prospers (see, e.g., Davis, 1988) as a policy instrument not because structural variables determine that result but because EIA affords such rich and diverse opportunities for political entrepreneurs to alter the circumstances of their existence.

In my view, the relationship of social structure to individual behavior, to initiative, or to volition to use Mann's words, is always mutual and reciprocal. Therefore, "the value of the concept of the entrepreneur," to borrow from Davis (1986:189), "is that it requires consideration of the interplay betweeen creative individuals that carry the process [of choice] and the constraints that both affect their choices *and in turn are affected by them* (Davis, 1986:189, emphasis added; see also Barth, 1967; Greenfield and Strickon, 1981; Elkin, 1980, 1987; Stone, 1987).

In this relationship, however, it is individuals who initiate political change, not groups, coalitions, agencies, networks, or other more aggregate but disembodied variables of a model of social structure. Beyond this, there is no expectation or necessity of equilibrium in a theory of entrepreneurial policy change, such as Taylor (1984) imagines or as appears in theories of economic change (Casson, 1982; Nelson and Winter, 1982). Relationships may take the form of exchange, as in Davis' (1986) model of constrained choice. More often, however, political relationships are far less symmetrical than the exchange metaphor implies, and they are much less stable (Kingdon, 1984; Browne, 1988).

Within this framework, a legal mandate, such as the EIA provision of NEPA, creates opportunities for enterprising people to cause change and is itself the product of creative destruction (Kutler, 1971), that is, of previous change opportunities already seized. It provides for what James Willard Hurst in a classic but sadly neglected study of nineteenth-century resource policy called "the release of energy" (Hurst, 1964; as well as, more recently, McEvoy and Scheiber, 1984; McEvoy, 1986; Scheiber, 1987).

This entrepreneurship is generally important, essential even, to accomplishing the political work without which the formulation, implementation, and enforcement of policy *all* would be impossible (see, for example, Long, 1949; Ostrom, 1953; Ostrom, 1965; Manley, 1968; Nonet, 1969; Bardach, 1972; Natchez and Bupp, 1973; Needleman and Needleman, 1974; Foley, 1975, Beer, 1976; Fox and Hammond, 1977; Malbin, 1977; Sigelman and Vanderbok, 1978; Derthick, 1979; Lewis, 1980; Nakamura and Smallwood, 1980; Rabkin, 1980; Nordlinger, 1981; Diver, 1982; Thompson, 1982; Miles and Bhambri, 1983; Hawkins, 1984; Chambers, 1985; Derthick and Quirk, 1985; Levin and Ferman, 1985; MacIntyre, 1985a, 1985b; Doig and Hargrove, 1987; Cayer and Weschler, 1988).

EIA is but one of a family of devices to encourage the creative, constructive, and controlled exercise of discretion in the civil service (Yates, 1982; West, 1985; Burke, 1986, Handler, 1986; Bryner, 1987; Gruber, 1987; but see also Freedman, 1978). As such, it both encourages and constrains a form of political entrepreneurship, administrative entrepreneurship, on the part of merit and political appointees in public agencies. It ought to be understood and appreciated, however, less as self-serving bureaucratic activism (Niskanen, 1971; Milward, 1980) than as responsible leadership (Chapman, 1984; Kellerman, 1984, 1986; MacIntyre, 1985a).

THE PRACTICE OF ENTREPRENEURSHIP

Whether practiced under the mandate of NEPA or one of the many state little NEPAs (McElfish, 1988), all the EIA tasks Taylor (1984) associates with analyst-advocates and with other employees of public agencies (engineers, resource specialists, managers, lawyers, and regional and national office staffs) are performed by these people acting, to a greater or lesser extent, as administrative entrepreneurs. They identify, estimate, and assess impacts. They help decide whether to conduct an assessment; whether assessments are to be challenged administratively, politically, or through the courts; and how much weight to give an assessment, along with other factors, in making a decision about a proposed policy, plan, or project.

Their performance of these tasks, often at the lowest levels of agency operations, constitute political work (Wandesforde-Smith and Kerbavaz, 1988; cf. Weinberg, 1987) just as much as the more frequently analyzed behavior of bureau chiefs, assistant secretaries, and others at the top of an organization (Heclo, 1977; Lewis, 1980; Kaufman, 1981; Doig and Hargrove, 1987; Lynn, 1987). Conceptually, the work is no different than that required to accomplish the seemingly grander policy changes sometimes called innovations (Polsby, 1984). This work is the product of a conscious strategy (Paluch, 1985; Pettigrew, 1987; Shover, Clelland, and Lynxwiler, 1986) in which the inevitable conflict between ecological and other forms of rationality is managed (Bartlett, 1986b).

In the face of environmental uncertainty, ambiguous goals and objectives, and changing circumstances, administrative entrepreneurs thus alter the structure of constraints on the exercise of choice. Their work takes advantage of windows of opportunity that come with electoral change or other political events (Wandesforde-Smith and Kerbavaz, 1988; more generally, Kingdon, 1984). It is also usually tied to that of other entrepreneurs in legislative and judicial arenas, as well as in other public agencies. And it may be undertaken at the instigation of or even in conjunction with entrepreneurial interest group leaders. Three important tasks each merit brief comment: building coalitions, making a case on the merits, and developing values.

Building Coalitions

Entrepreneurship in EIA to modify the constraints on choice is most visible when the work involves the successful preparation, review, and consideration of EISs or EIRs. This requires political as well as logistical and technical support. The legal structure of an EIA process usually places environmental analysts in public agencies, or allows them to conduct assessments that agencies must later formally approve. From either position, analysts must seek support for what they do by building coalitions, within their host agencies and outside. Some choose an inside track, some an outside track, and some pursue both simultaneously (Taylor, 1984:ch. 5). Whichever strategy they use, their tactics are tempered by the need to sustain continuing relations with other agency specialists and with agency managers. Continuing relations exerts a similar restraint at the stage at which EIAs are commented on externally.

The coalitions environmental analysts build as entrepreneurial actors trying to make EIA an effective instrument of policy change reflect a complex assortment of contingent factors, even extending to the environmental consciousness of agency managers and the public at large, the number and quality of the analysts drawn into the process, and procedural rules and informal expectations about when and how environmental impact information must be taken into account by decision makers. More powerful causes of variations in coalition building behavior and its consequences include the commitment of top agency leaders to environmental values, the precision of requirements for openly displaying impact data, and the personal attributes of the entrepreneurs themselves. These factors can clearly be seen at work in Taylor's (1984:198–231) unusually detailed analysis of EIA preparation and associated litigation in the Six Rivers National Forerst of northern California.

Not only is coalition building a central task for environmental analysts and for other EIA entrepreneurs, but it must be undertaken in strategic environments that vary significantly along several important dimensions from one agency to another. It is not always easy to tell, therefore, whether the skills and tactics of coalition builders have more effect on EIA outcomes than environmental variations until the nature and origins of the coalitions that sustain each assessment are explored.

Making a Case on the Merits

The practice of entrepreneurship also involves the strategic use of analysis, a process that Robyn (1987) calls making a case on the merits. This goes well beyond what Doig and Hargrove (1987) describe as the function of administrative entrepreneurs in enhancing the technical expertise of agencies.

In the context of EIA, making a case on the merits certainly involves assembling empirical evidence with strong credentials about the impacts of a project, and showing how the uncertainties they raise can be mitigated. Beyond tailoring the substantive case for protecting environmental values to the project at hand, however, the strategic use of analysis also requires "close coordination between the analytic shops and the political front line" (Robyn, 1987:239). An EIA entrepreneur's ability to accomplish that coordination may have as much or more to do with the influence analysis has on the outcome of a project as does the quality of the analysis itself, or the other resource and environmental contingencies assessed by Taylor (1984:ch. 6). The importance of this task and the difficulties of accomplishing it are superbly illustrated by Sproul (1986).

Again, the point is not that EIA affords opportunities for administrative entrepreneurship that have previously been unrecognized. Like coalition building, making a case on the merits has long been appreciated as a central task of civil servants. It is generally understood, in fact, as a manifestation of technical competence and expertise, the bedrock upon which favorable perceptions of the legitimacy of administrative actions rest in a democratic state. Chapter 14 in this book underscores this observation.

The point is that, to a degree not found with many other policy instruments, EIA affords rich and diverse opportunities for involvement in fitting the form and content of analyses to the political purposes the analyses serve. In addition, it affords such opportunities to line and staff people who work at the street level in public organizations, as well as to the top managers who are more usually the focus of analysis.

The intensity of this distribution of chances at all levels to create change is really what March (1984) had in mind, I think, when he associated how things happen in organizations with what he chose to call the density of administrative competence. I would rather say that an organization's ability to stimulate and guide change is a reflection of how entrepreneurial it is, and that that, to speak more precisely, really reflects the underlying distribution of individual opportunities for entrepreneurship. Whatever the distribution is called, EIA affects and enhances it, and that not only makes the process work but also keeps interest in using the process alive and vital, inside the agencies as well as outside.

Developing Values

Finally, entrepreneurship in EIA involves civil servants, again at all levels, in the affirmation and development of environmental values, such as those expressed in the opening policy sections of NEPA. Again, this is an aspect of the EIA process that is only implicit in Taylor's (1984) account. He observes, certainly, that all the actors in the process have values, and that their values coincide or conflict to some degree both with agency values and with NEPA. He never imagines, however, that the process can and will be used by the participants to advance their substantive values, probably because he assumes, for the purpose of analyzing his science-model of politics, that his actors are preoccupied with improving knowledge. The impression this leaves of environmental analysts in particular is that their values make them merely uncomfortable. They struggle, but only weakly, with the need, on the one hand, to gain concessions from managers by seeming to be organizational loyalists and with the desire, on the other hand, not to prostitute their own analytical or environmental values (Taylor, 1984:257–58).

I think entrepreneurial use of the EIA process to advance values goes much deeper and much further than this timid portrait suggests. Understanding how this happens is admittedly difficult because administrators, like judges (Mac-Intyre, 1985b), usually hide their role in making and changing policy—as one would expect them to do, given the premises of democratic theory. Certainly, in the case of prominent figures who provide leadership to public organizations for extended periods of time, one can expect to find well-developed and publicly articulated statements of the ideologies that motivate administrative entrepreneurs (see the individual analyses summarized by Doig and Hargrove, 1987).

I think it is also true, however, that values are at stake for everyone involved in the EIA process, from the earliest scoping meetings to frame the issues an EIA will address to the decision on an assessed project and any follow-up that occurs to monitor and manage impacts. And there are in the literature occasional glimpses of how, all along the way in this process, the development of values can affect and be affected by the people who take part (e.g., Fairfax and Andrews, 1979).

Moreover, the origins of entrepreneurial uses of EIA in the values of entrepreneurs, and in perceived disjunctures between their values and those of dominant social institutions, are unmistakable in other accounts. A California case is again instructive, for example, through the record Rossmann (Rossmann and Steel, 1982) makes of his role as special counsel to Inyo County in shaping the evolution of the county's long fight with the Los Angeles Department of Water and Power over the management of groundwater resources in the Owens Valley. Clearly, in this classic instance of the strategic use of litigation under California's EIA statute to force the pace and direction of policy change, strong beliefs about the substantive and procedural inadequacies of state water law and policy are the place where the story begins. It is a story that careful consideration of other accounts will make increasingly familiar (Perlstein, 1981; Nevins, 1984).

CONCLUSION

A strong case can be made that EIA is a useful, even powerful tool for adapting policy through analysis to a changing world. Over the last two decades, as the big questions about EIA have changed, appreciation for the range of factors that contribute to this outcome has steadily expanded. There is no question, for example, that EIA effectiveness is associated with changing political regimes and with the changing level of support for the EIA process among courts, chief executives, and senior agency managers that this implies. The way an EIA process is formally structured and the way structure taps informal incentives for administrative behavior are, equally clearly, important variables. Still to be squarely addressed is the question of how these abstract impersonal variables, like structure, exert their influence on the policy changes with which the day-to-day administrative practice of EIA can surely be associated. There is no intellectually satisfying way to tackle this problem without acknowledging the same human agency of causation already known to be at work in the processes of political interaction by which broad legislative agendas for the environment are framed and specific policies, including those for EIA, are set (Wandesforde-Smith, 1986). That acknowledgment is made here as a prelude to further exploration of the way specific individuals put their imprint on policy change by inventing and building coalitions, by making the case for change on the merits, and, above all, as Lynton Caldwell (1970) first imagined they would, by developing and affirming in EIA their environmental values.

NOTE

I appreciate the help of Morton Rothstein, in the Department of History, University of California, Davis, and the continuing exchanges I have about entrepreneurs with Angus MacIntyre, Centre for Resource Management, Lincoln College, Canterbury, New Zealand.

Bibliography

Abbott, John. 1979. "Radioactive Waste: A Technical Solution?" *Bulletin of the Atomic Scientists* (October):11–18.

Abracosa, R. 1987. "The Philippine Environmental Impact Statement System: An Institutional Analysis of Implementation." Ph.D. dissertation, Department of Civil Engineering, Stanford University, Stanford, CA.

ACIR (U.S. Advisory Commission on Intergovernmental Relations). 1979. *Citizen Participation in the American Federal System*. Washington, DC: Government Printing Office.

Anderson, F.R. 1973. *NEPA in the Courts*. Baltimore: Johns Hopkins University Press.

Anderson, G. William et al. 1982. *Rural Roads Evaluation Summary Report, A.I.D. Program Evaluation Report No. 5*. U.S. Agency for International Development, Washington, DC, March.

Andrews, Richard N.L. 1976. *Environmental Policy and Administrative Change*. Lexington, MA: Lexington Books.

Armstrong, Joe and W.H. Harmon. 1980. *Strategies for Conducting Technology Assessments*. Boulder, CO: Westview Press.

Arnstein, Sherry and Alexander N. Christakis. 1974. *Perspectives on Technology Assessment*. Workshop sponsored by the Academy for Contemporary Problems and the National Science Foundation. Jerusalem: Science and Technology Publishers.

Arterton, F. Christopher. 1988. "Political Participation and 'Teledemocracy.' " *PS: Political Science and Politics* 21 (Summer): 620–27.

Axinn, S. 1966. "The Fallacy of the Single Risk." *Philosophy of Science* 33 (1&2):154–62.

Baber, Walter, F. 1983. *Organizing the Future: Matrix Models for the Postindustrial Polity*. University: University of Alabama Press.

Baber, Walter. F. 1988. "Impact Assessment and Democratic Politics." *Policy Studies Review* 8 (Autumn): 172–78 and *Impact Assessment Bulletin* (3 & 4): 172–78.

Baldwin, John H. 1985. *Environmental Planning and Management*. Boulder, CO: Westview Press.

Barber, B. 1988. *The Conquest of Politics*. Princeton: Princeton University Press.

Bardach, Eugene. 1972. *The Skill Factor in Politics*. Berkeley: University of California Press.

Bardach, Eugene and Lucian Pugliaresi. 1977. "The Environmental Impact Statement vs. the Real World." *The Public Interest* 49:22–38.

Barth, F. 1967. "On the Study of Social Change." *American Anthropologist* 69:661–69.

Bartlett, Robert V. 1986a. "Rationality and the Logic of the National Environmental Policy Act." *The Environmental Professional* 8(2):105–11.

Bartlett, Robert V. 1986b. "Ecological Rationality: Reason and Environmental Policy." *Environmental Ethics* 8 (Fall):221–39.

Bartlett, Robert V. 1988. "Introduction: Policy and Impact Assessment." *Policy Studies Review* 8 (Autumn): 73–74 and *Impact Assessment Bulletin* 6 (3 & 4): 73–74.

Bartlett, Robert V. and Walter F. Baber. 1987. "Matrix Organization Theory and Environmental Impact Analysis: A Fertile Union?" *Natural Resources Journal* 27 (Summer):605–15.

Bartlett, Robert V. and Lynton K. Caldwell. 1983. "Science in the National Environmental Policy Act as Perceived by Agency Personnel." Pp. 123–373 in Lynton K. Caldwell et al., *A Study of Ways to Improve the Scientific Content and Methodology of Environmental Impact Analysis*. Springfield, VA: National Technical Information Service, No. PB 83–222 851.

Beaney, W.M. and E.N. Beiser. 1964. "Prayer and Politics: The Impact of *Engel* and *Schempp* on the Political Process." *Journal of Public Law* 12(2):475–503.

Becker, L. 1984. "Rights." Pp. 70–78 in L.C. Becker and K. Kipnis (eds.), *Property*. Englewood Cliffs, NJ: Prentice-Hall.

Beer, S.H. 1976. "The Adoption of General Revenue Sharing: A Case Study in Public Sector Politics." *Public Policy* 24:127–95.

Bentham, J. 1962a. *Principles of the Civil Code*. Pp. 297–364 in John Bowring (ed.), *The Works of Jeremy Bentham*, vol. 1. New York: Russell and Russell.

Bentham, J. 1962b. *Principles of Morals and Legislation*. Pp. 1–154 in John Bowring (ed.), *The Works of Jeremy Bentham*, vol. 1. New York: Russell and Russell.

Berger, T.R. 1977. *Northern Frontier, Northern Homeland: Report of the MacKenzie Valley Pipeline Inquiry*. Ottawa, Ontario: Ministry of Supply and Services.

Booth v. Maryland, 96 L. Ed. 2d. 440 (1987).

Booth, William. 1988. "Reintroducing a Political Animal." *Science* 241:154–58.

Braun, Ernst. 1984. *Wayward Technology*. Westport, CT: Greenwood Press.

Braybrooke, David and Charles E. Lindblom. 1963. *A Strategy of Decision*. New York: Free Press of Glencoe.

Brewer, G.D. and P. deLeon. 1983. *Foundations of Policy Analysis*. Homewood, IL: Dorsey Press.

Browne, W.P. 1988. *Private Interests, Public Policy, and American Agriculture*. Lawrence: University Press of Kansas.

Browning, R.P., D.R. Marshall, and D.H. Tabb. 1984. *Protest Is Not Enough*. Berkeley: University of California Press.

Bryner, G.C. 1987. *Bureaucratic Discretion*. New York: Pergamon.

Burdge, Rabel J. and Paul Opryszek. 1983. "On Mining Apples and Oranges: The Sociologist Does Impact Assessment with Biologists and Economists." Pp. 107–17 in Frederick A. Rossini and Alan L. Porter (eds.), *Integrated Impact Assessment*. Boulder, CO: Westview Press.

Burke, J.P. 1986. *Bureaucratic Responsibility*. Baltimore: Johns Hopkins University Press.

Burke, James. 1978. *Connections*. Boston: Little, Brown.

Butler, William B. 1987. "Significance and Other Frustrations in the CRM Process." *American Antiquity* 52:820–29.

Caldwell, Lynton K. 1970. *Environment: A Challenge to Modern Society*. New York: Natural History Press.

Caldwell, Lynton K. 1976. "The National Environmental Policy Act: Retrospect and Prospect." In *Workshop on the National Environmental Policy Act: A Report by the Environment and Natural Resources Policy Division, Congressional Research Service, U.S. Library of Congress*. Washington, DC: U.S. Congress, House Committee on Merchant Marine and Fisheries, 94th Cong., 2d sess.

Caldwell, Lynton K. 1978. "The Environmental Impact Statement: A Misused Tool." Pp. 11–25 in Ravinder K. Jain and Bruce L. Hutchings (eds.), *Environmental Impact Analysis: Emerging Issues in Planning*. Champaign-Urbana: University of Illinois Press.

Caldwell, Lynton K. 1979. "Is NEPA Inherently Self-Defeating?" *Environmental Law Reporter* 9(1):50001–7.

Caldwell, Lynton K. 1982. *Science and the National Environmental Policy Act: Redirecting Policy through Procedural Reform*. University: University of Alabama Press.

Caldwell, Lynton K. 1988. "Environmental Impact Analysis (EIA): Origins, Evolution, and Future Directions." *Policy Studies Review* 8 (Autumn): 75–83 and *Impact Assessment Bulletin* 6 (3 & 4): 75–83.

Caldwell, Lynton K. et al. 1983. *A Study of Ways to Improve the Scientific Content and Methodology of Environmental Impact Analysis*. Springfield, VA: National Technical Information Service, No. PB 83–222 851.

Canon, Bradley C. 1974. "Is the Exclusionary Rule in Failing Health? Some New Data and a Plea against a Precipitous Conclusion." *Kentucky Law Journal* 62 (1973–74):680–726.

Carley, M.J. and E.S. Bustelo. 1984. *Social Impact Assessment and Monitoring*. Boulder, CO: Westview Press.

Carpenter, Richard A. 1983. "Ecology in Court, and Other Disappointments of Environmental Science and Environmental Law." *Natural Resources Lawyer* 15(3):573–95. See also Commentary, 597–618.

Carter, Luther J. 1987. *Nuclear Imperatives and Public Trust: Dealing with Radioactive Waste*. Washington, DC: Resources for the Future.

Casson, M. 1982. *The Entrepreneur*. Oxford: Martin Robertson.

Cayer, N.J. and L.F. Weschler. 1988. *Public Administration: Social Change and Adaptive Management*. New York: St. Martin's Press.

Chambers, D.E. 1985. "The Reagan Administration's Welfare Retrenchment Policy: Terminating Social Security Benefits for the Disabled." *Policy Studies Review* 5:230–40.

Chapman, R.A. 1984. *Leadership in the British Civil Service*. London: Croom Helm.

Churchman, C.W. 1947. *Theory of Experimental Inference*. New York: Macmillan.

Clark, B.D., R. Bisset, and P. Wathern. 1981. "The British Experience." Pp. 125–153 in T. O'Riordan and W.D. Sewell (eds.), *Project Appraisal and Policy Review*. Chichester: Wiley.

Clark, B.D. et al. 1976. *Assessment of Major Industrial Applications*. London: Department of the Environment.

Clarke, Arthur C. 1967. *Voices from the Sky*. New York: Pyramid Books.

Clarke, Jeanne Nienaber and Daniel McCool. 1985. *Staking Out the Terrain: Power Differentials among Natural Resource Management Agencies*. Albany: State University of New York Press.

Clary, Bruce B. and Michael E. Kraft. 1988. "Impact Assessment and Policy Failure: The Nuclear Waste Policy Act of 1982." *Policy Studies Review* 8 (Autumn): 105–15 and *Impact Assessment Bulletin* 6 (3 & 4): 105–15.

Coates, Joseph F. 1976. "Technology Assessment—A Tool Kit." *Chemtech* 6(6):372–83.

Coates, Joseph F. 1987. *Technology Assessment: Anticipating the Consequences of Technological Choices*. A report prepared for the British Commonwealth Science Council. Washington, DC: J.F. Coates, Inc.

Coates, Vary T. and Thecla Fabian. 1982. "Technology Assessment in Europe and Japan." *Technological Forecasting and Social Change* 22:343–61.

Coggins, G.C. and C.F. Wilkinson. 1987. *Federal Public Land and Resources Law*, 2d ed. Mineola, NY: Foundation Press.

Cohen, B. and I. Lee. 1979. "A Catalog of Risks." *Health Physics* 36(6):707–22.

Colglazier, E. William (ed.). 1982. *The Politics of Nuclear Waste*. New York: Pergamon.

Cook, T.D. and D.T. Campbell. 1979. *Quasi-Experimentation*. Boston: Houghton-Mifflin.

Cooke, R.M. 1982. "Risk Assessment and Rational Decision Theory." *Dialectica* 36(4):330–51.

Council of the European Communities. 1985. "On the Assessment of the Effects of Certain Public and Private Projects." Pp. 40–48 in *Official Journal, L175, 28.5.85*.

Cowan, Ruth Schwartz. 1974. "A Case Study of Technological and Social Change: The Washing Machine and the Working Wife." Pp. 243–53 in Mary Hartman and Lois W. Banner (eds.), *Clio's Consciousness Raised: New Perspectives on the History of Women*. New York: Harper and Row.

Culhane, Paul J. 1987. "The Precision and Accuracy of U.S. Environmental Impact Statements." *Environmental Monitoring and Assessment* 8:217–38.

Darling, F. Fraser and John P. Milton. 1966. *Future Environments of North America*. Garden City, NY: Natural History Press.

Darst, Guy. 1986. "Environmental Groups Criticize Refuge Report." *Anchorage Daily News*, 16 December.

Davis, Joseph A. 1987. "Nevada to Get Nuclear Waste; Everyone Else 'Off the Hook.' " Pp. 3136–38 in *Congressional Quarterly Weekly Report,* 19 December.

Davis, S.C. 1988. "Common Wealth." *The Environmental Forum* 5 (July/August):10–13.

Davis, W.G. 1986. "Class, Political Constraints, and Entrepreneurial Strategies: Elites and Petty Market Traders in Northern Luzon." Pp. 166–94 in S.M. Greenfield and A. Strickon (eds.), *Entrepreneurship and Social Change.* Lanham, MD: University Press of America.

Denenberg, H. et al. 1964. *Risk and Insurance.* Englewood Cliffs, NJ: Prentice-Hall.

Department of the Environment. 1986. *Implementation of the Directive on Environmental Assessment. Consultation Paper.* London: Department of the Environment.

Department of the Environment. 1988. *Environmental Assessment: Implementation of EC Directive.* London: Department of the Environment.

Department of the Environment/Welsh Office. 1988. *Environmental Assessment.* Joint Circular DOE 15/88, WO 23/88. London: Her Majesty's Stationery Office.

Derthick, M. 1979. *Policymaking for Social Security.* Washington, DC: Brookings Institution.

Derthick, M. and P.J. Quirk. 1985. *The Politics of Deregulation.* Washington, DC: Brookings Institution.

DeSario, Jack and Stuart Langton (eds.). 1987. *Citizen Participation in Public Decision Making.* Westport, CT: Greenwood Press.

Dietz, Thomas and Alicia Pfund. 1988. "An Impact Identification Method for Development Program Evaluation." *Policy Studies Review* 8 (Autumn): 137–45 and *Impact Assessment Bulletin* 6 (3 & 4): 137–45.

Diver C.S. 1982. "Engineers and Entrepreneurs: The Dilemma of Public Management." *Journal of Policy Analysis and Management* 1:402–6.

Doig, J.W. and E.C. Hargrove. 1987. " 'Leadership' and Political Analysis." Pp. 1–23 in J.W. Doig and E.C. Hargrove (eds.), *Leadership and Innovation.* Baltimore: Johns Hopkins University Press.

Downey, Gary L. 1985. "Federalism and Nuclear Waste Disposal: The Struggle over Shared Decision Making." *Journal of Policy Analysis and Management* 5 (Fall):73–99.

Dryzek, John S. 1983a. "Ecological Rationality." *International Journal of Environmental Studies* 21:5–10.

Dryzek, John S. 1983b. "Present Choices, Future Consequences." *World Futures* 19:1–19.

Dryzek, John S. 1987. *Rational Ecology: Environment and Political Economy.* Oxford: Basil Blackwell.

Duncan, O.D. 1978. "Science Indicators and Social Indicators." Pp. 31–38 in Y. Elkana et al. (eds.), *Toward a Metric of Science: The Advent of Science Indicators.* New York: John Wiley.

Dunn, W.N. 1988. "Methods of the Second Type." *Policy Studies Review* 7 (Summer): 720–37.

Dunn, William N., Andrea M. Hegedus, and Burkart Holzner. 1988. "Science Impact Assessment and Public Policy." *Policy Studies Review* 8 (Autumn): 146–54 and *Impact Assessment Bulletin* 6 (3 & 4): 146–54.

Dunn, William N. and Burkart Holzner. 1987. "Introduction: Toward Knowledge Systems Accounting." *Knowledge: Creation, Diffusion, Utilization* 9(2):163–67.

Dunn, William N. et al. 1987. "The Architecture of Knowledge Systems: Toward Policy

Relevant Impact Indicators." *Knowledge: Creation, Diffusion, Utilization* 9(2):205–32.

Dutch Ministry of Education and Science et al. 1987. *Technology Assessment: An Opportunity for Europe.* The Hague: Ministry of Education and Science.

Eddy, D. 1982. "Probabilistic Reasoning in Clinical Medicine." Pp. 249–67 in D. Kahneman et al. (eds.), *Judgment under Uncertainty: Heuristics and Biases.* Cambridge, England: Cambridge University Press.

Egerton, J. 1981. "Appalachia's Absentee Landlords." *The Progressive* 45(6):42–45.

ELC-Electroconsult. 1976. "Lower Agno Development Plan: Multi-purpose Development Project—Preliminary Study." Manila.

ELC-Electroconsult and the Engineering Development Corporation of the Philippines. 1979. "San Roque Multi-purpose Project Feasibility Study Main Report." Manila.

Elkana, Y. et al. (eds.). 1978. *Toward a Metric of Science: The Advent of Science Indicators.* New York: John Wiley.

Elkin, S.L. 1980. "Cities without Power: The Transformation of American Urban Regimes." Pp. 265–93 in D.E. Ashford (ed.), *National Resources and Urban Policy.* New York: Methuen.

Elkin, S.L. 1987. *City and Regime in the American Republic.* Chicago: University of Chicago Press.

Ellul, Jacques. 1964. *The Technological Society.* New York: Random House.

Emmett, B. et al. 1978. "The Distribution of Environmental Quality." Pp. 361–376 in D. Burkhardt and W. Ittelson (eds.), *Environmental Assessment.* New York: Plenum.

Engineering Review. 1985. "Contract Archaeology Hits Paydirt." *Engineering Review* (25 April):20–24.

Environment Reporter. 1986a. "House Appropriations Passes $8.2 Billion for Interior, Other Agencies in Fiscal 1987." 26 September, p. 782.

Environment Reporter. 1986b. "Congressional Memo Says Energy Decision to Postpone Second Repository Siting Faulty." 7 November, pp. 1155–56.

Fairfax, Sally K. 1978. "A Disaster in the Environmental Movement." *Science* 199 (17 February):743–48.

Fairfax, S.K. and B.T. Andrews. 1979. "Debate Within and Debate Without: NEPA and the Redefinition of the 'Prudent Man' Rule." *Natural Resources Journal* 19:505–35.

Feibleman, James K. 1972. "Pure Science, Applied Science, and Technology: An Attempt at Definition." Pp. 33–41 in Carl Mitcham and Robert Mackey (eds.), *Philosophy and Technology.* New York: Free Press.

Feinberg, J. 1973. *Social Philosophy.* Englewood Cliffs, NJ: Prentice-Hall.

Feinberg, J. 1979. "The Nature and Value of Rights." Pp. 78–91 in David Lyons (ed.), *Rights.* Belmont, CA: Wadsworth.

Ferwerda, Vernon. 1976. *The Office of Technology Assessment,* ISTA Documentation Series No. 1. Troy, NY: Rensselaer Polytechnic Institute Center for Technology Assessment.

Finsterbusch, Kurt. 1984. "Statistical Summary of 52 AID Projects: Lessons on Project Effectiveness." Final report for the Office of Evaluation, Bureau for Program and Policy Coodination, Agency for International Development, Washington, DC, June.

Finsterbusch, Kurt, L.G. Llewellyn, and C.P. Wolf (eds.). 1983. *Social Impact Assessment Methods*. Beverly Hills, CA: Sage Publications.

Finsterbusch, Kurt and Warren A. Van Wicklin III. 1987. "The Contribution of Beneficiary Participation to Development Project Effectiveness." *Public Administration and Development* 7 (1):1–23.

Finsterbusch, Kurt and Warren A. Van Wicklin III. 1988. "Unanticipated Consequences of A.I.D. Projects: Lessons from Impact Assessment for Project Planning." *Policy Studies Review* 8 (Autumn): 126–36 and *Impact Assessment Bulletin* 6 (3 & 4): 126–36.

Finsterbusch, Kurt and Warren A. Van Wicklin III. 1989. "Beneficiary Participation in Development Projects: Empirical Tests of Popular Theories." *Economic Development and Cultural Change* (forthcoming).

Fischhoff, B. et al. 1978. "How Safe Is Safe Enough?" *Policy Sciences* 9(2):140–50.

Fischhoff, B. et al. 1980. "Facts and Fears." Pp. 192–207 in R. Schwing and W. Albers (eds.), *Societal Risk Assessment*. New York: Plenum.

Foley, H.A. 1975. *Community Health Legislation: The Formative Process*. Lexington, MA: Lexington Books.

Formby, J. 1987. "The Australian Government's Experience with Environmental Impact Assessment." *Environmental Impact Assessment Review* 7:207–26.

Foster, B.J. 1984. "Environmental Impact Assessment in the UK." *Zeitschrift fur Umweltpolitick* 4:389–404.

Fowler, Don D. 1982. "Cultural Resources Management." Pp. 1–50 in Michael B. Schiffer (ed.), *Advances in Archaeological Method and Theory*, vol. 5. New York: Academic Press.

Fox, H.W. and S.W. Hammond. 1977. *Congressional Staffs: The Invisible Force in American Lawmaking*. New York: Free Press.

Frank, P.G. 1980. "The Variety of Reasons for the Acceptance of Scientific Theories." Pp. 210–19 in E.D. Klemke, R. Hollinger, and A. Kline (eds.), *Introductory Readings in the Philosophy of Science*. Buffalo, NY: Prometheus.

Frankena, W. 1962. "The Concept of Social Justice." Pp. 9–15 in R. Brandt (ed.), *Social Justice*. Englewood Cliffs, NJ: Prentice-Hall.

Freedman, J.O. 1978. *Crisis and Legitimacy*. Cambridge: Cambridge University Press.

Friesema, H. Paul and Paul J. Culhane. 1976. "Social Impacts, Politics, and the Environmental Impact Statement Process." *Natural Resources Journal* 16 (April):339–56.

Fuller, G.I. 1986. *The Environmental Assessment. Proposals for Implementation*. Paper to CEMP conference, London, January.

Goldman, Sheldon and Thomas P. Jahnige. 1971. *The Federal Courts as a Political System*. New York: Harper and Row.

Goldsmith, R.I. and W.C. Banks. 1983. "Environmental Values: Institutional Responsibility and the Supreme Court." *Harvard Environmental Law Review*. 7:1–40.

Gormley, William T. 1987. "Institutional Policy Analysis: A Critical Review." *Journal of Policy Analysis and Management* 6(2):153–69.

Gould, Leroy C. 1983. "The Radioactive Waste Management Problem." Pp. 1–26 in Charles A. Walker, Leroy C. Gould, and Edward J. Woodhouse (eds.), *Too Hot to Handle? Social and Policy Issues in the Management of Radioactive Wastes*. New Haven: Yale University Press.

Graham, Stephen A. 1984. "The Nuclear Waste Policy Act of 1982: A Case Study in American Federalism." *State Government* 57:7–12.

Grant, George. 1986. *Technology and Justice*. Notre Dame, IN: Notre Dame Press.

Gray, Elizabeth Dodson. 1979. *Green Paradise Lost*. Wellesley, MA: Roundtable Press.

Greenfield, S.M. and A. Strickon. 1981. "A New Paradigm for the Study of Entrepreneurship and Social Change." *Economic Development and Cultural Change*. 29:467–99.

Griffin, Susan. 1978. *Women and Nature*. New York: Harper and Row.

Gruber, J.E. 1987. *Controlling Bureaucracies*. Berkeley: University of California Press.

Häfele, W. 1979. "Energy." Pp. 129–40 in C. Starr and P. Ritterbush (eds.), *Science, Technology, and the Human Prospect*. New York: Pergamon.

Haigh, N. 1984. *EEC Environmental Policy and Britain*. London: Environmental Data Services.

Handler, J.F. 1986. *The Conditions of Discretion*. New York: Russell Sage Foundation.

Harmon, P. and D. King. 1985. *Artificial Intelligence*. New York: John Wiley.

Harsanyi, J. 1975. "Can the Maximin Principle Serve as a Basis for Morality...." *American Political Science Review* 69(2):594–606.

Hart, H.L.A. 1979. "Are There Any Natural Rights?" Pp. 14–25 in David Lyons (ed.), *Rights*. Belmont, CA: Wadsworth.

Hawkins, K. 1984. *Environment and Enforcement*. Oxford: Clarendon Press.

Heclo, H. 1977. *A Government of Strangers*. Washington, DC: Brookings Institution.

Heymann, P.B. 1987. *The Politics of Public Management*. New Haven: Yale University Press.

Hoffman, W. and J. Fisher. 1984. "Corporate Responsibility." Pp. 211–20 in L.C. Becker and K. Kipnis (eds.), *Property*. Englewood Cliffs, NJ: Prentice-Hall.

Holzner, B., W.N. Dunn, and M. Shahidullah. 1987. "An Accounting Scheme for Designing Science Impact Indicators." *Knowledge: Creation, Diffusion, Utilization* 9(2):173–204.

Hood, C.C. 1976. *The Limits of Administration*. London: John Wiley.

Horberry, J. 1985. "The Accountability of Development Assistance Agencies: The Case of Environmental Policy." *Ecology Law Quarterly* 12(4):817–70.

Hospers, J. 1980. "What Is Explanation?" Pp. 87–103 in E.D. Klemke, R. Hollinger, and A. Kline (eds.), *Introductory Readings in the Philosophy of Science*. Buffalo, NY: Prometheus.

Hurst, J.W. 1964. *Law and Economic Growth*. Cambridge, MA: The Belknap Press of Harvard University Press.

Ingram, H.M. and S.J. Ullery. 1980. "Policy Innovation and Institutional Fragmentation." *Policy Studies Journal*. 8:664–82.

Interagency Review Group on Nuclear Waste Management. 1979. *Report to the President by the Interagency Review Group on Nuclear Waste Management*, March, TI29442.

James, W. 1951. *Essays in Pragmatism*. New York: Hafner.

Jenkins, B. 1983. "Models of Organizational Systems: Their Relevance to Organizational Effectiveness and Conflict." Masters of Administration thesis, Faculty of Economics and Politics, Monash University, Australia.

Johnson, Charles A. 1977. "The Implementation and Impact of Judicial Policies: A Heuristic Model." Pp. 107–26 in John A. Gardiner (ed.), *Public Law and Public Policy*. New York: Praeger.

Johnson, Charles A. and Bradley C. Canon. 1984. *Judicial Policies: Implementation and Impact*. Washington, DC: Congressional Quarterly Press.

Johnson, Janet Buttolph. 1985. "The Dynamics of Acid Rain Policy in the United States." Pp. 261–83 in Helen M. Ingram and R. Kenneth Godwin (eds.), *Public Policy and the Natural Environment*. Greenwich, CT: JAI Press.

Kahneman, D. and A. Tversky. 1982. "Availability: A Heuristic for Judging Frequency and Probability." Pp. 163–78 in D. Kahneman, Paul Slovic, and Amos Tversky (eds.), *Judgment under Uncertainty: Heuristics and Biases*. Cambridge, England: Cambridge University Press.

Kaplan, A. 1964. *The Conduct of Inquiry*. San Francisco: Chandler.

Karl, Barry D. 1987. "The American Bureaucrat: A History of a Sheep in Wolves' Clothing." *Public Administration Review* 47 (January-February):26–34.

Kaufman, H. 1981. *The Administrative Behavior of Federal Bureau Chiefs*. Washington, DC: Brookings Institution.

Kearney, Richard C. and Robert B. Garey. 1982. "American Federalism and the Management of Radioactive Wastes." *Public Administration Review* 42 (January-February):14–24.

Kearney, Richard C. and John J. Stucker. 1985. "Interstate Compacts and the Management of Low Level Radioactive Wastes." *Public Administration Review* 45 (January-February):210–220.

Kellerman, B. 1984. *Leadership: Multidisciplinary Perspectives*. Englewood Cliffs, NJ: Prentice-Hall.

Kellerman, B. (ed.). 1986. *Political Leadership: A Source Book*. Pittsburgh: University of Pittsburgh Press.

Kellert, Stephen R. 1978. *Policy Implications of a National Study of American Attitudes and Behavioral Relations to Animals*. Washington, DC: U.S. Fish and Wildlife Service.

Kennedy, William V. 1988. "Environmental Impact Assessment in North America, Western Europe: What Has Worked Where, How, and Why." *International Environment Reporter* 11(4):257–62.

Kettl, Donald. 1983. *The Regulation of American Federalism*. Baton Rouge: Louisiana State University Press.

Kingdon, J.W. 1984. *Agendas, Alternatives, and Public Policies*. Boston: Little, Brown.

Koppel, Bruce. 1988. "Ripples and Trickles: Impact Assessment and Policy Analysis in Asia." *Policy Studies Review* 8 (Autumn): 116–25 and *Impact Assessment Bulletin* 6 (3 & 4): 116–25.

Koshland, Daniel E., Jr. 1988. "Judicial Impact Statements." *Science* 239 (11 March):1225.

Kottack, Conrad Phillip. 1985. "When People Don't Come First: Some Sociological Lessons from Completed Projects." Pp. 325–356 in Michael M. Cernea (ed.), *Putting People First: Sociological Variables in Rural Development*. New York: Oxford University Press.

Kraft, Michael E. 1988. "Analyzing Technological Risks in Federal Regulatory Agencies." Pp. 184–207 in Michael E. Kraft and Norman J. Vig. (eds.), *Technology and Politics*. Durham, NC: Duke University Press.

Kraft, Michael E. and Bruce B. Clary. 1988. "Assessing Citizen Participation in Environmental Policy: The NIMBY Syndrome and Radioactive Waste Disposal." Paper presented at the annual meeting of the American Political Science Association, Washington, DC, September.

Kraft, Michael E. and Norman J. Vig (eds.). 1988. *Technology and Politics*. Durham, NC: Duke University Press.

Kruytbosch, C. and L. Burton. 1987. "The Search for Impact Indicators." *Knowledge: Creation, Diffusion, Utilization* 9(2):168–72.

Kunreuther, H. et al. 1987. "A Decision-Process Perspective on Risk and Policy Analysis." Pp. 260–74 in R.W. Lake (ed.), *Resolving Locational Conflict*. Rutgers, NJ: Center for Urban Policy Research.

Kutler, S.I. 1971. *Privilege and Creative Destruction*. New York: Norton.

Kweit, Robert and Mary Grisez Kweit. 1982. *Implementing Citizen Participation Programs in a Bureaucratic Society: A Contingency Approach*. New York: Praeger.

Landau, Martin. 1965. "*Baker v. Carr* and the Ghost of Federalism." Pp. 241–48 in Glendon Schubert (ed.), *Reapportionment*. New York: Charles Scribner's Sons.

Lave, L. 1979. "Discussion." Pp. 186–211 in Mitre Corporation (ed.), *Risk Assessment and Governmental Decision Making*. McLean, VA: Mitre Corporation.

Lawless, Edward W. 1977. *Technology and Social Shock*. New Brunswick, NJ: Rutgers University Press.

Lee, N. and C. Wood. 1976. *The Introduction of Environmental Impact Statements in the European Communities*. Brussels: Commission of the European Communities.

Levin, M.A. and B. Ferman. 1985. *The Political Hand*. New York: Pergamon.

Lewis, E. 1980. *Public Entrepreneurship*. Bloomington: Indiana University Press.

Lichtenberg, J. 1981. "National Boundaries and Moral Boundaries." Pp. 79–100 in P. Brown and H. Shue (eds.), *Boundaries: National Autonomy and Its Limits*. Totowa, NJ: Rowman and Littlefield.

Lindblom, Charles E. 1965. *The Intelligence of Democracy: Decision Making through Mutual Adjustment*. New York: Free Press.

Lindblom, Charles E. 1977. *Politics and Markets: The World's Political-Economic Systems*. New York: Basic Books.

Liroff, R.A. 1976. *A National Policy for the Environment*. Bloomington: Indiana University Press.

Logsdon, John M. 1970. *The Decision to Go to the Moon*. Chicago: University of Chicago Press.

Long, N.E. 1949. "Power and Administration." *Public Administration Review* 9:257–64.

Lovins, A. and J. Price. 1975. *Non-Nuclear Futures*. New York: Harper.

Lowrance, William M. 1976. *Of Acceptable Risk: Science and the Determination of Safety*. Los Altos, CA: William Kaufman.

Lynn, L.E. 1987. *Managing Public Policy*. Boston: Little, Brown.

Macaulay, S. 1963. "Non-contractual Relations in Business: A Preliminary Study." *American Sociological Review* 28:55–77.

Macaulay, S. 1985. "An Empirical View of Contract." *Wisconsin Law Review* 1985:465–82.

McElfish, J.M. 1988. "State Environmental Law and Programs." Pp. 6–1 to 6–35 in S.M. Novick, D.W. Stever, and M.G. Mellon (eds.), *Law of Environmental Protection*. New York: Clark Boardman.

McEvoy, A.F. 1986. *The Fisherman's Problem*. Cambridge, England: Cambridge University Press.

McEvoy, A.F. and H.N. Scheiber. 1984. "Scientists, Entrepreneurs, and the Policy Process: A Study of the Post–1945 California Sardine Depletion." *Journal of Economic History* 44:393–406.

Machlup, F. 1980. *Knowledge and Knowledge Production: Volume 1. Knowledge: Its*

Creation, Distribution, and Economic Significance. Princeton, NJ: Princeton University Press.

MacIntyre, A. 1985a. "Administrative Initiative and Theories of Implementation: Federal Pesticide Policy, 1970–1976." Pp. 205–38 in R.K. Godwin and H.M. Ingram (eds.), *Public Policy and the Natural Environment*. Greenwich, CT: JAI Press.

MacIntyre, A. 1985b. "A Court Quietly Rewrote the Federal Pesticide Statute: How Prevalent Is Judicial Statutory Revision?" *Law and Policy* 7:249–79.

MacRae, D., Jr. 1985. *Policy Indicators*. Chapel Hill: University of North Carolina Press.

MacRae, D., Jr. 1986. "Democratic Information Systems: Policy Indicators and Public Statistics." Pp. 131–168 in W.N. Dunn (ed.), *Policy Analysis: Perspectives, Concepts, and Methods*. Greenwich, CT: JAI Press.

MacRae, D., Jr. 1987. "Building Policy-Related Technical Communities." *Knowledge: Creation, Diffusion, Utilization* 8(3):431–62.

Macrory, R. 1986. *Environmental Policy in Britain. Reaffirmation or Reform?* Berlin: Wissenschaftszentrum.

Malbin, M.J. 1977. "Our Unelected Representatives: I. Congressional Committee Staffs: Who's in Charge Here?" *Public Interest* 47:16–40.

Mangun, William R. 1988. "Impact Assessment for Federal Wildlife Policy." *Policy Studies Review* 8 (Autumn): 84–94 and *Impact Assessment Bulletin* 6 (3 & 4): 84–94.

Manley, J.F. 1968. "Congressional Staff and Public Policy-Making: The Joint Committee on Internal Revenue Taxation." *Journal of Politics* 30:1046–67.

Mann, D.E. 1986. "Democratic Politics and Environmental Policy." Pp. 3–34 in S. Kamieniecki, R. O'Brien, and M. Clarke (eds.), *Controversies in Environmental Policy*. Albany: State University of New York Press.

March, J.G. 1984. "How We Talk and How We Act: Administrative Theory and Administrative Life." Pp. 18–35 in T.J. Sergiovanni and J.E. Corbally (eds.), *Leadership and Organizational Culture*. Urbana: University of Illinois Press.

Martin, James. A. 1977. "The Proposed 'Science Court.' " *Michigan Law Review* 75 (1977):1058–91.

Mason, R.O. and I.I. Mitroff. 1981. *Challenging Strategic Planning Assumptions*. New York: John Wiley.

Mason, Thomas W. 1988. "Economics and Impact Assessment: Ceteris Paribus or Mutatis Mutandis." *Policy Studies Review* 8 (Autumn): 165–71 and *Impact Assessment Bulletin* 6 (3 & 4): 165–71.

Masters, Roger and Arthur Kantrowitz. 1988. "Scientific Adversary Procedures: The SDI Experiments at Dartmouth." Pp. 278–305 in Michael E. Kraft and Norman J. Vig (eds.), *Technology and Politics*. Durham, NC: Duke University Press.

Maxey, M. 1979. "Managing Low-Level Radioactive Wastes." Pp. 410–17 in J. Watson (ed.), *Low-Level Radioactive Waste Management*. Williamsburg, VA: Health Physics Society.

Mazmanian, D. and J. Nienaber. 1979. *Can Organizations Change?* Washington, DC: Brookings Institution.

Mesthene, Emmanuel. 1970. *Technological Change: Its Impact on Man and Society*. Cambridge, MA: Harvard University Press.

Miles, R.H. and A. Bhambri. 1983. *The Regulatory Executives*. Beverly Hills: Sage.

Mill, J.S. 1986. *On Liberty*. Buffalo, NY: Prometheus.

Milward, H.B. 1980. "Policy Entrepreneurship and Bureaucratic Demand Creation."

Pp. 255–78 in H.M. Ingram and D.E. Mann (eds.), *Why Policies Succeed or Fail*. Beverly Hills: Sage.

Miranda v. Arizona, 384 U.S. 436 (1966).

Mitcham, Carl. 1985. "What Is the Philosophy of Technology?" *International Philosophical Quarterly* 25(1):73–88.

Mitroff, I.I. and L.V. Blankenship. 1973. "On the Methodology of the Holistic Experiment: An Approach to the Conceptualization of Large-Scale Social Experiments." *Technological Forecasting and Social Change* 4:339–53.

Mnookin, R. and W. Kornhauser. 1979. "Bargaining in the Shadow of the Law: The Case of Divorce." *Yale Law Journal* 88:950–97.

Molnar, Joseph J. and David L. Rogers. 1982. Pp. 95–108 in Dean E. Mann (ed.), *Environmental Policy Implementation*. Lexington, MA: Lexington Books.

Morell, David and Christopher Magorian. 1982. *Siting Hazardous Waste Facilities: Local Opposition and the Myth of Preemption*. Cambridge, MA: Ballinger.

Mulkay, M. 1979. "Knowledge and Utility: Implications for the Sociology of Knowledge." *Social Studies of Science* 9:63–80.

Mulvihill, R. et al. 1965. *Analysis of United States Power Reactor Accident Probability*, PRC R–695. Los Angeles: Planning Research Corporation. This is the update of US AEC report, WASH–740.

Nagel, Jack H. 1987. *Participation*. Englewood Cliffs, NJ: Prentice-Hall.

Nakamura, R.T. and F. Smallwood. 1980. *The Politics of Policy Implementation*. New York: St. Martin's Press.

Natchez, P.B. and I.C. Bupp. 1973. "Policy and Priority in the Budgetary Process." *American Political Science Review* 67:951–63.

National Academy of Sciences. 1957. Committee on Waste Management, *The Disposal of Radioactive Waste on Land*. Washington, DC: National Academy of Sciences, September.

National Science Board. 1987. *Science and Engineering Indicators—1987*. Washington, DC: Government Printing Office.

National Wildlife Federation. 1987. *The Arctic National Wildlife Coastal Plain: A Perspective for the Future*. Washington, DC: National Wildlife Federation.

Needleman, M.L. and C.E. Needleman. 1974. *Guerillas in the Bureaucracy*. New York: Wiley.

Nelson, R.R. and S.G. Winter. 1982. *An Evolutionary Theory of Economic Change*. Cambridge, MA: The Belknap Press of Harvard University Press.

Neuse, Steven M. 1983. "From Grass Roots to Citizen Participation: Where We've Been and Where We Are Now." *Public Administration Quarterly* 7 (Fall):294–309.

Nevins, H.S. 1984. "The Application of Emergency Exemptions under CEQA: Loopholes in Need of Amendment?" *Pacific Law Journal* 15:1089–1126.

Nicholls, William W., Jr., and Roland E. Smith. 1982. "The Impact of *Gideon v. Wainright* and *Miranda v. Arizona* in a State Appellate Court: The Conduit Is Not Passive." *Jurimetrics* 22 (Spring):307–25.

Niskanen, W.A. 1971. *Bureaucracy and Representative Government*. Chicago: Aldine.

Nonet, P. 1969. *Administrative Justice*. New York: Russell Sage Foundation.

Nordlinger, E.A 1981. *On the Autonomy of the Democratic State*. Cambridge, MA: Harvard University Press.

O'Hare, Michael, Lawrence Bacow, and Debra Sanderson. 1983. *Facility Siting and Public Opposition*. New York: Van Nostrand.

Okrent, D. 1980. "Comment on Societal Risk." *Science* 208 (442):372–75.

Organization of American States (Department of Regional Development, Secretariat for Economic and Social Affairs). 1984. *Integrated Regional Development Planning: Guidelines and Case Studies from OSA Experience.* Washington, D.C.: Organization of American States.

Ortolano, L., B. Jenkins, and R.P. Abracosa. 1987. "Speculations on When and Why EIA Is Effective." *Environmental Impact Assessment Review* 7:285–92.

Oskamp, S. 1982. "Overconfidence in Case-Study Judgments." Pp. 287–93 in D. Kahneman, P. Slovic, and A. Tversky (eds.), *Judgment under Uncertainty: Heuristics and Biases.* Cambridge, England: Cambridge University Press.

Ostrom, E. 1965. "Public Entrepreneurship: A Case Study in Ground Water Basin Management." Ph.D. dissertation, University of California at Los Angeles.

Ostrom, V. 1953. *Water and Politics.* Los Angeles: Haynes Foundation.

Otway, H. and M. Peltu. 1985. *Regulating Industrial Risks.* London: Butterworths.

Ouchi, W.G. 1977. "The Relationship between Organizational Structure and Organizational Control." *Administrative Science Quarterly* 22 (March):95–113.

Ouchi, W.G. 1978. "A Conceptual Framework for the Design of Organizational Control Mechanisms." Research Paper No. 434, Graduate School of Business, Stanford University, Stanford, CA.

Paluch, P.T. 1985. "Coping with Complexity: Bureaucratic Decisionmaking under the National Environmental Policy Act." Ph.D. dissertation, Michigan State University.

Pelto, Pertti J. 1973. *The Snowmobile Revolution: Technology and Social Change in the Arctic.* Menlo Park, CA: Cummings.

Peltu, M. 1985. "The Role of Communications Media." Pp. 128–48 in H. Otway and M. Peltu (eds.), *Regulating Industrial Risks.* London: Butterworths.

Perlstein, J.T. 1981. "Substantive Enforcement of the California Environmental Quality Act." *California Law Review* 69:112–88.

Peters, B.G. 1987. "Policy Design and the Development of Policy Indicators." *Knowledge: Creation, Diffusion, Utilization* 9(2):278–96.

Pettigrew, A.M. (ed.). 1987. *The Management of Strategic Change.* Oxford: Basil Blackwell.

Pfeffer, J. 1978. *Organizational Design.* Arlington Heights, IL: AHM Publishing Co.

Pfeffer, J. and G.R. Salancik. 1978. *The External Control of Organizations: A Resource Dependence Perspective.* New York: Harper and Row.

Pinch, Trevor J. and Wiebe E. Bijker. 1987. "The Social Construction of Facts and Artifacts: Or How the Sociology of Science and the Sociology of Technology Might Benefit Each Other." Pp. 17–50 in Wiebe E. Bijker, Thompson P. Hughes, and Trevor J. Pinch (eds.), *The Social Construction of Technological Systems: New Directions in the Sociology and History of Technology.* Cambridge, MA: MIT Press.

Polsby, N. 1984. *Political Innovation in America.* New Haven: Yale University Press.

Porter, Alan L. 1988. "Impact Assessment" (letter). *Science* 240 (29 April):587.

Porter, Alan L. et al. 1980. *A Guidebook for Technology Assessment and Impact Analysis.* New York: Elsevier North Holland.

Price, D. de Solla. 1963. *Big Science, Little Science.* New York: Columbia University Press.

Pritchett, C. Herman. 1948. *The Roosevelt Court: A Study in Judicial Politics and Values 1937–1947*. New York: Macmillan.

Project Impact Evaluation Reports. 1979–1986. Numbers 1–63, produced by the Office of Evaluation, Bureau for Program and Policy Coordination, U.S. Agency for International Development, Washington, DC.

Raab, L. Mark et al. 1980. "Clients, Contracts, and Profits: Conflicts in Public Archaeology." *American Anthropologist* 82(3):539–51.

Rabkin, J. 1980. "Office of Civil Rights." Pp. 304–53 in J.Q. Wilson (ed.), *The Politics of Regulation*. New York: Basic Books.

Rachels, J. 1980. "Euthanasia." Pp. 28–66 in T. Regan (ed.), *Matters of Life and Death*. New York: Random House.

Rakos, Christian, Ernst Braun, and Michael Nentwich. 1988. *Technikbewertung und Umweltvertraglichkeitsprufung*. Austria: Schriftenreihe der Forschungsinitiative des Verbundkonzern.

Raloff, J. and J. Silberner. 1986. "Chernobyl: Emerging Data on Accident." *Science News* 129(19):292–93.

Rapp, Friedreich. 1981. *Analytic Philosophy of Technology*, trans. by Stanley R. Carpenter and Theodore Lagenbruch. Dodrecht, Holland: D. Reidel.

Rasmussen, N. 1975. *Reactor Safety Study*, WASH–1400. Washington, DC: U.S. Nuclear Regulatory Commission.

Rawls, J. 1971. *A Theory of Justice*. Cambridge, MA: Harvard University Press.

Renwick, William H. 1988. "The Eclipse of NEPA as Environmental Policy." *Environmental Management* 12(3):267–72.

Richter, Maurice N. 1982. *Technology and Social Complexity*. Albany: State University of New York Press.

Riedel, James. 1972. "Citizen Participation: Myths and Reality." *Public Administration Review* 32 (May-June):211–20.

Robyn, D. 1987. *Braking the Special Interests*. Chicago: University of Chicago Press.

Rohr, John A. 1985. "Professionalism, Legitimacy, and the Constitution." *Public Administration Quarterly* 8 (Winter):401–18.

Rohr, John A. 1986. *To Run a Constitution: The Legitimacy of the Administrative State*. Lawrence: University Press of Kansas.

Rosenbaum, Walter. 1976. "The Paradoxes of Public Participation." *Administration and Society* 8 (November):335–83.

Rosenberg, Ronald H. 1981. "Archeological Resource Preservation: The Role of State and Local Government." *Utah Law Review* 4:727–802.

Rossmann, A. and M.J. Steel. 1982. "Forging the New Water Law: Public Regulation of 'Proprietary' Groundwater Rights." *Hastings Law Journal* 33:903–57.

Rothschild, Joan (ed.). 1983. *Machina ex Dea: Feminist Perspectives on Technology*. New York: Pergamon Press.

Rourke, Francis. 1984. *Bureaucracy, Politics, and Public Policy*, 3d ed. Boston: Little, Brown.

Rowe, P.G. et al. 1978. *Principles for Local Environmental Management*. Cambridge, MA: Ballinger.

Rybczynski, Witold. 1983. *Taming the Tiger: The Struggle to Control Technology*. New York: Viking Press.

Saaty, T.L. 1980. *The Analytic Hierarchy Process*. New York: John Wiley.

Sagoff, M. 1987. "NEPA: Ethics, Economics, and Science in Environmental Law."

Pp. 9–47 to 9–102 in S.M. Novick, D.W. Stever, and M.G. Mellon (eds.), *Law of Environmental Protection*. New York: Clark Boardman.

Sagoff, M. 1988. *The Economy of the Earth*. Cambridge, England: Cambridge University Press.

Sahal, Devendra. 1981. *Patterns of Technological Innovation*. London: Addison-Wesley.

Salisbury, David F. 1985. "Storing Nuclear Waste." *Christian Science Monitor*, 24–28 June.

Sanford, Robert M. 1984. "A Review of Archaeological Significance, Sites, and Legal Considerations." Master's thesis, SUNY College of Environmental Science and Forestry, Syracuse.

Sax, J.L. 1973. "The (Unhappy) Truth about NEPA." *Oklahoma Law Review* 26:239–48.

Scheiber, H.N. 1987. "Pacific Ocean Resources, Science, and Law of the Sea: Wilbert M. Chapman and the Pacific Fisheries, 1945–70." *Ecology Law Quarterly* 13:381–534.

Schelling, T. 1984. *Choice and Consequence*. Cambridge, MA: Harvard University Press.

Schick, Allen. 1976. "Congress and the 'Details' of Administration." *Public Administration Review* 36 (September-October):516–28.

Schick, Allen. 1981. "The Coordination Option." Pp. 85–113 in Peter Szanton (ed.), *Federal Reorganization: What Have We Learned?* Chatham, NJ: Chatham House.

Schoenbaum, T.J. 1985. *Environmental Policy Law*, 2d ed. Mineola, NY: Foundation Press.

Schubert, Glendon. 1965. *The Judicial Mind*. Evanston, IL: Northwestern University Press.

Scott, Russell. 1981. *The Body as Property*. New York: Viking Press.

Seidman, Harold. 1980. *Politics, Position, and Power: The Dynamics of Federal Organization*, 3d ed. New York: Oxford University Press.

Sheldon, Charles H. 1974. *The American Judicial Process: Models and Approaches*. New York: Dodd, Mead.

Shover, N., D.A. Clelland, and J. Lynxwiler. 1986. *Enforcement or Negotiation*. Albany: State University of New York Press.

Shrader-Frechette, Kristin. 1983. *Nuclear Power and Public Policy*. Boston: Reidel.

Shrader-Frechette, Kristin. 1984. *Science Policy, Ethics, and Economic Methodology*. Boston: Reidel.

Shrader-Frechette, Kristin. 1985. *Risk Analaysis and Scientific Method*. Boston: Reidel.

Shrader-Frechette, Kristin. 1988. "Producer Risk, Consumer Risk, and Assessing Technological Impact." *Policy Studies Review* 8 (Autumn): 155–64 and *Impact Assessment Bulletin* 6 (3 & 4): 155–64.

Shue, H. 1981. "Exporting Hazards." Pp. 107–45 in P. Brown and H. Shue (eds.), *Boundaries: National Autonomy and Its Limits*. Totowa, NJ: Rowman and Littlefield.

Sigelman, L. and W.G. Vanderbok. 1978. "The Saving Grace? Bureaucratic Power and American Democracy." *Polity* 10:440–70.

Simon, H.A. 1973. "The Structure of Ill-Structured Problems." *Artifical Intelligence* 4:181–201.

Skolimowski, Henryk. 1972. "The Structure of Thinking in Technology." Pp. 42–49 in Carl Mitcham and Robert Mackey (eds.), *Philosophy and Technology*. New York: Free Press.

Slovic, Paul and Baruch Fischhoff. 1983. "How Safe Is Safe Enough? Determinants of Perceived and Acceptable Risk." Pp. 112–50 in Charles A. Walker, Leroy C. Gould, and Edward J. Woodhouse (eds.), *Too Hot to Handle? Social and Policy Issues in the Management of Radioactive Waste*. New Haven: Yale University Press.

Slovic, Paul, Baruch Fischhoff, and Sarah Lichtenstein. 1980. "Facts and Fears: Understanding Perceived Risks." Pp. 181–214 in Richard C. Schwing and Walter A. Albert, Jr. (eds.), *Societal Risk Assessment: How Safe Is Safe Enough?* New York: Plenum Press.

Slovic, Paul et al. 1982. "Facts Versus Fears." Pp. 463–89 in D. Kahneman, Paul Slovic, and Amos Tversky (eds.), *Judgment under Uncertainty: Heuristics and Biases*. Cambridge, England: Cambridge University Press.

Spreiregen, R.D. 1971. "Perspectives on Regional Design." *American Institute of Architects Journal* 56 (October):20–22.

Sproul, C.A. 1986. "Public Participation in the Point Conception LNG Controversy: Energy Wasted or Energy Well-Spent." *Ecology Law Quarterly* 13:73–153.

Starr, C. 1972. "Benefit-Cost Studies in Sociotechnical Systems." Pp. 17–42 in Committee on Public Engineering Policy (eds.), *Perspectives on Benefit-Risk Decision Making*. Washington, DC: National Academy of Engineering.

Starr, C. 1976. "General Philosophy of Risk-Benefit Analysis." Pp. 1–30 in H. Ashley, R. Rudman, and C. Whipple (eds.), *Energy and the Environment*. New York: Pergamon.

Starr, C. and C. Whipple. 1980. "Risks of Risk Decisions." *Science* 208(4448):1114–19.

State of Maine. 1986a. *Governor's Task Force on High-Level Nuclear Waste, Comments on U.S. Department of Energy CRP Draft Area Recommendation Report*. Augusta, ME, 15 April.

State of Maine. 1986b. Advisory Commission on Radioactive Waste, *Comments on the U.S. Department of Energy CRP Draft Area Recommendation Report*. Augusta, ME, 15 April.

State of Nevada v. John Herrington (Secretary of D.O.E.) 777 Fed.2nd 529, 2 December 1985.

State of Tennessee v. John Herrington (Secretary of D.O.E.) 626 Fed. Supp. 1345, 5 February 1986.

Stegner, Wallace E. 1954. *Beyond the Hundredth Meridian: John Wesley Powell and the Second Opening of the West*. Boston: Houghton Mifflin.

Stein, C.S. 1957. *Toward New Towns for America*. New York: Reinhold.

Stein, R. and B. Johnson. 1979. *Banking on the Biosphere: Environmental Procedures and Practices of Nine Multilateral Development Agencies*. Lexington, MA: Lexington Books.

Stewart, R.B. 1985. "The Discontents of Legalism: Interest Group Relations in Administrative Regulation." *Wisconsin Law Review* 1985:655–86.

Stone, C.N. 1987. "The Study of the Politics of Urban Development." Pp. 3–22 in C.N. Stone and H.C. Sanders (eds.), *The Politics of Urban Development*. Lawrence: University Press of Kansas.

Stone v. Powell, 428 U.S. 465 (1975).

Sundquist, James. 1969. *Making Federalism Work*. Washington, DC: Brookings Institution.

Taylor, Serge. 1984. *Making Bureaucracies Think: The Environmental Impact Statement Strategy of Administrative Reform.* Stanford, CA: Stanford University Press.

Thompson, F.J. 1982. "Bureaucratic Discretion and the National Health Service Corps." *Political Science Quarterly* 97:427–45.

Thomson, J. 1986. *Rights, Restitution, and Risk.* Cambridge, MA: Harvard University Press.

Udall, Stewart L. 1963. *The Quiet Crisis.* New York: Holt, Rinehart and Winston.

Ulmer, S. Sidney. 1971a. *Courts as Small and Not So Small Groups.* New York: General Learning Press.

Ulmer, S. Sidney. 1971b. "Earl Warren and the *Brown* Decision." *Journal of Politics* 33 (August):689–702.

UNCSTD (United Nations Centre for Science and Technology for Development). 1988. *ATAS News: A Technology Assessment Supplement.* No. 2. New York: United Nations Centre for Science and Technology for Development.

U.S. Atomic Energy Commission. 1960. *Annual Report to Congress of the Atomic Energy Commission for 1959.* Washington, DC: Government Printing Office.

U.S. Congress. 1981. Committees on Energy and Natural Resources and Environment and Public Works Committee, U.S. Senate. *Joint Report on S1662,* 97th Cong., 1st sess., November 30.

U.S. Congress. 1985. Hearings before the Subcommittee on Energy Resources and Production, Committee on Science and Technology, *Nuclear Waste Policy Act of 1982: Progress and Problems,* 99th Cong., 1st sess., November 6–7.

U.S. Council on Environmental Quality. 1978. "Regulations for Implementing Procedural Provisions of NEPA." *Federal Register* 43:55978–56007.

U.S. Council on Environmental Quality. 1986. *Environmental Quality 1984.* Washington, DC: Government Printing Office.

U.S. Department of Energy. 1985. Office of Civilian Radioactive Waste Management, *Mission Plan for the Civilian Radioactive Waste Management Program,* 3 vols. Washington, DC: Department of Energy.

U.S. Department of Energy. 1986a. Office of Civilian Radioactive Waste Management, *Draft Area Recommendation Report for the Crystalline Repository Project,* vol. 1, DOE/CH–15(1). Washington, DC: Department of Energy, January.

U.S. Department of Energy. 1986b. Office of Civilian Radioactive Waste Management. *Multiattribute Utility Analysis of Sites Nominated for Characterization for the First Radioactive-Waste Repository—A Decision-Aiding Methodology,* DOE/RW–0074. Washington, DC: Department of Energy, May.

U.S. Department of Energy. 1986c. Office of Civilian Radioactive Waste Management, *Environmental Assessment: Reference Repository Location, Hanford Site, Washington,* DOE/RW–0070. Washington, DC: Department of Energy, May.

U.S. Department of Energy. 1987a. *General Guidelines for the Recommendation of Sites for Nuclear Waste Repositories,* Part 960, 10 CFR Ch. III (1–1–87 edition), 518–51.

U.S. Department of Energy. 1987b. Personal interviews with officials in the Office of Civilian Radioactive Waste Management, October. (Interviews were granted with a guarantee of confidentiality; therefore, the names of the officials are not included here.)

U.S. Department of Energy. 1987c. Office of Civilian Radioactive Waste Management, *Annual Report to Congress.* Washington, DC: Department of Energy, April.

U.S. Department of the Interior. 1979. Press release on Revised Predator Control Policy in the Western United States. Washington, DC, 9 November.

U.S. Fish and Wildlife Service. 1975. *Final Environmental Statement for the Issuance of Annual Regulations Permitting the Sport Hunting of Migratory Birds*. Washington, DC.

U.S. Fish and Wildlife Service. 1979. *Final Environmental Impact Statement on Mammalian Predator Damage Management for Livestock Protection in the Western United States*. Washington, DC.

U.S. Fish and Wildlife Service. 1986. *Final Environmental Statement on the Use of Lead Shot for Migratory Birds in the United States*. Washington, DC.

U.S. Fish and Wildlife Service. 1987a. *Arctic National Wildlife Refuge, Alaska, Coastal Plain Resource Assessment: Report and Recommendation to Congress of the United States and Final Legislative Environmental Impact Statement, 1987*. Washington, DC.

U.S. Fish and Wildlife Service. 1987b. *Final Impact Statement for Translocation of Southern Sea Otters*. Sacramento, CA.

U.S. General Accounting Office. 1985a. *Department of Energy's Initial Efforts to Implement the Nuclear Waste Policy Act of 1982*, GAO/RCED–85–27, January.

U.S. General Accounting Office. 1985b. *The Nuclear Waste Policy Act: 1984 Implementation Status, Progress, and Problems*, GAO/RCED–85–100, September.

U.S. General Accounting Office. 1987. *Nuclear Waste: Institutional Relations under the Nuclear Waste Policy Act of 1982*, GAO/RCED–87–14. Washington, DC.

U.S. Nuclear Regulatory Commission (NRC). 1975. *Reactor Safety Study* (NUREG–75/014), WASH 1400. Washington, DC: Government Printing Office.

U.S. Office of Technology Assessment. 1985. *Managing the Nation's Commercial High-Level Radioactive Waste*. Washington, DC: Government Printing Office.

Van Allen, James A. 1962. Paper in AAAA's "Symposium on the Integrity of Science," Philadelphia, 30 December 1962. *American Scientist* 53 (1965):177.

Vig, Norman J. 1988. "Technology, Philosophy, and the State: An Overview." Pp. 8–32 in Michael E. Kraft and Norman J. Vig (eds.), *Technology and Politics*. Durham, NC: Duke University Press.

von Thienen, Volker. 1983. *Technology Assessment and Social Science Research on Technology: A Bibliography*. Berlin: Wissenschaftszentrum.

Waldo, Dwight. 1955. *The Study of Public Administration*. New York: Random House.

Waldo, Dwight. 1972. "Developments in Public Administration." *Annals of the American Academy of Political and Social Science* 404 (November):217–45.

Walker, Charles A., Leroy C. Gould, and Edward J. Woodhouse (eds.). 1983. *Too Hot to Handle? Social and Policy Issues in the Management of Radioactive Wastes*. New Haven: Yale University Press.

Wandesforde-Smith, G. 1970. "National Policy for the Environment: Politics and the Concept of Stewardship." Pp. 205–26 in R.A. Cooley and G. Wandesforde-Smith (eds.), *Congress and the Environment*. Seattle: University of Washington Press.

Wandesforde-Smith, G. 1971. "The Bureaucratic Response to Environmental Politics." *Natural Resources Journal* 11:479–88.

Wandesforde-Smith, G. 1986. "Learning from Experience, Planning for the Future: Beyond the Parable (and Paradox?) of Environmentalists as Pin-Striped Pantheists." *Ecology Law Quarterly* 13:715–58.

Wandesforde-Smith, G. and J. Kerbavaz. 1988. "The Co-Evolution of Politics and Policy:

Elections, Entrepreneurship and EIA in the United States." Pp. 161–91 in P. Wathern (ed.), *Environmental Impact Assessment: Theory and Practice*. London: Unwin Hyman.

Warfield, P.N. 1976. *Societal Systems: Planning, Policy, and Complexity*. New York: John Wiley.

Wasby, Stephen L. 1970. *The Impact of the United States Supreme Court: Some Perspectives*. Homewood, IL: Dorsey Press.

Wathern, Peter. 1987. "The EC EIA Directive: Two Initiatives, One Issue." *Environmental Impact Assessment Review* 7:103–8.

Wathern, Peter (ed.). 1988a. *Environmental Impact Assessment: Theory and Practice*. London: Unwin Hyman.

Wathern, Peter. 1988b. "The EIA Directive of the European Community." Pp. 192–209 in P. Wathern (ed.), *Environmental Impact Assessment: Theory and Practice*. London: Unwin Hyman.

Wathern, Peter. 1988c. "Containing Reform: The UK Stance on the European Community EIA Directive." *Policy Studies Review* 8 (Autumn): 95–104 and *Impact Assessment Bulletin* 6 (3 & 4): 95–104.

Wathern, Peter et al. 1987. "Assessing the Environmental Impacts of Policy: A Generalised Framework for Appraisal." *Landscape and Urban Planning* 14:321–30.

Weinberg, M.W. 1987. "The Private Sector Political Entrepreneur: Bernard O'Keefe at EG&G." Pp. 343–68 in J.W. Doig and E.C. Hargrove (eds.), *Leadership and Innovation*. Baltimore: Johns Hopkins University Press.

Weinberg, Martha. 1977. *Managing the State*. Cambridge, MA: MIT Press.

West, W.F. 1985. *Administrative Rulemaking*. Westport, CT: Greenwood Press.

White, Lynn, Jr. 1974. "Technology Assessment from the Point of View of Medieval Historian." *American Historical Review* 27(1):1–13.

Wholey, Joseph. 1976. "The Role of Evaluation and the Evaluator in Improving Public Programs." *Public Administration Review* 36 (November-December):679–83.

Wilson, Woodrow. 1887. "The Study of Administration." *Political Science Quarterly* 2 (June):197–220.

Winner, Langdon. 1977. *Autonomous Technology: Technics-out-of-Control as a Theme in Political Thought*. Cambridge, MA: MIT Press.

Wolf, C.P. 1988. "Impact Assessment for International Development." Pp. 1–16 in *Proceedings of the 1987 Workshop of the International Association for Impact Assessment*, Barbados, West Indies. Vancouver, Canada: Federal Environmental Assessment Review Office.

Yates, Douglas, Jr. 1982. *Bureaucratic Democracy: The Search for Democracy and Efficiency in American Government*. Cambridge, MA: Harvard University Press.

Yngvesson, B. 1985. "Re-examining Continuing Relations and the Law." *Wisconsin Law Review* 623–46.

Zadeh, L.A. 1972. *Outline of a New Approach to the Analysis of Complex Systems and the Decision Process*. Berkeley, CA: College of Engineering, Electronics Research Laboratory.

Index

About the Contributors

RAMON ABRACOSA works in land and water resources management with a specialty in environmental impact assessment and planning. Dr. Abracosa's teaching experience includes work at the University of the Philippines and the University of California at Berkeley. He has consulted for several different natural resources groups and agencies in the Philippines.

WALTER F. BABER is visiting professor of public administration at San Diego State University. He is the author of *Organizing the Future: Matrix Models for the Postindustrial Polity* and articles on public administration, public policy, and impact assessment.

ROBERT V. BARTLETT is associate professor of political science at Purdue University. He is the author of *The Reserve Mining Controversy: Science, Technology, and Environmental Quality* and coauthor of *A Study of Ways to Improve the Scientific Content and Methodology of Environmental Impact Analysis*. He has written articles on the National Environmental Policy Act, ecological rationality, and environmental impact assessment, among other topics.

LYNTON K. CALDWELL is director of the Program in Science Policy Studies, Arthur F. Bentley Professor Emeritus of Political Science, and Professor Emeritus of Public and Environmental Affairs, Indiana University, Bloomington,

Indiana. He is the author of many articles and several books, including *Science and the National Environmental Policy Act: Redirecting Policy through Procedural Reform*.

BRUCE B. CLARY is professor of public policy and management at the University of Southern Maine. He holds a Ph.D. in political science from the University of Southern California and taught previously at North Carolina State University, Portland State University, and the University of Wisconsin–Green Bay. He has published widely on environmental policy, citizen participation, state and local government, intergovernmental relations, natural hazards policy, and technology assessment.

JOSEPH F. COATES is president of J.F. Coates, Inc., which specializes in futures research and technology assessment. He teaches graduate courses in technology assessment and futures research at The George Washington University. He was formerly assistant to the director of the Office of Technology Assessment. At the National Science Foundation he established and directed the first program in technology assessment.

VARY T. COATES is a project director at the Office of Technology Assessment, U.S. Congress. Formerly associate director of the Program of Policy Studies in Science and Technology at The George Washington University, she is now a member of the adjunct faculty of that university. She is current president of the International Association for Impact Assessment and U.S. editor of the international journal, *Project Appraisal*.

WILLIAM N. DUNN is a professor in the Graduate School of Public and International Affairs and the School of Library and Information Science, University of Pittsburgh, and director of the Program for the Study of Knowledge Use. He is codirector of the NSF-sponsored project titled "The Impact of Science on American Society." He has authored and edited books, articles, and government reports in areas of public policy analysis, science policy, planned social change, and research utilization. His publications include *Public Policy Analysis* (1981), *Values, Ethics and the Practice of Policy Analysis* (1983), and *Policy Analysis: Perspectives, Concepts, and Methods* (1986). He is immediate past president of the Policy Studies Organization and editor-in-chief of *Knowledge in Society: The International Journal of Knowledge Transfer*.

KURT FINSTERBUSCH is an associate professor of sociology at the University of Maryland. He has authored *Understanding Social Impacts, Social Research for Policy Decisions* (with Annabelle Bender Motz), and *Organizational Change as a Development Strategy* (with Jerald Hage). Two of his recent articles coauthored with Warren Van Wicklin III are "The Contribution of Beneficiary Participation to Development Project Effectiveness,'' in *Public Administration and Development,* and ''Beneficiary Participation in Development Projects: Empirical Tests of Popular Theories,'' in *Economic Development and Cultural Change.*

ANDREA M. HEGEDUS is completing her doctoral studies at the Graduate School of Public and International Affairs, University of Pittsburgh, with a specialization in public policy research and analysis. She is currently on the faculty of the Graduate School of Public Health at the University of Pittsburgh. In the past year she served as a Health Policy Fellow at the Health Policy Institute, Graduate School of Public Health, University of Pittsburgh, and as a visiting scientist with the Pennsylvania House of Representatives. Her research interests include biomedical science policy, technology assessment, and the social impact of science. Ms. Hegedus is the managing editor of *Knowledge in Society: The International Journal of Knowledge Transfer.*

BURKART HOLZNER is professor of sociology and director of the Center for International Studies, University of Pittsburgh. He is director of the NSF-sponsored project titled ''The Impact of Science on American Society.'' His books include *Reality Construction in Society* and (as coauthor) *Knowledge Application: The Knowledge System in Society, Identity and Authority, Directions of Change: Modernization Theory, Research and Realities,* and *Organizing for Social Research.* His articles and essays have dealt with issues in sociological theory, sociology of knowledge, comparative science development, research organizations, and knowledge utilization.

W.D. KAY is an assistant professor of political science at Northeastern University. He is currently writing a book on public policy and technological development.

MICHAEL E. KRAFT is a professor of political science and the Herbert Fisk Johnson Professor of Environmental Studies at the University of Wisconsin–Green Bay. During the spring semester, 1988, when this chapter was prepared, he was a visiting distinguished professor at the La Follette Institute of Public Affairs at the University of Wisconsin–Madison. He is the coeditor with Norman Vig of *Environmental Policy in the 1980s: Reagan's New Agenda* (1984) and *Technology and Politics* (1988).

WILLIAM R. MANGUN is associate professor and director of the Master of Public Administration Program at East Carolina University. Formerly he served as project manager for policy analysis and national surveys of the U.S. Fish and Wildlife Service, Washington, D.C. Professor Mangun is the author of *The Public Administration of Environmental Policy* and the coauthor of *Nonconsumptive Use of Wildlife in the United States* and *Managing the Environmental*

Crisis. He has published numerous articles and book chapters on environment-related topics such as wildlife valuation, funding of wildlife programs, outdoor recreation, hazardous waste management, acid rain, and air and water pollution control.

THOMAS W. NEUMANN is the supervisory archaeologist for Goodwin & Associates Archaeological Consultants. He has a Ph.D. in anthropology and has consulted on impact assessments for the past fifteen years.

WILLIAM W. NICHOLLS, JR., has worked for a major southeastern bank and has served as a member of the faculty at Texas Tech University. Since September 1985 he has been trial court administrator of the third judicial district of the state of North Carolina. Author of several articles on judicial politics and policy, he holds a Ph.D. in political science from the University of Kentucky.

LEONARD ORTOLANO, UPS Foundation Professor of Civil Engineering at Stanford University, is a specialist in water resources and environmental planning. Professor Ortolano has written numerous articles on environmental assessment, and he is the author of a widely used textbook, *Environmental Planning and Decision Making.*

JAMES F. PALMER is a senior research associate with the faculties of landscape architecture and environmental studies at SUNY College of Environmental Science and Forestry. He holds a Ph.D. in forestry with an emphasis on environmental planning and behavioral research. On behalf of the college, he conducts research on environmental policy and visual impact assessment.

ROBERT M. SANFORD works for the state of Vermont as a land use permits administrator. Formerly he worked for six years as a consulting archaeologist in central New York. He has an M.S. in environmental planning and is a doctoral candidate in environmental science at SUNY College of Environmental Science and Forestry.

KRISTIN SHRADER-FRECHETTE holds an undergraduate degree in mathematics and physics and a Ph.D. in philosophy and philosophy of science. She has authored more than seventy articles and five books in the areas of philosophy of physics, philosophy of economics, environmental ethics, and science/technology policy. Currently graduate research professor of philosophy at the University of South Florida, she has held professorships at the University of California and the University of Florida. Editor of the Oxford University Press monographs on "Environmental Ethics and Science Policy," her current research, on using ecology as a basis for environmental policy, is funded by the National Science Foundation.

WARREN A. VAN WICKLIN III is a doctoral candidate in the political science department at the Massachusetts Institute of Technology. He has coauthored articles on the role of beneficiary participation in development projects. His research interests include private voluntary organizations and U.S. foreign aid policy toward Central America and the Caribbean.

GEOFFREY WANDESFORDE-SMITH teaches environmental policy and law in the Department of Political Science and the Division of Environmental Studies at the University of California at Davis. He has written extensively on EIA, particularly in California, and is cochair of the editorial policy committee of the *Environmental Impact Assessment Review*.

PETER WATHERN received a B.Sc. from the University of London and a Ph.D. from Sheffield University. He formerly was a senior fellow at the Wissenschaftszentrum, Berlin. Currently, he is a lecturer in applied ecology and director of postgraduate EIA studies in the Department of Biological Sciences, University College of Wales, Aberystwyth.

Policy Studies Organization publications issued with Greenwood Press/Quorum Books

Intergovernmental Relations and Public Policy
J. Edwin Benton and David R. Morgan, editors

Policy Controversies in Higher Education
Samuel K. Gove and Thomas M. Stauffer, editors

Citizen Participation in Public Decision Making
Jack DeSario and Stuart Langton, editors

Energy Resources Development: Politics and Policies
Richard L. Ender and John Choon Kim, editors

Federal Lands Policy
Phillip O. Foss, editor

Policy Evaluation for Local Government
Terry Busson and Philip Coulter, editors

Comparable Worth, Pay Equity, and Public Policy
Rita Mae Kelly and Jane Bayes, editors

Dimensions of Hazardous Waste Politics and Policy
Charles E. Davis and James P. Lester, editors

Small Business in a Regulated Economy: Issues and Policy Implications
Richard J. Judd, William T. Greenwood, and Fred W. Becker, editors

Rural Poverty: Special Causes and Policy Reforms
Harrell R. Rodgers, Jr., and Gregory Weiher, editors

Fundamentals of the Economic Role of Government
Warren J. Samuels, editor